Our Women Are Free

Our Women Are Free

Gender and Ethnicity in the Hindukush

Wynne Maggi

Ann Arbor
THE UNIVERSITY OF MICHIGAN PRESS

A CIP catalog record for this book is available from the British Library.

Library of Congress Cataloging-in-Publication Data

Maggi, Wynne, 1966–
    Our women are free : gender and ethnicity in the Hindukush /
Wynne Maggi.
        p.   cm.
    Includes bibliographical references and index.
    ISBN 0-472-09783-0 (cloth : alk. paper) — ISBN 0-472-06783-4
(paper : alk. paper)
        1. Women, Kalash.   2. Gender identity—Hindu Kush Mountains
Region (Afghanistan and Pakistan)   3. Ethnicity—Hindu Kush
Mountains Region (Afghanistan and Pakistan)   I. Title.

DS380.K34 M34   2002
305.42'09581—dc21   2001041477

For Lilizar and the children of Rumbur,
And for Ariel and Emma.
May you live meaningful lives.

With inspiration from Priscilla Beal and Saras Gula Aya

Contents

List of Illustrations   ix

List of Tables   xi

Pronunciation Guide   xiii

Acknowledgments   xix

Introduction: A Women's March   1

Chapter 1. Getting There   11

Chapter 2. The Invisible Landscape   44

Chapter 3. Women's Work   73

Chapter 4. Fashion   94

Chapter 5. The Kalasha Bashali   117

Chapter 6. Marrying   167

Conclusion: Bringing Back the Sun   213

Glossary   221

Notes   229

References   245

Index   263

Illustrations

Fig. 1. Map of the Kalasha valleys   15

How Onjesta/Pragata Space Works in Chet Guru

Fig. 2. Men   51

Fig. 3. Nonmenstruating women   52

Fig. 4. Before the *ḍhak bónyak* ceremony   53

Fig. 5. After the *ḍhak bónyak* ceremony but before the
gul parík ceremony   54

*How Menstruating Women Navigate the
Onjesta/Pragata Landscape*

Fig. 6. Mentruating women staying at Chet Guru
rather than living in the *bashali*   55

Fig. 7. Menstruating women living in the *bashali*   56

Fig. 8. Floor plan of a Kalasha house   59

How Onjesta and Pragata Spaces Change over Time

Fig. 9. Menstruating women staying at home in 1985   64

Fig. 10. Menstruating women staying at home in 1995   65

Fig. 11. A Kalasha *suṣútr*   100

Fig. 12. A Kalasha *kupás*   101

Photographs following page 106

Kalasha villages built into the steep valley walls

Grom village in Rumbur Valley

Kalasha women clean wheat

A goatherd watches over his flock

A young man makes cheese in the high pastures

A woman makes an unleavened morning bread

A baby boy celebrating fall by eating grapes

A Kalasha man

Women singing lighthearted songs during the Chaumos winter
solstice festival

A young girl learning to sew

Wives of Chitrali officials with Kalasha women

Female relatives from different villages catch up at a
Chaumos gathering

A girl washing her headdress near the river

A woman in the bashali offering the first peek at her
newborn baby

Three cousins begin their daily laughter and mischief

Tables

1. Goat Ownership and Agricultural Productivity   85
2. Number of Adult Women per Household and
   Agricultural Productivity   87
3. Average Reproductive Career of Menopausal Women   134
4. Reproductive History of Pilin Gul   136
5. Reproductive History of Khoshma Gul   137
6. Reproductive History of Sawarash   138
7. Kalasha Marriages   173

Pronunciation Guide

Kalashamon, the Kalasha language, is unwritten. Transcriptions of Kalasha words in this book follow the system devised by Trail and Cooper (1999), and this pronunciation guide is adapted from their *Kalasha Dictionary*. Transcriptions are broadly phonetic, sometimes phonemic. Many Kalasha sounds have no corresponding English sound.

Klasha Sound	American English Sound	Explanation
´		This mark over a vowel means that the word should be stressed on that syllable.
a	a	Low to mid central vowel. Pronounce like "a" in "father." If the "a" occurs in an unaccented syllable, it is pronounced like the "a" in "about."
ã		All vowels written with a tilde above are nasalized.
ạ		All letters written with a dot beneath are retroflex.
ạ̃		All vowels written with a dot as well as a tilde are both nasalized and retroflex.
aw	ow	Diphthong. Pronounced like English word "cow."
ay	I	Diphthong. Pronounced like English word "sky."

b	b	Voiced unaspirated bilabial stop. Pronounced like the "b" in "bit."
bh		Voiced aspirated bilabial stop.
č		Voiceless unaspirated palatal affricate. Pronounced like "ch" in the English word "cheese," but not aspirated.
čh	ch	Voiceless aspirated palatal affricate. Pronounced like the "ch" in "cheese."
c̣		Voiceless unaspirated retroflex affricate.
c̣h		Voiceless aspirated retroflex affricate.
d	d	Voiced unaspirated dental stop. Pronounced like the "d" in "dog."
ḍ		Voiced unaspirated retroflex stop. Pronounce like the "d" in "dog," but with the tongue tip farther back in the mouth.
dh		Voiced aspirated dental stop. Pronounced like the "d" in "dog," but aspirated.
ḍh		Voiced aspirated retroflex stop.
dz	dz	Voiced unaspirated dental affricate. Pronounced like the final two sounds in "adds," but with the tongue against the back of the front teeth.
e	e	Mid-front vowel. Pronounced like the "e" in "best."
ey	a	Diphthong. Pronounced like the English word "say."
g	g	Voiced unaspirated velar stop. Pronounced like the "g" in "girl."
gh		Voiced aspirated velar stop.
h	h	Voiceless. Pronounced like the English "h."
i	ee	High front vowel. Pronounced like the "ee" in "feet." If the "i" occurs in an unaccented syllable, it is pronounced like the "i" in "fit."

ǰ	j	Voiced unaspirated palatal affricate. Pronounced like the "j" in "judge."
ǰ̣		Voiced unaspirated retroflex affricate.
ǰh		Voiced aspirated palatal affricate.
k	k	Voiceless unaspirated velar stop. Pronounced like the "k" in "skin."
kh	k	Voiceless aspirated velar stop. Pronounced like the "k" in "king."
ḷ	l	Dental lateral (velarized). Pronounced like the "l" in "tool," but tongue touches the back of the front teeth.
l	l	Palatal lateral. Pronounced like the "l" in "leap," but made a bit with the tongue blade rather than the tongue tip.
m	m	Bilabial nasal stop. Pronounced like the "m" in "money."
n	n	Dental nasal stop. Pronounced like the "n" in "no," but the tongue tip touches the back of the front teeth.
ŋ	ng	Palatal nasal stop. Pronounced like the "ng" in "sing."
o	o	Mid to high back vowel. Pronounced like the "o" in "go." If it occurs in a closed syllable (between two consonants), it is pronounced like the "oo" in "foot."
p	p	Voiced unaspirated bilabial stop. Pronounced like the "p" in "spin."
ph	p	Voiceless aspirated bilabial stop. Pronounced like the "p" in "pin."
r		Alveolar tap. Just a tap of the tongue tip against the front of the palate.
s	s	Voiceless alveolar fricative. Pronounced like the "s" in "sing."
ṣ		Voiceless retroflex fricative. Pronounced like "s," but the tongue tip touches farther back in the mouth.

š	sh	Voiceless palatal fricative. Pronounced like the "sh" in "sheep."
t	t	Voiceless unaspirated dental stop. Pronounced like the "t" in "stare," but the tongue tip touches the back of the front teeth.
ṭ	t	Voiceless unaspirated retroflex stop. Pronounced like the "t" in "stare," but the tongue tip touches farther back in the mouth.
th	t	Voiceless aspirated dental stop. Pronounced like the "t" in "tear," but the tongue touches the back of the front teeth and there is a puff of air.
ṭh	t	Voiceless aspirated retroflex stop. Pronounced like the "t" in "tear," but the tongue touches farther back in the mouth and it is aspirated.
ts	ts	Voiceless unaspirated dental affricate. Pronounced like the "ts" in "Betsy."
tsh		Voiceless aspirated dental affricate. Pronounced like the "ts" in "Betsy," but aspirated.
u	oo	High back vowel. Pronounced like the "oo" in "too."
w	w	Bilabial semivowel/glide. Pronounced like the "w" in "water."
y	y	Palatal semi-vowel/glide. Pronounced like the English word-initial "y" in "you."
z	z	Voiced alveolar fricative. Pronounced like the "z" in "zebra."
ẓ		Voiced retroflex fricative. Pronounced like "z," but the tongue tip touches further back in the mouth.
ž		Voiced palatal fricative. Pronounced like the "z" in "azure" or the "s" in "television."

Place Names

I have written place names as they are commonly pronounced in English. Kalasha pronunciation is as follows:

Ayun	ẽhẽ
Badtet	baṭét
Balanguru	balangurú
Birir	biríu
Bumboret	mumurét
Chet Guru	čhet gurú
Chitral	čhetráw
Kalashagrom	kaḷása grom
Kort Desh	koṭ deš
Rumbur	rukmú

Acknowledgments

This project has made my life richer and my world bigger. I am grateful for the support and encouragement of many friends and colleagues, here and in Pakistan.

First and foremost, of course, I want to thank my'friends, who feel like family, in the Kalasha valleys. Many of those who have been most important to me cannot be named here, as they figure in this book. They will know who they are and how much I care for and appreciate them. On Kagayak, the night when the white crow carries prayers to Balumain, the last night of the winter solstice festival, Saras Gula Aya sang a prayer for me: "Whatever my daughter's purpose here, may she do it fully." This book feels like a completion of my work in the valleys, but the generosity and good-heartedness, the stories, the friendship, and the beauty of so many of you continue to transform my life. I think I am a better person, a better anthropologist, and a better mother for having lived with you.

I am grateful to many institutions and the people behind them for the financial support that made this project possible. My research was assisted by a grant from the Joint Committee on South Asia of the Social Science Research Council and the American Council of Learned Societies with funds provided by the Andrew W. Mellon Foundation and the Ford Foundation. Additional support was provided by the American Institute of Pakistan Studies, the National Science Foundation, the Wenner-Gren Foundation, the Louis Dupree Prize, a P.E.O. Scholar Award, a Fulbright student grant, and an Emory University Graduate Fellowship.

In Chitral, Mr. Heider, Mr. Babu, and Rashid made us feel welcome at the Mountain Inn and kept our mail for us. I miss drinking tea in your beautiful garden, encircled by roses and rings of snow-capped mountains. The English teachers at Sayurj Public School brought us into their house and visited us at ours. Thanks especially to Katie and Crispin, who made even the dreariest days of the Hindukush winter more fun. Vachel Miller visited me several times in Rumbur and is remembered by my Kalasha family (and by me) for the joyful and appreciative way he embraces life.

Sher Afzal Lal became our special friend, indeed our brother. His home in Chitral became our home and his family our family. Thank you, Afzal, for integrating us into your world—for showing us Chitral and upper Chitral, for teaching us some Khowar, for helping us appreciate Chitrali music (tip-top, tip-top) and culture and food, and for making us part of your family. Thanks also to Nawshad, my special friend.

Dr. Peter Dodd and Erica Dodd and the staff of the Fulbright house at the U.S. Educational Foundation in Pakistan helped Steve and me negotiate the bewildering world of visas and permits and provided a home base in Islamabad. Thanks to Lorraine Sakata, Debbie Grammar, Bill Belcher, Ashley Barr, Andrew Wilder, Rauf Yusufzai, and Adam Nayar for their generosity, good humor, and friendship.

Birgitte Glavind Sperber was an inspiration in commitment and enthusiasm, and I thank her for her friendship and for introducing me to her friends in Pakistan and Denmark. It was Birgitte who first drew my attention to the theme of Kalasha women's freedom. Augusto Cacopardo, Peter Parkes, and Elena Bashir gave me good advice and warm encouragement from the outset. Elena Bashir also reworked my Kalasha transcriptions, checking every word. I can't thank her enough for this. Nigel Allan gave me Nalgene bottles, bedsheets, and a solar shower on my way into the field, bought me drinks on my way out of the field, and commented generously on the final manuscript. Maureen Lines first brought us into the valleys and is inextricably bound up with our experience of Chitral and Kalashadesh. She caused me to think hard about the role of anthropologists and to fight for what I believe in.

This book began as a Ph.D. dissertation for Emory University. My dissertation committee, Joyce Burkhalter Flueckiger, Peggy Barlett, Margaret Mills, and Fredrik Barth, challenged and encouraged me throughout this process. Thanks to each of you for reading and commenting on many drafts, for allowing me to find my own voice, and for making this work far better for your criticisms and insights. My dissertation adviser, Bruce Knauft, was unfailingly supportive and always available. I hope that I will be able to give as freely of my time and intellectual energy to my own students and colleagues as Bruce does to his. Also, thanks to Holly Wardlow, Nancy Lowe, Nancy Smith, Jennifer Phillips Davids, Marian Maggi, Steve Byers, Cathy Comstock, Mari Yerger, Matsheliso Molapo, Cameron Hay Rollins, John Wood, Alex Hinton, Gayatri Reddy, Don Donham, and Charles Nuckolls, each of whom read and commented on various chapters along the way. Priscilla Beal, Marie Venner, and Nancy Smith painstakingly edited and commented on the final manuscript, a true testimony to friendship. John Harrison, Ken Hall, and Tiffany Aranow lent their artistic talents. Ingrid Erickson, my acquisitions editor, was supportive and responsive and wonderful in every way. I am also grateful to Margaret Mills, Fredrik Barth, Laura Ahearn, Donna Murdock, Unni Wikan, and one anonymous reviewer for careful readings of the entire manuscript, encouragement, and helpful and explicit criticism.

My family and friends in Colorado also deserve many thanks. Marian Maggi's interest in my work was a source of strength and stamina. I am happy that I could share this part of my life with her. She came to visit us in Pakistan, read every page of my field notes and every page of this book (indeed several drafts), and watched my kids so I could write. My brother, Gary Maggi, loaned me his computer when mine crashed. My dad bought me a new computer, and offered to pay for babysitters during the last critical months of writing. Gary and Misha Maggi and Jan and Ron Byers and Janie Patterson helped with much appreciated babysitting.

And, finally, Steve. Thank you for your willingness to follow me someplace cold and far away and inconvenient and for eating boiled goat though you are a vegetarian, for shoveling snow and chopping wood and making fires, for drawing maps and doing surveys and taking pictures, for staying up all night with me at funerals and festivals, for not blaming me for forever compromising your digestive system, for remembering things I forget, for animated conversations, for computer tech support, and for your cheerful willingness to make so many sacrifices for this book. And thank you for your constant companionship.

A Women's March

There should have been a festival, but there was a war. It was a small war, to be sure, but Rumbur Valley is a small place, so it seemed big to us. I remember feeling disoriented and exhausted and cold. It was the middle of December, and the sharp mountains of the Hindukush cast long, dark shadows over the narrow valley until midday. Usually in the winter we'd pass time over endless cups of too sweet tea, waiting for the few hours of sun before creeping outside. That morning, though, I stood shivering on the roof of the house of our Kalasha family in Kalashagrom village. I watched as men from the valley, both Muslim and Kalasha, streamed up the steep scree slopes to defend the holly oak and cedar forests above Rumbur against a thousand men from the town of Ayun, who had come demanding rights to cut firewood and receive royalties for logging. The Ayuni side of the mountain is barren, and for generations Ayuni people had been taking wood from the forests above the Kalasha valleys. This conflict was the culmination of fifteen costly years of battle in court, as the Kalasha and their Muslim neighbors who share the valleys organized to prevent the dangerous acceleration of logging in their forests. In this place, where wood is scarce yet everything is cooked and heated and built with wood, where the sale of cedar brings untold riches to outside contractors, and where increasing deforestation brings devastating landslides, the forests are worth fighting for. The men from Rumbur carried guns I hadn't even known they had.

Women were all out of place too, having wrapped up babies and bread and run home to their natal villages to check on brothers and fathers and to gather news. My friend Wasiara Aya,[1] the oldest daughter of our family, came storming into the village. She was crying and frightened and angry. Wasiara Aya stood on the roof with the other women who had gathered there, and she shouted at the men. I didn't speak Kalasha well yet and couldn't understand. It didn't seem appropriate to ask. We could hear shots on the ridge just over the village. Everyone was crying. We saw Saras Gula Aya (Saras Gul's mother) heading straight up the mountain. A while later a Kalasha man caught up with her and escorted her back. She told us she had heard the shooting and went to put a stop to it or to help. Her daughter-in-law, Bayda Aya, seemed pleased that she had made the attempt. "But what can we do?" she said, "It is men's work, men's war." We went inside to wait.

We waited for three days. No one knew anything or, rather, everyone claimed to know a different piece of something. Each day the *dič*—the heart of the Chaumos (*čaumós*) winter solstice festival—was postponed. Everything and everyone should have been thoroughly washed and ritually purified, houses and roofs swept clean, and things foreign—including Muslim neighbors—banned from the villages (Loude and Lievre 1984, 1988; Cacopardo and Cacopardo 1989). Chaumos is a special time out of time, when the Kalasha are as Kalasha as they imagine they once were, a time when great care is taken to do everything just right. It should be a week of abandoned dancing, of endless eating, of laughter and bawdy singing and banter, and very little sleep. The *dič* should have begun just as the sun set on the high pomegranate tree (*dáim hútala*) on the ridge above the valley. The sun would "sit in its winter house" for seven days before beginning its yearly trek back down-valley. Mushiki, Wasiara Aya's eighty-some-year-old aunt, was greatly upset about the delay and said over and over that nothing would grow and the goats wouldn't prosper and there would be illnesses and other terrible misfortunes. Others agreed with her but were more immediately worried about the gunfire echoing down from the ridge.

The next morning the women in my family told me that soon women from all over the valley would assemble and march to Kort Desh, a small hamlet about half a mile down-valley from our village, where they were to meet with the district commissioner (D.C.). My husband Steve and I should come along, they said. As always in those early days of fieldwork, we waited and waited and suddenly were late. Saras Gula Dada (Saras Gul's father), Mir Beck, a powerful and respected Kalasha elder, came bursting in. He exclaimed that I must represent all the women to the D.C. I should tell him that the women were terrified that their sons and husbands would be killed (this was true), that gunfire had been coming directly into the village (this was not true), and that the D.C. must do something or all the Kalasha in Rumbur would be wiped out and the villages burned (this was likely not true, but it felt true at the time). The D.C. would listen to me because I was American and had *páwa* (power), Mir Beck insisted. I said that I was just there to watch. The march had already started, he pointed out. He said there was no time to argue about it, so I must do as he asked. Saras Gula Aya was ready with her shawl and pushed us before her toward the steep shortcut. Lilizar, who was twelve, sprinted ahead. Mir Beck called out that it would be faster to take the regular trail. Husband and wife argued for a while, until, exasperated, she gave in and we all went running down the main path, Mir Beck shouting last minute instructions behind us. When we reached Badtet village, we saw the eighty or so women from the up-valley villages already walking down the road across the river. They all wore their *kupás*, the elaborate, heavy, cowrie shell and bead-laden headdresses that are saved for festivals and funerals and special occasions and excursions. With them were a couple of Kalasha men and two young boys. "I knew we should have gone the other way," Saras Gula Aya gasped as we ran to catch up. "I don't know why I always listen to him."

I had misunderstood or been misinformed that the women were heading for Kort Desh. In fact, they planned to walk all the way to Chitral—a much different matter. Chitral is the seat of the district government, the hub of political and economic activity for the whole region. Most women had never been outside of the valleys before, let alone to Chitral, so walking twenty miles to get there was no empty gesture and took enormous courage. The walk itself was dangerous since we would have to pass right through Ayun, the large village of the men who had invaded the valley. The tension between the two communities was so high that it seemed unlikely that we would pass through without incident. Lilizar, who was very brave at twelve, proclaimed that any Kalasha woman could take on any Ayuni woman since Kalasha women were *mezbút*, sturdy from work and walking, while Muslim women just sat in their houses getting fat.

Despite, or perhaps because of, the danger, joining the march was important. Over the next year, I would see that Saras Gula Aya usually sent her daughters-in-law on errands and necessary social visits around the valley, while she volunteered to watch the grandchildren. But on this day she insisted on going herself. Along the way we saw Sumali, who was sobbing uncontrollably because her mother had forbidden her to go further, saying she was too sickly and wouldn't make it. Another woman said her heart hurt and was crying as she explained, "I wanted to go along, I thought I could walk, but I can't." I put my arms around her and supported her for a while, and then her friends took turns and she was able to continue.

All along the way they prayed. Their prayers were a strange and effective blending of Muslim and Kalasha traditions, a sincere calling out to God but performed so that both their concern and their devotion would be understandable to onlookers. All Kalasha people know that the constitution of Pakistan guarantees the rights of minority groups to freely practice their religion, but since Kalasha religion is so denigrated and misunderstood in the area they "translated" their religion in such a way that Muslim onlookers would see it as a true religious expression. As they walked, they prayed as local Muslims do, holding their palms open as if they were reading from the Koran and stroking their "beards," crying out, "Oh my God, you know who is in the right! You know that we poor Kalasha are trying to hold our Chaumos for you!" I had never seen Kalasha people pray like this before, and I haven't since—usually prayers on behalf of the whole community are made by men who offer meat or walnuts or bread at altars, while the area is made pure with the smoke of juniper or hollyoak branches. In places where the road widened, the whole procession paused. The boys who had come along ran to the river to wash their hands, and then they lit juniper branches and purified the area with smoke. Men held up their hands and called out traditional Kalasha prayers. The women, meanwhile, knelt in a large group and continued praying, as if they were reading from the Koran. As we neared the police check post where the river forks, this was repeated more frequently. The police, who had been yelling for us to go back and alternately threatening and cajoling those they knew well, stood at a respectful distance and watched.

When we were in sight of the police check post, all the women hunted around for long sticks, which I assumed were for walking since we had come a few miles and had many more to go. The police were blocking our path, shouting that we had to go back. Steve and I tried to look invisible but to no avail. The police superintendent marched directly to me, grabbed my arm, and insisted that I come inside and call the district commissioner. I knew better and argued that I had no idea what was going on, that the Kalasha should represent themselves to the D.C., that I was only an anthropologist. Since the superintendent spoke very little English and I spoke little Chitrali or Urdu, my protestations were in vain, and he literally dragged me into the office. I told the D.C. what was going on, and he asked me all sorts of questions designed to make me feel small and stupid. He told me to tell the women to go home, that he would come to visit them later. I said that no one seemed to be taking orders from anyone, let alone me, and that they had come all this way just to talk to him and seemed seriously to be heading for his office. He said to tell them he would be right there.

In the meantime, the marchers had been in no mood to wait. The police had tried to impede their progress and had lowered the gate to barricade the road. Steve, who had been outside the whole time, told me that the women had pushed right up to the gate and begun hitting the police with their sticks—not viciously, but certainly not in jest either. They broke through the roadblock, and the police raised the gate and let them pass. They continued down the road to Ayun, fifteen or twenty policemen trailing behind them, yelling at them to sit down and wait for the D.C., alternately threatening them and offering to make tea. Barzangi and Sarawat Shah, two young Kalasha men, showed up and tried to take control and stop the women too. But Dajela Aya and her friends took their sticks and soundly whacked the presumptuous young men, forcing them to retreat into a cornfield where the women continued throwing rocks at them.

No one stopped, but in the confusion the coherence of the group broke down, and the story begins to come to an anticlimactic ending. Some women thought they should wait for the D.C. Others said that he was lying and they should continue. The marchers straggled along for a couple of miles, when finally, just as we reached the outskirts of Ayun, an official representing the D.C. showed up. He singled out Bibi Shan, one of only two Kalasha girls who had received any high school education, and talked exclusively with her. Bibi Shan happily assumed a position of authority and agreed with the official that she should be the only one to go to Chitral and represent the other women to the D.C. Of course, she said, Steve and I should come

along also. We refused. Finally, just as Bibi Shan was preparing to get
into the official's jeep, one old woman stepped up and asked her who
had made her their *gadérak* (the term for respected Kalasha male elders who mediate in disputes). After this, the official offered to take
ten women. I stood back, a little disappointed in their civil disobedience tactics, knowing that the official's offer to take representatives
was only an attempt to diffuse the energy of the marchers, and that
only solidarity would be effective, but I held my tongue. Everyone
became indecisive, and the group broke down entirely, with some
women waiting to go to Chitral, some walking on, some turning back.

Just then the assistant commissioner (A.C.), second in command
under the D.C., whipped up in his sporty red Toyota, and everyone
came rushing back. He stormed out of his jeep, sought out Steve and
me, and began berating us in English. He was very angry that we
were involved in all this, he said. Didn't we know how dangerous
this was? What if we were killed? If one of these "subjects" were
killed, it would be a "normal" death and they could deal with it, but
if we were hurt it would be very serious and our government and
theirs would be really upset. We begged him to listen to the women
who had come so far to plead their case. We asked him to speak in
Khowar (the language of Chitral in which all Kalasha are bilingual) or
at least to speak with Bibi Shan. He said he was there because of us,
not because of them. I felt embarrassed later when I had to tell my
friends what he had said.

Takat Jan, the elected representative of the Kalasha, was with the
A.C. Takat Jan told the women that the war was over, and that the
Ayunis had gone home, and anyway their going on would serve no
useful purpose since the D.C. spoke no Khowar. He himself would
have to translate for them, and he had already told the D.C. of their
views. Everyone turned back and started the long uphill walk home,
splitting into little groups of two or three.

Over the next several weeks, more police would be posted in
Rumbur. While there was still considerable tension, the battle over
firewood and logging rights continued in the courts rather than with
guns.[2] Chaumos was late and the celebration subdued. Some women
commented that all their efforts had been for nothing. Some said that
at least the D.C. would know that they were seriously concerned. I
didn't know what to make of the disheartening truncation of what
had seemed to me a brave and important effort. Perhaps, I thought, it
had all been for nothing.

But over the course of the next two years, when my friends would illustrate for me why and how it was that Kalasha women were "free" (*azát*)—and this was a favorite topic of conversation, mine as well as theirs—they would remind me of this walk.

And so I open with this story because it is where I began and because I kept being brought back to it. It happened early in my fieldwork, when the theme of women's "freedom" had not yet begun to crystallize. Later this theme would help to guide me through women's stories and through the complex unfoldings of everyday life in the valleys. With time, and now distance, too, I have finally come to understand why my Kalasha friends spoke of this march as an enactment of women's freedom. At first I saw only the tangled knots of ethnic conflict, the translation of Kalasha rituals into gestures more likely to be understood by Muslims as "religious," my own bumbling participation, the conflicts between men and women, and especially the eventual anticlimactic dissolution of the whole march. I found it hard to detect much that resonated with what I thought of as free. Slowly, I began to see that complications, context, restrictions, resistances, possibilities, and consequences are all braided into the trope of women's freedom. This book is about what it means to Kalasha women to be free and what women's freedom means to being Kalasha.

In the following chapters, I follow the concepts of Kalasha women's freedom and "choice" across several diverse arenas, attending especially to the ways in which these concepts are experienced and used by women.

Chapter 1, "Getting There," introduces the historical and cultural "ethnoscape" (Appadurai 1990) in which the Kalashi live and describes the way in which women's freedom acts as a central ethnic marker for the entire Kalasha community. In this chapter, I unpack the women's march to Chitral, which illustrates both the power of and limitations on Kalasha women's freedom. Finally, I locate the concept of Kalasha women's freedom within anthropological theories of agency.

Chapter 2 offers a demonstration of how Kalasha women's freedom "works" through an examination of how women actively participate in shaping the landscape they move through and live in. Central to Kalasha cosmology are the concepts of *onjesta* (*ónǰeṣṭa*) and *pragata* (*prágata*), which have been glossed in English as "pure" and "impure." The world of Kalashadesh is divided into things and places

that are onjesta and those that are *pragata,* and there is much concern
about the separation of the two and endless discussions about the
transgressions of the boundaries between them. Women are associated with and responsible for the *pragata* and men with the *onjesta.*

While female "impurity" has often been taken as the antithesis of
women's freedom, I argue that *pragataness* is not a construct of denigration imposed upon them but is shaped by women's active agency.
Rather than being defined by the *pragata* spaces with which they are
associated, women define and redefine these spaces as they negotiate
their identity as Kalasha women. Finally, I suggest that the attention
paid to boundaries between *onjesta* and *pragata* spaces within the
Kalasha community suggests long-standing insecurity about larger
ethnic boundaries—particularly the difficult relationship with the
larger Muslim world in which they are embedded.

In chapter 3, "Women and Work," I describe the ways in which the
kind of work Kalasha women do, the responsibilities they undertake in
terms of production and distribution, their movement through and
creative shaping of the landscape they live in, underpin (and limit) the
agency women claim in other arenas of their lives. Kalasha men and
women do very different kinds of work—work that takes them in
different directions, requires different skills, and encourages different
sorts of sociality. In turn, what Kalasha women (and men, too, of
course) are thought to be *able* to do is in large part understood through
what they *do* do.

Although land is "owned" by men, and passed to sons through
their fathers, women organize and perform most of the work on the
land, while men are primarily responsible for herding animals. Women
often describe places in the valleys by listing the women who worked
there in the past and the improvements each made to the land. A
family's fortune depends on the resourcefulness and dedication and
effort of adult women (all of whom marry into the family). Much of
what supports women's claims of "choice" in other spheres of their
lives comes from their substantial contributions to subsistence and the
freedom of movement they need to get their work done.

The fourth chapter describes how the continually evolving forms
of Kalasha women's fashion function as a material symbol of women's
agency. Women's elaborate costumes are central markers of Kalasha
ethnicity, both within and beyond the Kalasha community. While
many other aspects of traditional Kalasha culture—rules about mar-

riage, merit feasting, religious rites, and so on—seem to be waning, women's dresses are becoming, if anything, ever more elaborate and central to the Kalasha identity as a unique people. While the clothing may look the same to outsiders, in fact each woman's dress is an important expression of her individual identity. Her choice of colors, combinations, patterns, and the amount of decoration and her careful attention to detail allow for her creative expression of self—yet the result is a constellation of features that is also an evocative symbol of the identity of the Kalasha collective. Through their continual attention to and elaboration of their dress, Kalasha women are not simply "wearing" ethnicity but are actively involved in making culture.

Chapter 5 focuses on women's community and culture within their *bashali* (*bašáli*), or menstrual house. Once a widespread feature of many different cultures, menstrual houses were among the first institutions that many native peoples relinquished upon contact with outsiders from the West. As a result, there is surprisingly little documentation of the range of structures and meanings through which menstrual houses must have been organized. This study of the Kalasha bashali offers a rare ethnographic account of women's lived experience in a particular menstrual house. It is clear to me that speculation about menstrual houses as oppressive institutions designed by men could not be further from the truth (at least in this case).

The *bashali*, as the most *pragata* space in the valleys, and the place where the pragata is managed through women's own active agency, is one of the most important Kalasha institutions. The importance of the bashali in women's lives goes beyond its ritual significance in Kalasha cosmology. In this chapter, I argue that the *bashali* is an important center for female culture and community. Far from being a prison in which women are separated from the community and rendered powerless to act, the structure of the institution itself contributes to women's agency, both personally and collectively. Specifically, the *bashali* provides women with space from which to act—to be creative and religious, to be part of the larger community of women, and to make personal decisions about marriage and reproduction away from the intense social pressure of village life.

The right to elope with a man other than the one to whom your parents have "given" you—to go *aḷasíŋ* (or to choose not to)—is the prototypic act that defines Kalasha women's "freedom." This freedom is always configured against the ground of an equally compelling discourse: respect for and devotion to one's family and partriline. Chapter 6 is structured around two of my friends' stories of their own experiences of marrying. Interrupting their narratives are theoretical and ethnographic sections that unwrap the simultaneous constraints on and possibilities for women's agency (following Ahearn 1994) that are implicit in their stories.

In the concluding chapter, I weave together common themes from previous chapters through an analysis of the Hawyashi (*hawyáši*) ritual—a women's march that every year brings spring back after the seemingly interminable winter. In so doing, I offer an interpretation of what Kalasha mean when they say "our women are *free*," suggesting a specifically Kalasha understanding of women's agency.

Chapter 1

Getting There

It is nearly impossible to get to the Kalash valleys in northwestern Pakistan, either geographically or intellectually, without first passing through Chitral, the district capital. On days when there is no wind or rain or snow, there is a breathtaking flight from Peshawar to Chitral on a Fokker Friendship. (On days when there is wind or rain or snow— and there often is—you brace yourself for a nauseating twelve-hour ride in a rickety passenger van at speeds that seem impossible given the number of switchbacks, potholes, and hashish cigarettes smoked by the driver.) But on happy days when the weather is fair, for forty-five astonishing minutes the landscape of the North West Frontier Province unfurls beneath you. Flat agricultural plains, dotted with brick facto-ries and water buffalo, suddenly tilt skyward. The plane follows the mountainous teeth of the Hindukush, which guard the Lowari Pass. The Hindukush is the youngest mountain range in the world and looks as if it has just been torn from the imagination of some young god who didn't have the patience to soften the jagged edges. Once through the pass, the plane slips between 20,000-foot peaks that shelter hundreds of tiny valleys in their folds. Three of these are the Kalasha valleys of Rumbur (*rukmú*), Birir (*biríu*), and Bumboret (*mumurét*).

The narrow pass suddenly opens to Chitral's rich plains. In sum-mer, clothed in fields of the greenest wheat and rice and corn, the city looks like an emerald set securely in a ring of pronged peaks. At the heart of Chitral is a bazaar, a narrow, dusty strip of shops. Each store sells some unexpected combination of, among other things, sweaters, auto parts, biscuits, vegetables, meat, medicine, beads, paper prod-ucts, cloth, and souvenirs (rugs, rocks, and jewelry from Afghanistan; the Chitrali cap, the regional hat worn by almost all men in the North

West Frontier Province; and fake Kalasha headdresses). Looming over the bazaar is Tirich Mir, which rises to 25,229 feet (7,690 meters). Both Kalasha and Muslim Chitralis believe that Tirich Mir is the home of fairies.

A long and difficult history, complemented by a fragmented topography, has resulted in great regional ethnic diversity.[1] Chitral and the areas immediately surrounding it are mostly populated by Khowar-speaking peoples. There are also Kohestani people (Barth 1956; Keiser 1971, 1986), Pakhtuns (Barth 1959, 1981a, 1985; Lindholm 1981, 1982; Grima 1992), refugees from Afghanistan, and Indic-Gujar transhumants who travel through seasonally with their flocks and have begun to buy land and farm in recent generations. Uniting these diverse people is a common faith in Islam. Chitral is one of the most religiously conservative districts in Pakistan. Most people scrupulously fast during the month of Ramadan and pray five times each day—or, like my friend Nazir, at least on Fridays. Long before the most enthusiastic rooster has risen, the call to early morning prayers echoes from each of Chitral's many mosques.

For outsiders, much of Chitrali life is obscured by the eight-foot-high mud or cement walls, which shield colorful gardens and intimate family life from the eyes of strangers or, rather, of strange men.[2] Chitrali culture, like many conservative Islamic societies, makes a strict division between male public and female or familial private space. While the division between public and domestic has received two decades of criticism as reductive (Moore 1985:21–24),[3] in Chitral, these categories are meaningful descriptions of a social world that is divided in two—a division that is far more pronounced than in less conservative, more cosmopolitan areas of Pakistan. One sees women outside in Peshawar shopping, their heads and upper bodies covered with a large white *dupáta*, or shrouded in a form-concealing dark Afghan *burqua*. But not in Chitral. The feeling that male public spaces are no place for women is so strong that even my most liberal male Chitrali friends would never think of accompanying their sisters or wives or daughters to the bazaar or polo field or other male gathering spots. Chitrali women themselves would not think of going anyway, for keeping strict purdah is a powerful expression of women's social morality and devotion to Islam. As I grew accustomed to the ethos of Chitrali life, even I, a foreign woman for whom all manner of allowances are made, began to feel uncomfortable. I began to feel that the

old mullahs, who would berate me when my less than skillfully managed *dupáṭa* slid from the top of my head, were right: I was out of
place.

To get to the Kalasha valleys from Chitral, you can hire a private
jeep for twenty dollars or pile into one of the several cargo jeeps that
run back and forth several times a day for two dollars. Just south of
Chitral, the town of Ayun with its many rice fields fills the basin
below the mountains that encircle the valleys. Like Chitral, Ayun
presents a partial face to the outsider, and only the dusty edges of
richly textured lives are visible. Ayun's wide bazaar is built over what
was an old polo field. The now flea-infested hotel was once a viewing
platform for Chitrali princes. The jeeps swerve around the dozens
of look-alike dogs, who somehow manage to sleep undisturbed in the
middle of the road.

Spring graced Ayun weeks before the first pear tree bloomed in
Rumbur. Their corn and wheat harvests foreshadowed ours. I learned
to take careful note of what was being planted or harvested as I rode
through so I could report to my Kalasha friends. I took special care to
peek behind the heavy wooden doors into Mr. Jinnah's garden. Mr.
Jinnah, a self-proclaimed friend of the Kalasha, loved to dance and
came enthusiastically to Kalasha celebrations. Jinnah always encouraged us to stop for tea in his rose garden. Behind the high wooden
gates of his family compound, he cultivated a colorful paradise of
everything from mountain wildflowers to his delicate and tempera-
mental "green rose."

Yet in Ayun I also tangibly felt the years of quiet (and sometimes
not so quiet) animosity and disdain many Ayunis held for the Kalasha.
The several times I walked through Ayun wearing my Kalasha dress,
when snow prevented jeeps from entering the valleys or when walking
to a festival in Birir with Kalasha friends, Ayuni children streamed
behind me throwing small stones and chanting derisively "Hey,
Kalash', Kalash'."[4] (When I was wearing American or Chitrali clothing,
they'd follow behind chanting the less offensive "one pen, one pen."
Many tourists come to Pakistan equipped with cheap pens to give to
children instead of money or candy. Over the course of the years I lived
in the valleys, Kalasha children learned to beg from tourists as well but
upped their requests to "two pen, two pen.") From Ayun, the winding
road forks up into the three Kalasha valleys, Birir to the south and
Rumbur and Bumboret to the north.

As Ayun disappears behind the cliffs, the world dries out. There are no trees, no flowers, no grass, only the river below, and the sharp gray and red and tan shale walls rushing to the sky above. The river bends, and the cliffs follow, casting sharp shadows so that one bursts from cool shade into bright, hot sun and back with every turn of the road. Finally, the valley forks again; Bumboret River and Rumbur River, always strikingly different colors, join, and at just this spot is the check post (*dubáč*). A wooden sign proclaims "Wel Come," and uniformed border police rush out of the small police station to check cars headed for Bumboret or for Rumbur, where I spent most of my time. The first time I approached the check post I bristled at the militarization and the officious document checking and fee collecting (foreigners pay fifty rupees to visit the valleys and Pakistanis pay ten). But later I would look forward to this stop as the first place where I would collect news to take "home" with me. Policemen were both Kalasha and Muslim, from both Rumbur and Bumboret, and were unfailingly hospitable. And since they saw everyone who came and went they knew everything—who'd had a baby, who was sick, who was going to Peshawar, who had eloped with whom.

Fifteen years ago, the only way to get into Rumbur was to walk. Even then, there were tourists and anthropologists, but they were fewer and of a hardier sort. Now a jeep road is etched tenuously into the side of the rather unstable and mostly vertical cliffs that form the mouth of the valley. Slowly the valley starts to open up, and a patch-work of green fields and little congregations of houses and stables begin to nest in the tiny alluvial plains against the valley walls. The valley bottom looks verdant and sculpted, lush against the pale moun-tainsides above, filled with walnut and fruit trees that serve as arbors for huge, twisting grapevines. The houses furthest down-valley be-long to Chitrali Muslims who migrated into the valley two or three generations ago. Their houses are properly walled off from view, but even so women often peep out from the gates to see who is coming and children spill into the road. Just around the next bend, at Kort Desh, are the first Kalasha houses.

Being an anthropologist, or at least wanting to be an anthropolo-gist, I was determined to resist the wholesale romanticism that drips from guidebooks and tourist propaganda about the Kalasha. And yet the first time I rounded that corner I had to agree with the other tourists in my jeep (I remember being slightly annoyed, in fact, that

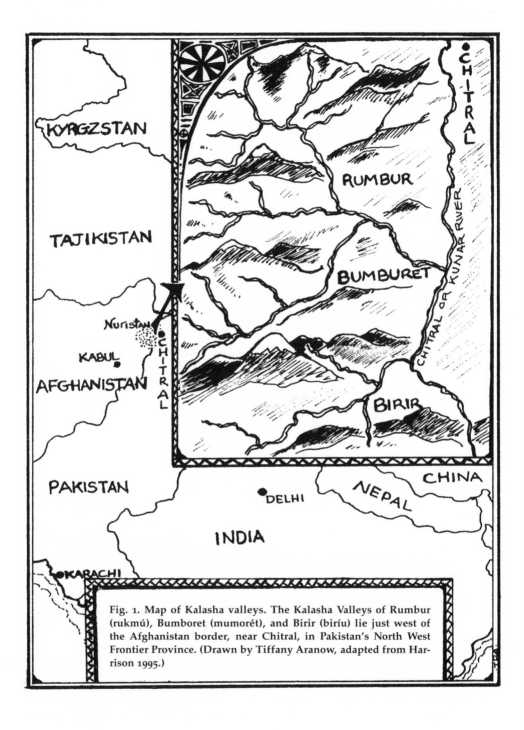

Fig. 1. Map of Kalasha valleys. The Kalasha Valleys of Rumbur (rukmú), Bumboret (mumorét), and Birir (biríu) lie just west of the Afghanistan border, near Chitral, in Pakistan's North West Frontier Province. (Drawn by Tiffany Aranow, adapted from Harrison 1995.)

there *were* other tourists in my jeep since, as I said, I so wanted to be an *anthropologist*) that everything seemed to relax somehow. The landscape seemed to breathe a heavy sigh. Suddenly there were women everywhere—women chatting in the shade with their friends, working in their fields, walking from village to village. Coming from Chitral, Kalasha women's bright dresses, elaborate headdresses, and pounds of beautiful beads seemed all the more striking. When we left the jeep to explore, we found that the patched fields are fed by an elaborate irrigation system. Kalasha children led us by the hand to a lovely place where their mothers were shaking mulberries onto a blanket. We were invited to share tea with them.

I was instantly infected with the romanticism I had come determined to resist. Two years of valley life convinced me that Kalashadesh is not Shangri-La:[5] I saw what one inevitably sees in any community—sickness, conflict, violence, and death. But still I contend that the Kalasha valleys—both the place and the people living there (and not just the women, the men, too)—*are* charming. The Kalasha enjoy their lives and cultivate graciousness, joyfulness, and generosity. They think their valleys and the high mountain pastures surrounding them are lovely, and they are. They participate enthusiastically in a rich ritual life. They think their women's clothing is the most beautiful way of dressing in the world. And, as one schoolboy said to me that first summer I was there, showing off his newly acquired English and his nuanced understanding of the way into an anthropologist's heart, "Sister, we love our religion." I felt, and still feel, an overwhelming sense of gratitude that the muse of ethnography led me to this gentle and interesting people.

My ethnographic muse was Fredrik Barth. He had visited the valleys in the 1950s while he was doing his doctoral field research among the Swat Pathan (1956, 1959, 1981, 1985). He said that when he got tired of the continual drama of Pakhtun honor he took a long trip and visited the Kalasha, where his mentor, Georg Morgenstierne, had worked in 1929. The Kalasha were hospitable and liked to laugh. Fredrik was offered bread and milk and honey. While he was there, he witnessed a young woman eloping from the menstrual house. He said women kept little stores of toiletries hidden in the rocks by the river. He gave me some black and white photographs he had taken, in which women wearing cowry shell headdresses look unabashedly into his camera. I wanted to know more about these women, about their menstrual house, about their lives. I started digging through the existing literature. I was disappointed. While there are plenty of *pictures* of Kalasha women, there is very little of substance or detail *written* about them. (Although for young anthropologists finding significant gaps in the literature is exciting as well.)

The Project

After a three-month pilot study in the summer of 1992, I planned a careful research design that would "evaluate the thesis that gendered meanings and practices vary systematically across social arenas." I had hypothesized that "male insistence on female impurity and its entrainments in female subordinate practice will be most emphasized in community ritual practice, less evident in village and household relations, and strongly countered with female-centric ideology and expressions of women's power and autonomy in the menstrual house." I am surprised now to realize that this structure could have worked and that my initial hypothesis, clothed though it is in thick anthrojargon, is correct: Kalasha women do act differently toward one another and toward men in these three contexts, and these differences could be measured empirically. So the problem was not that my initial research questions were untenable. It was that no one besides me (and other anthropologists) thought they were especially interesting.

My Kalasha friends, both men and women, brushed aside my questions about "female subordinate practice." They were resolutely uninterested in issues of gender "equality" or "women's power and autonomy." It wasn't that these issues were not important. And it certainly is not the case that men and women live in balanced harmony.[6] But rather, for Kalasha people, comparing the relative positions of men and women—ritually, socially, politically—is not very interesting, is not a focus of identity for Kalasha, as it is for many Westerners. On the other hand, the related concepts that Kalasha women are "free" (*azát*) and have "choice" (*čit*)—especially compared to women from neighboring communities—are compelling concerns (Wikan 1990, 1992). The idea of women's "freedom" emerges spontaneously in conversation, explains a wide range of behaviors and motivations, and touches the heart of individual women's identities and the collective identity of the Kalasha community.

Over and over Kalasha men and women say, to one another and to anthropologists and filmmakers and tourists, "Our women are free" (*hóma istríža azát ásan*). "Women's choice" (*istrížan čit*) is also a common topic of conversation among Kalasha people—interesting to them (and to me) for the way it makes their social world both more complex and less predictable and the way it sets them apart from their non-Kalasha neighbors. In the following chapters, I follow the way these concepts play through several diverse arenas, attending especially to the ways these concepts are experienced and used by women. In attempting to unravel what is meant by *freedom* and *choice*, I hope to unwrap an indigenous theory of women's agency—a set of pathways and rights through which each Kalasha woman defines herself through the actions she takes or doesn't take, the choices she makes or doesn't make. The implications for women's choice go beyond the shaping of individual lives, also contributing broadly to the flexibility, fluidity, and dynamism of many dimensions of collective Kalasha life.

Before I begin, I want to sketch the history of Kalasha relationships with the peoples who live around them, for it is always implicitly in relation to their ethnoscape (Appadurai 1990) that women's freedom is meaningful and effective.

A Brief Tour of the Kalasha Ethnoscape

The literature about the Kalasha is historically deep, but not very "thick" in the Geertzian sense. Anthropologists, and the colonial explorers who preceded them, have been writing about the Kalasha for over a hundred years.[7] Most researchers have concentrated their efforts on descriptions of Kalasha religion. As Peter Parkes noted at the 1993 conference on the Kalasha, together, anthropologists probably know more about Kalasha religion than any single Kalasha person. The Kalasha have also hosted scholars interested in linguistics, merit feasting, material culture, and development.

Nuristan

Due to a tragic historical "accident," the Kalasha have received more than their share of ethnographic attention. The Kalasha valleys lie on the eastern periphery of a cultural area once known as Kafiristan (from the Arabic *k'afir*, or "infidel," hence "land of the nonbelievers"— obviously not an indigenous term). A number of independent tribes lived in the nearly impenetrable mountains of the Hindukush extending east from the Kalasha valleys into what is now Afghanistan. Since almost nothing was known of Kafiristan (and thus everything imaginable was possible), it was the perfect setting for Rudyard Kipling's story "The Man Who Would Be King," in which two British scoundrels set off to make themselves kings of Kafiristan, a wild and mysterious place. (John Huston's film adaptation starring Sean Connery and Michael Caine was filmed in the Atlas Mountains of Morocco.) In 1888, Kipling described the country to his vast readership through one of the ill-fated protagonists (the one who lost his head, as it turns out) like this:

> They call it Kafiristan. By my reckoning it's the top right-hand corner of Afghanistan, not more than three hundred miles from Peshawur. They have two and thirty heathen idols there, and we'll be the thirty-third and fourth. It's a mountainous country, and the women of those parts are very beautiful. (1953:169, quoted in LaRiche 1981:6)

In 1889, only a year after the publication of Kipling's story, George Scott Robertson (who later became Sir George Scott Robertson) made a preliminary expedition to the Kam tribe of Kamdesh in Bashgal Valley. A year later he returned to live among the "Kafirs" for over a year. Although his ultimate goal was to figure out how best to secure British India's North West Frontier against possible invasions by the Russians, he was also fascinated by these "wild and interesting people" and was a thorough (if not at all reflexive) ethnographer and a poetic writer. Robertson described societies with complex social organizations and distinctive religions. Powerful men competed with one another for positions of rank through lavish "feasts of merit" (1896:449–59). The facades and interiors of buildings were covered with beautiful, elaborate carvings, symbols that represented the rank and accomplishments of the inhabitants.[8] Each tribe worshiped a distinct but related pantheon of gods and goddesses (381–415, 376–77), and believed in spirits and fairies (1896:412–13). According to Parkes, their religion "appears to have preserved many archaic features that seemingly date from the

time of the earliest Aryan migrations into North-West India" (1983:2).
The tribes were often at war with one another. Men who were ruthless
warriors were much respected. Victors characteristically cut off the ears
of their defeated enemies as trophies. Livestock raiding was a practiced
art form.

In 1895, British representatives, wishing to create a buffer between British India and Russian expansion in Central Asia, drew the
famous Durand Line on a map, separating the North West Frontier
from Afghanistan. The British ceded territory west of the Durand Line
(territory that they did not in fact control), to the amir of Afghanistan,
Abdur Rahman.[9] (Not surprisingly, there were no representatives of
Kafiristan present at the signing.) Durand himself had mused ten
years earlier, "I have always been a little afraid of the Amir turning
our breechloaders upon the independent tribes, and especially upon
the Kafirs" (see Jones 1974:2–20). His fears were well founded. In the
winter of 1895–96, Abdur Rahman led his army into Kafiristan and in
only forty days ruthlessly conquered the non-Muslim communities,
slaughtering and relocating tens of thousands and forcibly converting
the rest to Islam. Male children were taken and educated to become
mullahs. Other Afghans were settled in the valleys. The Amir's son,
Habibullah, finished the job by allowing those who converted to Islam to keep their land, while those who stubbornly held to their
religion had their lands confiscated (Gregorian 1969:181–82; LaRiche
1981:1). Kafiristan, Land of the Infidels, was then renamed Nuristan,
Land of Light. The inhabitants of present-day Nuristan are called (and
also call themselves) Nuristanis.[10]

The Durand Line also divided the Kalasha from the "Kafirs" in
larger Kafiristan. The then five[11] small Kalasha valleys fell under the
protection of British India, and so were spared the Amir's religious
zeal. Yet even before the Durand Line split them off from neighboring
communities, the Kalasha appear to have lived on the periphery of this
larger world, culturally as well as geographically. It seems clear that the
Kalasha were not held in high esteem by their fellow non-Muslims
(Loude and Lievre 1988:6). Robertson was not much impressed with
the Kalasha, calling them a "most servile and degraded race" and explaining that they were "not the true independent Kafirs of the Hindu-
Kush, but an idolatrous tribe of slaves subject to the Mehtar of Chitral,
and living within his borders" (1896:4). As Albert Cacopardo notes,
Robertson, in this much-criticized comment, was only reflecting the

opinions of neighbors on both sides of the present border (1991:279). Kalasha were considered easy prey by neighboring Kati peoples, who both raided their livestock (in fact there was an attempted raid while I was there during the summer of 1995) and captured them as prisoners (Holzwarth 1993). Two Kati men, Tak and Shamlar of Kamdesh, who answered a questionnaire about their culture (through a Muslim interpreter) in about 1835, reported that "All Kafirs together are called 'Kalasha' [i.e., Kalasha was the generic term for all the Kafir tribes], and offered without being asked that the so-called Kalasha of Chitral are not 'true Kafirs.'"[12] It is an ironic twist of history that, although they were apparently peripheral to Kafiristani culture and scorned by many "true Kafirs," Kalasha have come to be the only living heirs to what was once a huge and diverse cultural area.

In fact, Kalasha mythology and ancestor legends predicted that this would be so.[13] Kalasha histories about the origins of ritual practices are quite detailed, and almost all trace back to the glory days, twelve to fourteen generations beyond living elders, when the famous Kalasha kings, Rajawai and Bulasing, controlled most of Chitral as well as part of Bashgal Valley in Kafiristan. Almost every major religious institution in Kalasha culture—from the women's menstrual house to the location of ritual altars to specific rites and sacrifices— was introduced during this period under the inspired revelations of Nanga Dehar, the most famous Kalasha shaman-prophet. Nanga Dehar accompanied King Rajawai on his frequent excursions into Kafiristan. In trance, Nanga Dehar was made to understand, by the gods of Kafiristan, that the entire region would eventually be converted to Islam. The gods wished to have their altars transported to the Kalasha valleys so that they would continue to receive their necessary offerings. Nanga Dehar arranged for shrines to be built in their honor and instructed the ancestors of the Kalasha in the proper way to perform religious rites (Parkes 1991, 1983:16–18; Wazir Ali Shah 1974:70).[14]

Borrowings from Nuristan continue today. Peter Parkes (personal communication) has noted that even in 1975 the Kalasha had an "inferiority complex" in relation to neighboring Nuristani tribes. Kalasha would often comment that this or that aspect of their culture was inferior in comparison. I heard similar comments twenty years later, though I would have to qualify this by saying that such comments were almost exclusively made by men and referred specifically to aspects of war, religious practice, merit feasting, or building techniques.[15] After recounting for me a very accurate history of the amir's conquest of Kafiristan, Baraman, the most respected *kasí*, or ritual and historical expert in Rumbur Valley, pronounced "the Kafirs of Kafiristan were always 'above us' (*hóma pi tára*) in both purity (*ónjeṣṭa*) and strength." He explained that merit feasting was a tradition in Kafiristan that the Kalasha had "brought back," and he went on to recount which aspects of which feasts had been instituted by whom (see also Klimburg 1995). Nuristani craftsmen, renowned for their beautiful woodworking, are often hired to decorate Kalasha houses. Women buy the conical baskets that they use to carry everything from babies to pears to firewood from Nuristani craftswomen. Nuristanis also make most *kálun*, the traditional soft-soled shoes once commonly worn and still important for burial dress (replaced for everyday wear with plastic slippers made in China or Power brand tennis shoes).

Yet fear and general mistrust of Nuristanis also continues into the present. Baraman, for example, added that as well as being "stronger and more pure" the Kafirs of Kafiristan were also evil and killed and stole often and for sport (in comparison with the Kalasha, who, like the *aŋglís* (English, a reference to Westerners in general), are "more gentle and honest." Today, women bristle when unknown Nuristani men walk by, and with reason: a young Kalasha girl was attacked and nearly raped by a Nuristani man while I was there, an occurrence that women considered not uncommon. A tragic bombing that killed a beloved young man is widely believed to have been committed by a Nuristani. And raids and attempted raids on Kalasha livestock in the high pastures are commonplace. Counterbalancing this picture, true though it is to the Kalasha stereotype of Nuristanis, are fictive kinship relationships that have endured though generations, close friendships and trusting trading relationships, and a mutual interest in preserving the forest in their valley.

Chitral

The relationship of Kalasha to Chitralis is no less complex or ambivalent. The Kalasha rulers Raja Wai and Bula Singh were defeated by the first Muslim kings of Chitral, the Rais, between the fourteenth (Wazir Ali Shah 1974:70) and the sixteenth century (Siiger 1956:33; Loude and

Lievre 1988:21).[16] The Rais were succeeded by the Katur dynasty toward the end of the sixteenth century. The Katur princes, or Mehtars, further developed the feudal order begun under the Rais, and Chitral emerged as the most powerful principality in the region (Parkes 1983:21–22; Biddulph 1986:66–68). The Kalasha therefore have been a subject people to Chitrali rulers for the last three to five hundred years.[17] The Kalasha received some protection as dependents of the Mehtars from both the raids of the Afghan Kafirs and the incessant proselytizing of Islamic missionaries and for the most part were left to govern their own internal affairs. Parkes (1995) has speculated that Kalasha "pagan" beliefs were tolerated because they were often consulted as diviners by Chitrali rulers. Like other Katur subjects, Kalasha were forced to pay substantial tribute in honey, walnuts, and livestock to Chitrali overlords. One male from each household was required to perform arduous corvée labor several days each month. Young women and children were sometimes sold into slavery. The proceeds from these sales were used to pay for foreign luxuries (Durand 1899:51–52, cited in Parkes 1983:22).

This oppression, still remembered bitterly by the older generation, continued until the Kalasha and other subject peoples in Chitral were freed from serfdom in the early 1950s (Parkes 1994:159). Baraman (an elder respected for his amazing command of historical details), after recounting for me the names of the last ten Mehtars recalled that while all the Mehtars had exploited them some were more cruel than others. The last Mehtar wasn't so bad, he said. He required his subjects to pay heavy taxes to him in goats and grain and honey, and ten men were sent to do corvée labor in a rotation of nine or ten days. (This was at a time when the population of the valley was much smaller, and so this was a considerable burden.) Baraman said proudly that he himself was willful and disobedient: he was put in jail twenty-six times for refusing to pay as much as was required, though he always tried to pay something.

Even after they were released from serfdom, Kalasha were required to pay heavy taxes to the Chitrali Mehtar. They continued to suffer sometimes brutal attempts at forced conversion by Muslim neighbors. Kalasha say they were poor and *sadá* (simple, straightforward, honest) and *jangalí* (from the jungle, hillbillies) and were often taken advantage of by "clever" Chitralis (Parkes 2000). Many people were forced to sell valuable resources for very little; there is a well-known modern myth about a man who traded a productive walnut tree for a Chitrali hat.

In 1969, Chitral District was officially incorporated into the nation of Pakistan. Because Chitral is classified as a disadvantaged region, the people of Chitral District (including the Kalasha) do not pay national taxes, although they receive government services in the form of schools, roads, police, and medical clinics. The Kalasha are still relatively disadvantaged politically as one of Pakistan's few non-Muslim minorities, although they are protected by Pakistan's constitutional commitment to freedom of religion. (The women's march to Chitral demonstrated that they are well aware of this right.) Kalasha men and women vote in national, regional, and local elections and have representatives at the district level. Kalasha candidates have campaigned (thus far unsuccessfully) for a minority seat in the National Assembly.

But as significant as the changes in the last thirty years have been, Kalasha experience with and relations to the administration in Chitral remain much the same. As Parkes noted,

> The distant D.C. (district commissioner) may have replaced the Mehtar, but government officials come from the same families as the wazirs, the court advisors, of former years. Local princes can no longer call upon the free labour of the Kalasha, but they retain their importance as contractors, for example, over the new roads and irrigation projects that are now reaching these valleys. Old networks of dependence continue to dominate their relations with a "foreign" world into which they have long been partially incorporated. (1983:23)

Muslim Neighbors and Kalasha šek

Kalasha relations with the Muslim world are complicated because Kalasha and Muslims live together in the same valleys and even in the same families. Although the center of each of the three Kalasha valleys is primarily populated by Kalasha people, Chitralis (whom the Kalasha call *pátua*) and Gujar families also own houses and fields. In Rumbur Valley in 1995, there were eight families of Kho-speaking Chitralis and four Gujar families living near, but not in, the main villages.[18] Both Muslims and Kalasha own shops in the small bazaar in the center of the valley. There are two mosques in Rumbur.

Usually people treat one another in a "neighborly" way, borrowing sugar or walnuts, helping with harvesting, dropping in for visits. Our Gujar neighbor was known to be an excellent herbalist, and many Kalasha women sought her advice. My Kalasha "aunt" was also a renowned healer, practiced in the art of *khet thek,* in which smoldering threads of special bark are applied to specific points on the body. Muslims as well as Kalasha asked for her services. Kalasha also ask Muslim *daṣmán,* Muslim mullahs, to write specific prayers that are made into necklaces and thought to bring health or make someone fall in love. Kalasha and Muslim children play together. But there was also suspicion and disrespect between the communities. In private, people from each community harbor negative stereotypes about the other. Kalasha complained that their Muslim neighbors were constantly trying to talk them into converting. The deep ambivalence, but also the interdependence, of these communities was illustrated for me when the village mosque burned down.

In the middle of a dark, quiet summer night, shrieking Kalasha children began beating on the doors and windows of my room. Outside on the porch women and children were singing and dancing. The mosque across the river was burning down. The men in the family had already left to help put out the fire. The dancing subsided, and everyone stared at the horrible blaze. What a shame, *kía darkár,* the women said, shaking their heads. They said they hoped no one had been hurt. I noticed that Bayda Aya was crying. Then they all broke out dancing again. When the fire was finally out, and the men had returned, saying no one had been injured, we all went to bed. During the next week, all the neighboring Kalasha men dropped their own work to help rebuild the mosque. Women baked and sent bread. Many Kalasha families donated money to help pay for the reconstruction.

In addition to Muslim neighbors, almost all Kalasha have Muslim family members. Of the 848 people in the Kalasha community in 1995, 84, almost 10 percent, had converted to Islam or had been born in the valleys to parents who had converted before they were born. Converted Kalasha are called Kalasha *šek.* During the two years I lived in the valleys, there were fifteen conversions to Islam in all three Kalasha valleys. In my valley, Rumbur, there were two. The Kalasha population is growing, as their birth rate far outstrips the rate of conversion to

Islam. Still, from a Kalasha perspective every conversion feels like a threat to their whole way of life. News of a conversion ripples within minutes down the length of the valley. And while converted relatives are eventually reintegrated into valley life, families are initially grief stricken.

Most unmarried Kalasha *šek* continue to live in the same houses as their Kalasha relatives. Eleven Kalasha families shared their houses with a sibling, parent, or grandparent who was Muslim. One older Kalasha woman, who is blind and childless, lives with her dead husband's second wife's son and his family, all of whom are *šek*. Married *šek* commonly set up their own households, often on land outside of the village near the river or slightly down-valley (because these places are less *onjesta* and Muslims are explicitly *pragata*). There were ten households of Kalasha *šek* in Rumbur in 1995. Kalasha *šek* participate in the everyday and economic life of the community and maintain obligations to their Kalasha lineages (*kam*), although they no longer take part in most Kalasha rituals. They are also integrated into the social world of the other Muslims living in the valley. At feasts, Kalasha take care that some animals are slaughtered by a Muslim so that the meat is *halal*, permissible for Muslims to eat, and *šek* relatives can share the meal. Kalasha women who are having difficult births often are taken to *šek* houses (rather than to the *bashali*) so that they can be attended by doctors (since men are not allowed in the menstrual house). Many Kalasha *šek* try to marry their children to other *šek* rather than to Muslims from outside the Kalasha community.

Every *šek* has a personal and poignant story about how and why he or she converted. Some tell of being tricked with promises of health or fortune. One old woman says that when she was a young woman her husband was "tricked" into converting and then she was coerced with force and cruelty (*zor kay, zúlum kay*). Young couples sometimes convert if their families won't allow them to marry. Young Kalasha sometimes fall in love with someone Muslim and convert so they can marry. Kalasha claim that there are financial incentives to convert, but I had no way of confirming this directly. Many of the conversions while I was there were among young people, usually schoolboys who learn about Islam as one of the required subjects in school. Many *šek* say they converted out of genuine religious conviction or revelation. A teenage boy who had attended high school told me, "I have read all the spiritual books—Christian, Bahai, Hindu, and

Islamic. The Koran is the most beautiful. My family just doesn't understand." Whatever the reason, each person's decision to convert is final. For a *šek* to change his or her mind and become Kalasha again is thought to be impossible. And yet, among Kalasha, there is likely to be an imagined exception for each impossibility. In Bumboret Valley, a myth (at least to me it sounds like myth, though many swear it is the truth) circulates about a Kalasha man who converted to Islam and then became Kalasha again. This man is said to have converted under duress and then spent a number of years across the border in Nuristan. He wanted to come back to Bumboret, but the Nuristanis knew that he was thinking of becoming Kalasha again, so they kept guard over him, blocking the bridge that was his only way out. Every night, he tried, and for many nights he failed. One night, all the guards fell asleep, and he stole over six sleeping bodies and went back over the mountains to his home village. There the elders and all the men of the community held a ceremony for him, sacrificing a one-year-old male goat, sprinking him with the blood, and purifying him with juniper. He knew that the Muslims would try to kill him at night for converting back to Kalasha, so he had a coffin built, and every night he closed the lid and slept inside. He was never discovered by his tormentors. Years later, when he was very ill, he told his son that when he died he shouldn't bother making another coffin for him, as he had been sleeping quite comfortably in this one for many years. "Just bury me in it," he said.

Foreign Relations: Tourists and Anthropologists

There has been another player on the Kalasha ethnoscape. For more than a hundred years, Europeans have been peering into the valleys. Following the famous Siege of Chitral in 1885 (Robertson 1898), the British named the fourteen-year-old boy Shuja-ul-Mulk as Mehtar, and established a permanent garrison in Chitral. From then on, British political officers governed the region and more or less controlled the Mehtars. Aside from Robertson's account, I could find very little written about British relations with the Kalasha, although British control of the border spared the Kalasha the fate of the Kafirs in Afghanistan.

The first anthropologists arrived in the valleys in the 1920s, and, as noted earlier, the Kalasha have received a steady stream of ethnographic attention ever since. The presence of foreign tourists has increased dramatically in the past decade.[19] Most are European, but tourists from Australia, North America, Japan, and more rarely the Middle East or South America also wander through. I never saw tourists from elsewhere in South Asia, Africa (except white South Africans, who do seem to travel widely in South Asia) or the former Soviet Union or China. In 1995, fourteen hundred foreign tourists passed through the check post on their way to the Rumbur or Bumboret Valley. Most tourists go to Bumboret, a larger and more scenic valley. Most come for day trips, but some spend several nights in the valleys.[20] Some tourists are so drawn by the beauty of the valleys and the warmth of the people that they stay all summer and return almost every year. One Japanese woman married a Kalasha man and now lives with his extended family. In addition to tourists and anthropologists, foreign aid organizations have funded numerous small development projects in the Kalasha valleys (Parkes 2000), and the directors of two organizations are well-known personalities throughout the valleys.

The effects of foreign involvement in the valleys are multiple, contradictory, sometimes alarming, and sometimes funny.[21] Yet despite the presence of tourists during the summer months, and of a constant succession of anthropologists and development workers, I would still argue that the "tourist gaze" (Urry 1990) has not yet pierced as deeply into the heart of Kalasha culture as it has done in many other tourist destinations (cf. Selwyn 1996; Greenwood 1989; Boissevain 1996; Adams 1996). MacCannell (1992), for example, has argued that the penetration of tourism is everywhere so all-encompassing that there are no "primitives" left in the world, only "ex-primitives" playing the part of primitives in order to satisfy the desires (and capture the dollars) of tourists who come dreaming of a premodern, authentic Other.[22]

To this, I think most Kalasha would say (if they had read enough anthropological theory to use the jargon) that they have a sophisticated understanding of the idea of "authenticity," that part of being Kalasha means bringing new people and ideas in and making them their own. I often heard Takat Jan, for example, reassuring tourists worried about the new mini–hydroelectric plant (built in 1995) that electricity won't destroy Kalasha culture but it will help them see better at night. In fact, rather than playing the part of primitives (or rather "pagans," as tourist literature on the Kalasha valleys promises) for tourists, Kalasha tend to pull foreigners into their own cultural fantasies and use them toward their own political ends.

An interesting fictive kinship has developed between Kalasha and the foreigners who are so fascinated with them. As with much contemporary "ethno-tourism," tourists come to the valleys (or rather they pause there, as these small valleys are always a stop on a larger journey and rarely a final destination) looking for "authenticity,"[23] for a way of life that seems somehow less commodified, less fragmented, less harried, and more social than their own. Westerners have been quick to recognize their authentic/original selves in the Kalasha. Some come seeking the descendants of Alexander the Great, some one of the lost tribes of Israel, and one traveler even waxed poetic about how they reminded him of the Whos in Dr. Seuss's Whoville—that is, they reminded him of the best of what we imagine ourselves capable of being. This imagined sameness is cultivated by Kalasha people, who also search for reflections of themselves in their visitors, though for different reasons.

Because the Kalasha are a tiny population whose religion and customs stand out in relief against the Islamic background of the rest of Central Asia, foreigners (who are mostly non-Muslim themselves) coming into the valleys find themselves in the somewhat unique postcolonial position of working with or visiting a community that identifies *with* rather than *against* them. If foreigners are looking to Kalasha for confirmation of their own essential (or potential) goodness and wholeness, Kalasha look to foreigners for confirmation that Kalasha culture is good in contrast to the daily barrage of hellfire and damnation promised by their Muslim neighbors. Countless times my Kalasha friends said something like this to me or to other visitors: "We are all Kafirs [nonbelievers], after all. We are all one *kam*, one lineage."[24]

One example, of almost daily possible examples, occurred early in my fieldwork. My friend Wasiara Aya and I were sitting on little stools outside her guesthouse in Rumbur Valley. She was using her most animated gestures to help me learn Kalasha. I had been staying with Wasiara Aya and her family for the first several months of my fieldwork. We were both laughing at my silly mistakes when Abdul Salam and his friend, Mohammed Asam, came up the stairs. My husband and I had visited their home in Urtsun when I was conducting a pilot study the previous summer. Urtsun is inhabited by a population of people who converted from Kalasha to Islam only a few decades ago (Aug. Cacopardo 1991). Abdul Salam had given me an enthusiastic tour of his valley, pointing out the ruins of Kalasha shrines and the women's menstrual house. The men good-naturedly joined in the language lesson, and Wasiara Aya made a game out of sorting out the differences in dialects spoken in the two valleys.

Then, out of nowhere, Mohammad Asam turned to Wasiara Aya and asked why she and the other Kalasha don't convert to Islam so they could go to heaven rather than burn in hell. I hadn't been in the valleys long enough to realize that this sort of pointed proselytizing is commonplace. Wasiara Aya turned to me and said, "Why should we convert, *ne bāba* (right sister)? Kalasha is a good religion, a free religion (*azát masaháp*), *ne bāba*?" To the men she said, "Everyone comes here to see us. You don't even have any hotels in Urtsun. *amerikáy* (Americans), *pharansí* (French), *aŋglís* (English), *kanadá* (Canadians), *japaní* (Japanese)—they all like Kalasha. No one comes to see you. Kalasha is good, isn't that right, sister?" The appreciation of foreigners, the imagined kinship propagated on both sides, contributes to the sense, held by all Kalasha I know, that they are special and that their culture is valuable.

Identity, Ethnicity, and Gender

I hope that this brief cultural and historical tour has conveyed the sense, keenly felt by Kalasha themselves, that they are a tiny minority community treading water in a vast and compelling sea of Islam, which threatens daily to flood into their valleys. They have struggled for centuries to preserve their cultural identity in the face of "chronic . . . oppressive subordination" (Parkes 1994:159). This continual pressure has had a profound effect on the ethos of Kalasha life. Peter Parkes, following Mary Douglas, has diagnosed the Kalasha community as an "enclave culture" (cf. Castile and Kushner 1981). He writes:

> The societal institutions of enclaves are expressly modified to ensure communal solidarity in the face of an encompassing and alien social universe, being particularly adapted to discourage the "defection" of internal members to this more dominant exterior environment, as irrevocably occurs through Kalasha conversions to Islam. The religious culture of enclaves also tends to be preoc-

cupied with exacting ritual criteria of purity and pollution (Parkes 1987), serving to demarcate a distinctive group boundary that defines insiders from outsiders; and the political institutions of enclaved societies are similarly instituted in contrastive opposition to the "hierarchical" polities in which their communities are encapsulated. In other words, enclaves are determinedly *egalitarian* in principle, where all members are supposedly alike in status and moral evaluation. (Parkes 1994:159–60)[25]

If you ask most any Kalasha adult whether the community will be practicing its religion in ten or twenty years, the answer will be "probably." "What about 50 years from now, or a hundred?" you ask. And they'll answer, "Who knows? Who knows? We hope so." The persistence of their cultural identity is not something that can be taken for granted but something that is won daily. Kalasha ritual life is focused explicitly on maintaining the purity (*ónjeṣṭa*) of their people, and their valley, against the impure (*prágata*) world outside. And the rhetoric of Kalasha political life often repeatedly emphasizes the fact that "'all Kalasha are poor, all are equal' in contrast to the hereditary status grading characteristic of surrounding Muslim peoples in Chitral" (160).

I would take Parkes's argument one step further by noting that every aspect of this cultural work of defining and maintaining ethnic boundaries, and of generating solidarity through a commitment to egalitarian principles, is inextricably bound up with gender. Kalasha women have come to represent Kalasha ethnicity in the way they dress, behave, and interact with men.

Two generations ago, Kalasha men wore clothing that marked them as distinctively Kalasha. Today Kalasha men are almost indistinguishable from their Muslim neighbors, while women continue to wear almost all the distinctive physical markers of Kalasha ethnicity. When a Kalasha woman converts to Islam, she immediately changes her clothing, tearfully gives her headdress and beads to her female relatives, and unbraids her hair. While there is no scriptural basis in the Koran for these changes (since Kalasha women's clothing is already quite modest and their heads are covered at all times), women's dress is the central marker of Kalasha ethnicity. It is unthinkable that a Muslim woman would dress in Kalasha clothing (I discuss this in detail in chapter 3).

Kalasha "exacting ritual criteria of purity and pollution" are inher-
ently gendered. The Kalasha ritual world assigns both Muslims and
Kalasha women to the realm of the impure. So it is women who are
responsible for maintaining the purity of the valleys by means of their
conscientious attention to boundaries between pure and impure.
Thus, they also symbolically maintain the "group boundary that defines insiders from outsiders."

Finally, when asked what differentiates them from their Muslim
neighbors, Kalasha people almost always remark that "Our women
are free (*hóma istríža azát ásan*)." While clearly different from "egalitarian principles" (freedom in this sense in fact has nothing to do with
equality), the concept of Kalasha women's freedom gives women
great latitude in determining the course of their own lives—sexually,
emotionally, and ritually. This concept is both a core marker of
Kalasha ethnicity and an important incentive for women not to "de-
fect" from the community by converting to Islam.[26] At the same time,
the ever-present knowledge that women *could* leave the community
serves to strengthen community commitment to the constellation of
rights and responsibilities involved in women's freedom—even when
these directly contradict an also present value of respecting men's and
familial authority.

That gender and ethnicity are intertwined is not unique to the
Kalasha. There is a large body of both theoretical and ethnographic
works that deal with the embedded nature of gender,[27] the inability to
disentangle gender theoretically from the lived experience of other
aspects of identity—ethnicity, race, class, age, religion, sexual orientation, and so on.[28] But in the Kalasha valleys ethnic boundaries are so
near and so clear, and gender is so important to their maintenance,
that the mutual construction of gender and ethnicity is explicit in a
way it is not in many other places.

Our Women Are Free

During the winter, Steve and I lived in Kalashagrom village, which is
perched atop a steep hill, so we could see all the other villages in
Rumbur, the road and the river below, and the snow-covered peaks
that rise to 17,000 feet in the background. Steve shoveled snow and
chopped firewood for our family, did our laundry, and wrote poetry
and an autobiographical novel. I did "fieldwork." This meant, as far as

my Kalasha family could discern, that I spent all my time gossiping and drinking tea with our neighbors. My favorite neighbor, Mushiki, was eighty years old, or so she claimed. *Mushiki* means "alfalfa," an old-fashioned name that suits her, although everyone addresses her with a more respectful term such as *mother* or *great-aunt*. Her clear blue eyes were nearly completely blind. She loved babies, and her nephews' wives would drop their infants off with her while they went to braid their hair or to the mill to grind grain. They would return with news they had picked up while they were out, so Mushiki kept an intricate command of valley politics and intrigue, even though she never left her house. She would make sharp, sweeping pronouncements on everything from national politics (men should look out because a woman, Benazir Bhutto, sat on the throne now) to local culture ("girls these days don't know how to sing—why, when I was a girl, my friends and I used to sing and dance for days"), but her favorite topic was ethnicity.

One afternoon, Siasat came over with her new baby girl. I handed the baby to Mushiki backward from the way she had expected, and since she couldn't see she scooped up the swaddled bundle and gave the baby's feet an affectionate kiss and nuzzle. Everyone laughed. Mushiki laughed so hard she almost fell off her stool, baby and all. Then Siasat said she had come bearing bad news. She'd just returned from visiting her mother in Birir Valley, and two more Kalasha had converted to Islam. Mushiki shook her head, saying that she just didn't understand how women could do this. "They don't think!" she exclaimed. "They don't think, and then it is too late." Then she turned to me and said, "We Kalasha are free. We women go where we want. We go to Birir, to Bumboret, to Balanguru, to Chet Guru. We go to Peshawar if we want to." I interjected that it appeared to me that women had to ask permission from their husbands to travel, but she insisted that this wasn't true. Of course, they probably would ask their husbands, but they didn't have to, and if he said no they still *could* go, though probably they *wouldn't*. "So even without permission Kalasha women go where they want. *Pátua* (Chitrali Muslims) are bad. They don't let women out of the house. They can't go visiting. Women cover their faces, and if other people see their faces they will be killed. Not so with the Kalasha. The Kalasha religion is a free one. We say '*móa* (mother's brother),' 'brother,' 'son-in-law,' so we are free [in other words, Kalasha women have relationships with men that are not suspected of being sexual in nature]. *Pátua* don't. They can't even go to their own brothers' houses. We Kalasha go *alasíŋ* (elope) if we don't like our husbands. Those 'shit-eating' [stupid—as in stupid enough to eat shit instead of food] *šek* [Kalasha who have converted to Islam] are very jealous."

This book is an attempt to unwrap what Mushiki meant by "Our women are free" (*hóma istríža azát ásan*),[29] a refrain that is echoed again and again by Kalasha men and women both. At the time that I noted down this conversation, I hadn't realized that this would become the focus of my work for the next several years. In fact, I remember I almost didn't bother taking notes—the sentiments Mushiki expresses are so common that they had become a cliché to me in a very short time. When I look at them now, after having spent years trying to understand what Kalasha women do and why they do it, I am amazed that Mushiki captured, in a few short sentences, almost everything that I have to say about what I have begun to call an "ethnotheory of Kalasha women's agency."

Throughout this work, I have glossed the Kalasha word *azát* as the English word *free*. In doing so, I know that I run the risk that readers will carry into this discussion their own cultural associations of *freedom* with lightness, boundlessness, and independence rather than interdependence. I know too that *freedom* conjures up all sorts of unsavory associations with unreflective patriotism or naive feminism. And yet I want to rescue the word and use it, even though it is out of vogue. For one thing, I think *free* really works as a translation for *azát*, at least for one particular meaning of that word in English. You cannot use the word *azát* to describe something that is "empty"—as in the English "free from infection," nor can you use it to signify something that doesn't cost anything. However, if you catch a bird in a trap and then release him, he would be *azát*, free. You are also "freed" from prison. A woman whose husband marries a second wife is *azát*—she can choose to stay with him if she wants to or she can leave him and her husband then forfeits the bridewealth his family paid hers when they were first married. (In either case, the children are "his," so it's not a decision without consequences.) *azát* then carries the meaning of the English word *free* as in "released from restriction"—but always within it is the assumption that those restrictions were there, were real. If women are "free," it is because they *are also* bounded—by traditions and rules, in marriages, by where they should and shouldn't go and what they should and shouldn't wear. Being free for them means being free to step outside the boundaries of those rules—or to choose not to do so—but it doesn't mean that there are no restrictions, no frame, no norms, no expectations, no consequences.

It isn't only that Kalasha women are self-possessed and active. Like all humans, some are and others are less so. Like all of us, most are sometimes but not all the time. I take for granted that individual Kalasha women have "agency" in this more general sense. They negotiate the nooks and crannies of their world in many and varied ways; they do things, and what they do makes a difference. Rather, women's freedom among Kalasha refers to a particular constellation of rights and abilities that are claimed by Kalasha women as a group—because they are women and, more specifically, because they are Kalasha women.

As Mushiki points out, Kalasha women's freedom involves the ability to travel freely and widely, or at least the ability to think of yourself as being able to travel freely and widely if you really, really want to. It is the freedom to be "seen" in a cultural milieu where women from neighboring cultural groups take pride in being out of sight. It is about the freedom to have relationships with men that are not immediately assumed to be sexual in nature. It is the freedom to make choices about sexuality and marriage, although these decisions are always difficult. It is *not* limitless freedom but rather the freedom to choose, sometimes, to step beyond limits. It is also the freedom to *choose* to live *within* cultural norms, and thus to embrace rules not as something imposed from without but as something that you, too, have played a part in creating.

The women's march to Chitral detailed in the prologue was characterized by Kalasha women as an enactment of this freedom. In these few dramatic hours, many of the assumptions implicit in the trope of women's freedom were made visible, as were the limits on that freedom. First and foremost, by leaving the valleys in the midst of a war, women were exercising what they see as a fundamental right—the right to exit an intolerable situation. That this exit was made by physically walking out of the valleys is important, for freedom almost always involves embodied action. While men may make speeches, give

their word, and issue orders, women act—in fact, usually they *walk*—
and this freedom of movement is important to their identity as Kalasha
women.

Further, and this, too, is important, it was not only women who
were involved in the march. Later I was told that the march was in
fact organized by men, who thought eighty Kalasha women walking
to Chitral would be an effective form of civil disobedience. (It would
have been if CNN had been there.) Men and boys were essential for
the ritual component of their march as well. Women's freedom is a
value that is shared by men and women, not a value that women
cultivate at the expense of men.

The march also emphasized the role Kalasha women play in the
cultural work of representing and maintaining Kalasha ethnicity—
through their dress, their behavior, and especially the way they relate
to Kalasha men—as well as inherent contradictions of that work. Every woman on the march remembered to wear her heavy *kupás* headdress, which is saved for festivals or funerals or other special religious
occasions or excursions. They were keenly aware of their visual impact, and, although it was cold, they consciously pulled down their
woolen shawls so that their *kupás* were visible as we passed the few
tiny Muslim settlements down-valley from the Kalasha villages. The
conservative Islamic milieu of northern Pakistan serves as the foil
against which Kalasha ethnicity is reflected back as bold, strong (as
Lilizar put it), attractive, and slightly shocking. But the Kalasha are not
isolationists, and they also want to be understood and respected by
their neighbors. They do want to be seen but as more than spectacle
and costume. So, while the marchers took the regionally shocking
action of walking, unescorted by husbands, and unveiled, down the
road toward Chitral, they also modified their religious gestures so that
they would be understandable to their Muslim audience. They wanted
to be seen as serious and pious so their neighbors and Chitrali officials
would understand that they were marching on behalf of the right to
worship.

This story also points out my own role, witting and unwitting, in
Kalasha women's exercise of freedom. Early in my research, I was
ejected from a self-absorbed period of gnawing guilt at not "doing"
anything to "help" the Kalasha by some sharp words from one of
most respected and educated (and funny, smart, and sexist) men in
the community. When I asked him what I could do to "help," he

proceeded to speculate about Western women. Why was it, he asked, that they went crazy with loneliness when they grew older and either kept hundreds of chickens or cats or dogs or felt compelled to go and "save" some poor people somewhere? To me, he advised, "Write a book about us. Make a movie. Write ten books—we don't care. If you want to live here, come! Live in my house. We'll give you food. We'll even give you land. But please don't save us." I recommitted myself to the role of participant/observer, and, until the women's march, I really thought I could simply watch and listen with attention and compassion and my presence wouldn't matter much. (Of course, I knew better theoretically, but then I knew many theoretical things before I went to the field.) But Steve and I were quickly drawn in, and it was impossible to be disinterested, impossible not to change things by our very presence. As I write this book, I am keenly aware that my friends must have tried to represent themselves to me using images and ideas they thought I would understand and admire. While it is true that Kalasha people never seemed to tire of talking about women's freedom, it is also true that they knew that *I* never tired of talking about it. Surely my questions about and interest in Kalasha women's freedom must have influenced the way they represented themselves to me. And possibly, at least among my closest friends, my presence may have affected the way they think about themselves and their lives.

Western women have become a new point of comparison against which Kalasha women measure themselves. My intimate involvement in the lives of my family and friends brought this comparison into even sharper focus. One day, when Wasiara Aya was visiting me at her father's house in Kalashagrom, she remarked, "Wynne, I have never been jealous of anyone before in my life, but when I see you and other *aŋglís* (English—the Kalasha gloss for all foreigners) women traveling around the world, going wherever you want to go, I feel jealous." Wasiara Aya and her sisters-in-law embarked on a discussion about whether or not *aŋglís* were freer than Kalasha. Was it really true, they asked me, that *aŋglís* women give wealth to marry their husbands? Barzangia Aya, who had been listening in on our conversation, jumped in. She said that it wasn't that *aŋglís* were freer than Kalasha but that in addition to freedom *aŋglís* had "power" (*pawa*). (I don't know when this word entered the Kalasha language, but I suspect it was introduced by anthropologists.) Everyone is afraid of *aŋglís*, she

said, even the government of Pakistan. No one would dare to hurt
anglís. This isn't true of Kalasha women, who do feel vulnerable outside of their familiar valleys.

In other words, Kalasha women find themselves bounded on all
sides by a larger geopolitical world in which their agency is not
taken seriously, where they are neither effective nor safe. Chitrali
authorities assumed that Steve and I had organized this march, taking for granted that Kalasha were not active, bold, or intelligent
enough to take such an action on their own. They also assumed that
Steve and I were not so naive as to be ignorant of the fact that
foreigners are forbidden to take part in political marches in Pakistan.
They were wrong on both counts. The assistant commissioner arrived saying he was worried that Steve or I might be killed, but the
women's concerns were roundly dismissed.

The final, anticlimactic dissolution of the march points to another
limitation on women's freedom. Individual women usually act alone
(indeed, the ability to do so is part of what defines Kalasha women's
freedom). The concept of women's freedom is entirely without connotations of women's solidarity. When pressured by the authorities, the
group fractured and each woman made up her own mind about
whether to go on or go back.

Implicit in all these freedoms, as you can see in Mushiki's remarks,
is a specific comparison with women from surrounding Islamic communities. The ability to make these choices and do these things is therefore
an important—I would even claim that it is the most important—
ethnic marker. I want to make it clear that I know (and Kalasha women
know, too) that neighboring Muslim women have agency—that is,
they work to define their lives in active ways, they resist or actively
embrace the structures they live in, they have affairs, use veiling to
their advantage, influence choices about their weddings, and travel
about. The difference is this: Kalasha women think of themselves as
people who move about, and claim the right to do so, whether they
take advantage of it or not. Chitrali women think of themselves as
people who stay put, while in fact they move around an awful lot.
Kalasha women think of themselves as being free to make decisions
about marriage, although they recognize that in fact situations are
often defined for them and there is sometimes little latitude. Chitrali
women think of themselves as having marriages that are arranged,
while in fact girls have a lot of say in who they are given to (while

Kalasha girls do not). Kalasha women think of themselves as people who are seen, although many also value privacy. Chitrali women value the strict purdah they keep, although they, too, find ways of making themselves visible. In other words, discourse about women's agency is moral discourse in which definitions of gender come to define the claims of ethnic superiority or difference.[30] And in the case of the Kalasha the claim that women's freedom is what makes Kalasha different from Muslims helps to shore up women's freedom when it is challenged.

And it often *is* challenged. When my colleague, Joyce Flueckiger, first read a draft of one of my early chapters, she said that she liked it but she didn't *believe* it—as someone who grew up in and writes about and studies South Asia, it sounded too romantic. For a while, I didn't get it. I believed that I had described women's lives as "truly" as I was able. Since then, I realize that I often do the same thing Kalasha women do—assert their freedom, their ability to make choices, without explaining the background of undeniable male privilege and authority (in a region where male privilege is taken as God given) against which women's freedom is configured.

In scoring the Sherpas on a scale of gender inequality across world cultures, Sherry Ortner has recently pronounced them "pretty good," noting that it is "notoriously difficult to assign a score of degree of gender equality or inequality in a particular society" (1996:186). Following her lead, I would also score the Kalasha as "pretty good" in comparison with other world cultures and "really quite good" on a scale of gender inequality in the conservative milieu of northern Pakistan. Kalasha women enjoy a great deal of respect from men in everyday interactions. They make major economic contributions to their families, and their contributions are acknowledged. Kalasha men are not "macho," and women are not sexually preyed upon. But Kalasha culture is certainly not egalitarian. Kalasha culture accords all positions of formal political and religious authority to men. Men own all the land and animals. They have the right to demand deference from women. They are served first, they eat more and better, and if there is only one chair a man will usually sit in it. Men's names are remembered through the generations. I don't think any Kalasha person would claim that men and women are "equal," and it seems to me that men clearly have the lion's share of overt power and prestige.

Yet Kalasha culture accords women the right to interrupt this

flow of male privilege. Kalasha women's freedom involves the structural freedom to resist—it doesn't mean that there is no need to resist.
It is not some decontextualized freedom from male influence that an
abstract and idealized notion of freedom might suggest. But it is freedom nonetheless. And this freedom matters, and changes things, for
men and women both.

Freedom and Agency

In many ways, Kalasha people's concern with women's freedom com-
plements the emerging theoretical orientation in the 1980s and 1990s
toward issues of "agency." Sherry Ortner has outlined a clear (but
diverse) trend across the social sciences toward theories and methods
that foreground "practice"—that is, toward increased theoretical interest in action and interaction, in the people doing the acting and inter-
acting, and on the (intended and unintended) effects of all this action
on the reproduction of or changes in "the system" (1984, 1996). Although theories of practice are multistranded, they are linked in the
understanding that concern with agency is a necessary counterpart
(and not an alternative) to the study of systems or structure.

Within anthropology, attention to agency has followed several
paths to its position as a current node of theoretical discourse. The
British sociologist Anthony Giddens has developed and promoted an
approach to understanding the interplay between structure and
agency (1977, 1979, 1984). Giddens has stated simply that "agency
refers to doing" (1984:10), and he has been especially interested in the
unintended consequences of social action (Knauft 1996:108).

At the same time that Giddens's earliest works on agency
emerged, Pierre Bourdieu's *Outline of a Theory of Practice* (1977) was
revised and translated into English. Bourdieu's theory of practice uses
a Marxist critique to analyze (and criticize) the structures of inequality,
both material and symbolic, that organize the subjective world of
actors. Bourdieu emphasizes that this order "played itself out in real
practices and real time to create real inequalities among real people"
(Knauft 1996:112).

An indigenous commitment to attention to action and agency
developed within anthropology in what was called transactionalism.
Fredrik Barth (1966, 1981b, 1987, 1993, 1994), for example, has long
been developing generative models through which the structures of

social life are revealed as emerging through the practices (and interpretations of these practices) of people "who have multiple simultaneous purposes and know that so do their fellow villagers" (1993:156). Barth stresses, "I am in no way arguing that formal organization is irrelevant to what is happening—only that formal organization is not *what is happening*" (157).

Recently, Sherry Ortner has offered up what she calls a "new and improved brand of practice theory"—a "Feminist, Minority, Postcolonial, Subaltern, etc., Theory of Practice." She suggests that it is useful to replace the focus on structures with the looser concept of "serious games" and argues that:

> If we take the methodological unit of practice as the game, rather than the "agent," we can never lose sight of the mutual determination(s) of agents and structures: of the fact that players are "agents," skilled and intense strategizers who constantly stretch the game even as they enact it, and the simultaneous fact that players are defined and constructed (though never wholly contained) by the game. (1996:19–20)

In other words, embedded in working theories of agency, from Bourdieu's conception of "habitus," to Barth's generative models of social life, to Ortner's "serious games," to the Kalasha conception of "freedom," are understandings of the limits to and constraints on that agency. Kalasha suffer no delusions that they can make the world anew, or destroy it. Yet there is general understanding that individual women have the capacity to significantly rearrange their physical, ritual, and social worlds in specific ways.

Feminist anthropologists have made specific and important contributions to broader understandings of gendered agency (Kratz 2000; Finn 1995; Moore 1994; Ortner 1996; MacLeod 1992; Ahearn 1994). As Henrietta Moore has noted, there is an "established link between gender difference and types of agency" (1994:50) and an understanding that in non-Western cultures gender and agency do not necessarily link up in the expected "male is to female as active is to passive" (Gardiner 1995:2). Sherry Ortner has further developed this linkage in the introduction to *Making Gender* (1996), in which she addresses the question of how to think about women's relationship to a masculinist social order. She stresses that it is important to look at women as agents without assuming *either* that women identify wholly with the hegemony (and thus their agency is effaced) *or* that women are engaged in wholly different projects (and thus are not affected by the social world they live in) (16).

I agree with Ortner that it is important to avoid stumbling into these either/or traps—indeed, throughout this work I have attempted to find the very balance she proposes. Yet I think she would agree that what she is suggesting is not new, though the language needed to talk about what we are doing may be. Ethnographic approaches that looked seriously at women's lived experience and action in the world, as well as the constraints on and effects of women's action, were common well before agency jargon spread throughout the discipline.[31] Indeed, Louise Lamphere insists that one of the original impulses for *Woman, Culture, and Society* (1974), perhaps the pioneering feminist anthology, was to "delineate the ways in which women are actors even in situations of subordination" (1995:96).[32]

Among Kalasha, both women and men are hyper-aware of women's agentive power—within a society that is clearly dominated by men in many respects. The understanding that Kalasha women are "active" (following Hobart 1990, in which he defines *active* as not necessarily rushing about but "liable to act") significantly undercuts and indeed defines men's (and familial) authority over women. Women's freedom also influences the "ethos" of Kalasha social life. Finally, most Kalasha women have a sense that their lives have become what they are through the series of choices and commitments they themselves have made (although there is also a complicated mix of fatalism involved that counters this claim).

I have already addressed the way in which women's freedom extends beyond women's personal relationships and self-concepts to become a central marker of Kalasha ethnicity for both men and women.[33] In this small world, where ethnic boundaries loom so large, gender and agency are inextricably and explicitly bound up with ethnicity. It is impossible to talk about one concept without drawing in the others. Women's claims to freedom are strengthened through their ties with Kalasha ethnicity: since men see women's freedom as a marker of their own ethnic identity, they often feel compelled to support it even as they sometimes also resent the concomitant insecurity and lack of control that women's freedom brings into men's lives.

Finally, while the concept of agency has become increasingly nuanced and analytically powerful in recent works (Ortner 1984, 1996; Karp 1995; Mannheim 1995; Gardiner 1995; Hornsby 1993; Sangari 1993, among others), much theoretical literature on agency is terribly dry and distant. Recent ethnographies have begun to breathe life back into theoretical abstractions by focusing on the way agency is experienced by individuals at specific times and places.[34] In particular, I think careful ethnography can detail the culturally specific ways agency is always structurally rooted. More importantly, sensitive ethnography can show us what it *means*, how it *feels*, to live in a particular place, situation, and time and with particular others. In this book, I follow the concept that "our women are free," a compelling concern (Wikan 1990, 1992) of Kalasha people that cuts through many dimensions of their lives. In so doing, I offer a specifically Kalasha understanding of women's agency, women's freedom—freedom constrained by cultural assumptions of male privilege, by deeply felt commitments to others that make acting only for oneself impossible, and by their location in a larger geopolitical world that does not take Kalasha women's agency seriously. But Kalasha women's freedom, limited though it is, holds open a path of resistance, prevents closure, and, through this creative and constant turning over of things, contributes to the dynamism and flexibility of Kalasha culture.

Chapter 2

The Invisible Landscape

When tourists first enter Kalashadesh, many exclaim that the relaxing atmosphere of the valleys washes over them, as if the welcoming smiles of Kalasha men and women soften the air itself. Yet the landscape here—however inviting—is more complex than these idyllic impressions make it seem.[1] One dripping wet, tearful, confused English tourist was brought to my room one day. The woman said she had seen a group of Kalasha women and their infants outside of a little house across from the Exlant Hotel, where she was staying. She took her camera and went for a visit, not knowing that this was the *bashali* (*bašáli*), or menstrual house, an impure (*prágata*) space from which you can't leave without a thorough washing. The Kalasha women were not friendly and yelled at her. They insisted that she wash with soap in the cold river. She washed with her clothes on, which made them laugh—which made her cry. They even dunked her camera in the water, which made her angry. And she was ashamed, too, because she realized that she had crossed into some place where she wasn't supposed to be. Knowing something about the nature of taboos, she hoped there wouldn't be any supernatural repercussions.

The purpose of this chapter is to describe how the invisible, gendered landscape of the Kalasha valleys works and through this description to provide a concrete example of what Kalasha mean when they say women are free. As I noted earlier, most of the anthropological work done in the community has focused on Kalasha religion and ritual practices. I found, though, that the majority of Kalasha people were singularly uninspired to talk about gods and goddesses and myths, that this specialized knowledge is known only by a few experts (who are happiest to talk to you if you want to pay them) and a few custom (*dastúr*) enthusiasts (who talk and talk even when you and everyone else wish they wouldn't). But everyone is interested in one pair of cosmological concepts, the *onjesta* (*ónjesṭa*) and the *pragata* (*prágata*), which are usually glossed in English as the "pure" and the "impure." The world of Kalashadesh, as the three valleys are called, is divided into things and places that are more or less *onjesta* and those that are more or less *pragata*. There is much concern about the separation of the two and endless discussions about transgressions of the boundaries between them.

It took me a long time to come to an understanding I felt comfortable with about what *onjesta* and *pragata* mean. I spent a lot of time asking about definitions, and my "informants" were not very cooperative. They seemed basically uninterested in the questions I was asking and a little perturbed by my bone-headed persistence. "Why do you keep asking that?" they would say. "You already understand." And then they would patiently recount, you go here, you don't go there, you do this, you don't do that. And I would gasp, "I know all that, but why, why, why?" They would sigh and politely brush me off, saying, "Why don't you go ask *kazí* X [a ritual expert renowned for making up elaborate stories for the benefit of anthropologists]? He'll make something up for you." Or they'd simply say, "Here, cut up this onion."

The most thorough attempt to describe the geography of *onjesta* and *pragata* focused on what I will call the "altitude hypothesis," the idea that "pure" male things and places are located in the mountains, while "impurity" and danger emanate from women and the low-lying places associated with them and their work as the primary agriculturalists (Parkes 1983, 1990b). According to Peter Parkes (1983), the Kalasha place high cultural value on pastoralism and the "ideal" cooperative, social world men achieve while living in the high pastures. Therefore, this pastoral world and the things in it are associated with the *onjesta*, the pure. Women, because they divide the solidarity of the men who compete for them, disrupt this ideal world of unfettered male bonding and so are relegated to (and contained within) the impure, along with Muslims, outsiders, and evil spirits, who are similarly disruptive and dangerous.

While Parkes makes a compelling case, there are three problems with his interpretation for the perspective I want to develop here.

First, it assumes that men are the makers of Kalasha culture and that male values alone determine the entire cosmology that compels and organizes everyone's lives. Second, from my informants' accounts, the geography of *onjesta* and *pragata* is simply far more complex and flexible than the altitude hypothesis would predict. Finally, it is impossible to see such a system being generated by the actions of real people who use it and change it as they navigate their world.

Like the English tourist in the opening anecdote, during my first months in the valleys I also tripped over invisible, seemingly arbitrary boundaries. Determined to learn the rules of this complex, "serious game" (Ortner 1996), I visited every village and summer settlement and mapped out who could go where and when. I found that I could easily predict the broadest outlines of the *onjesta/pragata* landscape using the schema Parkes describes—generally, higher places are more *onjesta* than lower places, ritual altars and stables are *onjesta*, and areas near Muslim settlements are *pragata*, as are the menstrual house and areas where women wash, braid their hair, and so on. But I also found that the "micro" landscape—the world Kalasha people move through as they work their fields, visit their neighbors, mill their grain, wash themselves, and chase after their children—is more complicated, more finely graded, and far less predictable than these general "rules" imply. Further, the *onjesta/pragata* landscape was not static but shifted perceptibly, demonstrably, and frequently. This dynamism is not generated by formal rules or beliefs but through the daily enactment of Kalasha commitment to women's freedom.

Female impurity has often been taken as the antithesis of women's freedom in the sense that it is assumed that this identity and the restrictions that go with it are imposed rather than embraced or selected. Yet for Kalasha women *pragataness* is not a construct of denigration imposed upon them, but a concept shaped by women's own active agency. As I detailed in the previous chapter, Kalasha women's agency, which they conceptualize as being free (*azát*) or having choice (*čit*), runs through many dimensions of their lives.[2] It includes especially freedom of movement within the valley and the right to sometimes choose not to follow certain cultural expectations. Customs relating to *onjesta* and *pragata* are no exception. Rather than being defined by the *pragata* spaces with which they are associated, women define and redefine these spaces as they negotiate their identity as Kalasha women. And, as with other dimensions of Kalasha women's freedom, here, too, gendered agency is bound up with ethnicity. Attention to boundaries between *onjesta* and *pragata* spaces within the Kalasha community suggests long-standing insecurity about larger ethnic boundaries—particularly the difficult relationship with the larger Muslim world in which the Kalasha are embedded.

Onjesta and Pragata spaces

Kalasha people have very few myths that are commonly shared (Parkes 1991), but everyone knows this one: when Nanga Dehar—the greatest Kalasha shaman, an amazing *mišári moč* (man mixed with the fairies) who initiated most rituals and taboos and to whose actions you can trace most of the "whys" of Kalasha custom—first directed his people to settle in Rumbur he stood on the high passes that separate the valleys from Afghanistan. Entering a trance, he shot two arrows, one red and one black. Then he directed the Kalasha to find the black arrow and there to make an altar to Sajigor. Also called *déwa dur* (the house of god), this most *onjesta* place could only be entered by men. Where they found the red arrow, they were to make a *bashali*, which would become the most *pragata* place in the valley and would be used only by women and then only when menstruating or giving birth (Sperber 1992b:12).[3]

Men are thus explicitly associated with the *onjesta* and women with the *pragata*. The most fully *onjesta* places include the important ritual altars at all times, the goat stables during the purest time of winter, and the altar to the goddess Jestak located in the back of every family house. Also *onjesta* is the honey from domestic bees and the meat of male goats born in a Kalasha flock. Things that are special or unpredictable are also said to be *onjesta*—a double-headed stalk of wheat or a woman who gives birth to twins.[4] The most *pragata* things or places include death, the *bashali* or menstrual house, and especially menstrual blood and the blood of parturition (a euphemism for both kinds of blood is simply *pragata*). Sexual intercourse itself is not *pragata* unless it happens at an inappropriate time or place. All Muslims are considered *pragata*, and Kalasha people and places are defined as *onjesta* against the Islamic world that surrounds them. The point of most Kalasha rituals and customs is to avoid the "mixing" (*mišári hik*) of *onjesta* and *pragata* things and places since it is the careful separation of the two that fosters prosperity and fertility. Although blame for unfortunate events is usually only attributed in retrospect, the consequences of mixing are unpredictable and could include the unleashing of nasty spirits, landslides, floods, or a variety of illnesses and possessions.

In accordance with much of the Kalasha ethos, there are few absolutes and lots of gaps and cleavages that are subject to individual interpretation. Places where women never go are completely *onjesta;* the *bashali,* where men never go, is completely *pragata.* Everything and everywhere else falls somewhere in the middle. Villages, for example, are *onjesta* in comparison with the *bashali* grounds but *pragata* in comparison with the high pastures. And while the high pastures are quite *onjesta* they are not completely *onjesta* because Kalasha women go there once a year and female tourists often trek there. *Onjesta* and *pragata* spaces also shift seasonally. During the winter months, stables near villages are very *onjesta,* while during the summer months they are not. Summer lands up-valley are also *onjesta* in winter, so women do not go there then. Women quite plainly state that they are *pragata,* a comment that always implies comparison with men, who are said to be *onjesta,* although there are times when both women and men are more or less *pragata* or *onjesta.* In the menstrual house, women take care not to eat food that has been set on the floor or the beds and therefore might have touched menstrual blood. Even in the most *pragata* place in the valley then, there are still degrees of *pragataness.*

The English glosses "purity" and "impurity" are misleading because these words commonly involve judgments about sexuality, cleanliness, and relative worth in the eyes of God. In Kalasha thought, the concepts do not imply moral judgments, nor are they tied to honor, shame, or prestige. Kalasha do not rank one another, or their patrilineal clans (*kam*) in terms of relative purity. This is strikingly different from descriptions of other South Asian communities, where ideas about purity seem to organize and legitimate caste and class hierarchies.[5] Further, the prestige of individual Kalasha men is not dependent on the purity of the women in their families, in contrast to the way the status or honor of men in many Muslim, Hindu, and Christian communities is directly related to the purity, especially the sexual purity, of their wives and sisters (Rozario 1992).

Onjesta and *pragata* are explicitly gendered. But rather than simply providing cultural metacommentary on the natures of men and women these concepts seem to me to define a common project in which both Kalasha men and women are engaged: the ordering of the world such that little pockets of space are held back from the swirling insecurity and change that pushes in on them from all sides. Although this is a generalization Kalasha people themselves are not willing to make, I believe *pragata* things, including Muslims, introduce unpredictability and change.[6] An *onjesta* Kalashadesh is not one in which there is no *pragata* but rather a place where the *pragata* is managed and contained.

Onjesta and Pragata Spaces and Women's Agency

Rather than being defined by the *pragata* world with which they are associated, Kalasha women themselves actively redefine the *pragata* spaces in which they live and work.[7] Kalasha men and women experience the landscape differently and have different sorts of responsibilities for maintaining it. Men do not "generate" *onjesta* with their mere presence but through deliberate ritual action. Men have the exclusive privilege (and it does seem like a privilege) of actively attending to *onjesta* spaces by making occasional offerings and sacrifices at *onjesta* ritual altars and goat stables and at special times such as festivals, planting, harvest, or when a major transgression demands a purification. Men and women are both affected by the occasional *pragata* associated with the death of a clan member or spouse, and the observance of *šok* (mourning customs), though inconvenient, is considered a caring sign of respect for the loved one. While men deal with *onjesta* and *pragata* only periodically, women's bodies are inextricably bound up with *pragata*. Women therefore assume the complicated, everyday responsibility for maintaining the boundaries between the *onjesta* and the *pragata*. The presence of any woman in a very *onjesta* place, such as the ritual altar at Sajigor, causes that place to become *pragata*. Each woman avoids other spaces in the valleys depending on the phase of her menstrual and reproductive cycle. Women's agency therefore involves watchful awareness of where they are, what they are doing, and what state they are in.

For men, *onjesta* and *pragata* spaces and the responsibility they take for them are relatively straightforward. Men are involved in the creation or reparation of more *onjesta* spaces through blessings and prayers made with juniper smoke or the blood of a sacrificed animal.

Men can recast the geography of *onjesta/pragata* through ritual action
(e.g., by performing a ceremony whereby the *bashali* grounds are
moved so that the old *bashali* house can be rebuilt), but the landscape
does not change simply by means of their everyday movement in it.
In fact, because men move freely through the valley, the always
graded landscape of *onjesta/pragata* hardly affects their day to day
movements at all. Men purify themselves by washing before performing a sacrifice and are supposed to wash after having sex before they
enter the goat stables. Beyond this, there is for them only one absolute: men avoid crossing the invisible boundary onto the *bashali*
grounds, although there is no fear or dread about the place, only a
vague interest in its secrets and a definite interest in its occupants,
who are all the more attractive for their inaccessibility.[8]

Women's experience of *onjesta/pragata* space is fluid, local, individual—tied directly to women's bodily movements about their everyday world. Women physically navigate and organize the shifting
gray spaces between these two extremes, paying attention to where
they wash their faces and bodies, where they braid their hair, where
they go, how they dress, where they urinate, and how they deal with
menstruation. The customs women observe vary depending on location and a woman's own reproductive status. For each lifecourse event,
there is a different set of spaces to avoid and practices to follow. The
onjesta/pragata landscape is differently contoured if you are still a
premenarchal child, or a menstruating woman, have just had a baby,
have had the *ḍak bónyak* (back swaddling) ceremony for your newborn
at one month, or have had the *gul parík* (going with/to the flowers)
blessing ceremony for your infant at three or more months (which
releases women entirely from their association with the intense *pragata*
of childbirth), or if you have gone through menopause (see figs. 2–5).
Kalasha women now choose whether they will stay in the village when
they are menstruating (fig. 6) or live in the *bashali* (fig. 7). The *onjesta/
pragata* landscape is quite different for each choice.

These spaces are extremely local and always potentially change-
able. Most women know well the land that they move through every
day, but they don't necessarily know how space is organized in, say,
the next village or across the river. Most men know very little about
the intricacies of even their own property. And even women who
live together disagree about the exact layout of their land, as boundaries and associated practices are constantly changing as individual

How *Onjesta/Pragata* Space Works in Chet Guru

The *onjesta-pragata* landscape changes throughout the course of women's lives. Figures 2 through 7 are maps of part of the Chet Guru summer village, comparing spaces avoided by women during various life course events. Chet Guru lies near the river, down-valley from the main Kalasha villages and the *bashali.* The small squares represent individual families' houses (those at the top are stables), and fields are marked out with dotted lines. Women avoid crossing boundaries into areas considered *onjesta* (marked with diagonal lines) or *pragata* (crosshatched). All women, menstruating or not, are careful to avoid the ritual altar (*jač*) above the goat stables and the *ónjesta wão* at the back of each house.

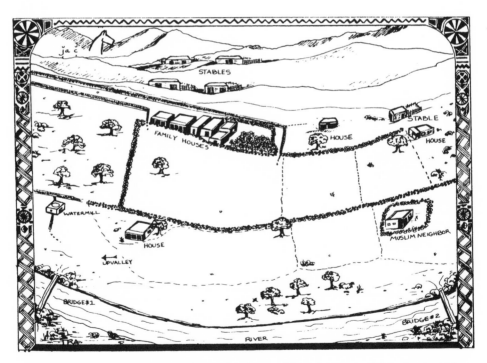

Fig. 2. Men. Men move freely about Chet Guru without having to think about which places are more or less *onjesta.*

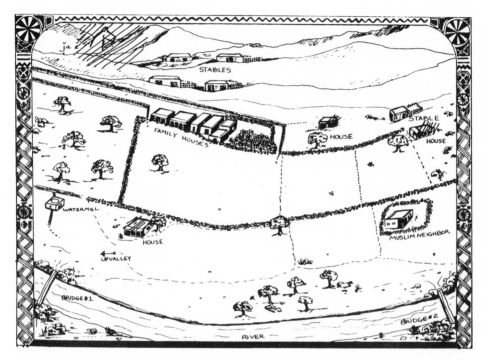

Fig. 3. Nonmenstruating women. Women who are not menstruating avoid walking above the ritual altar on the hillside (*ǰač*) and do not step across the *ónǰeṣṭa wāo* at the back of each house. All women avoid entering the goat stables above the family houses until the *istám sáras* ritual in late March, when the goddess Goshedoi (who presides over milk and the birth of baby goats) replaces Surisan (who protects the stables during the *onjesta* time from Chaumos until spring).

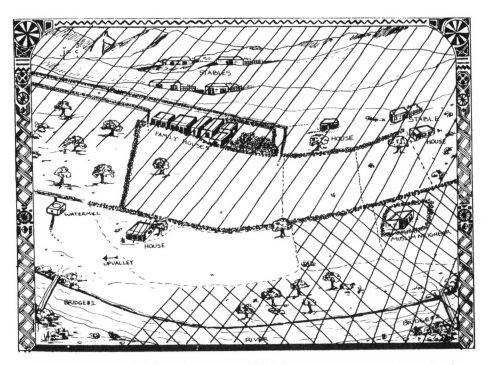

Fig. 4. Before the *dhak bónyak* ceremony. Childbirth is very *pragata,* so immediately
following the birth of a child women are careful to remain in *pragata* spaces. Women
stay in the *bashali* with their newborns for twelve to twenty days. Then, after both
mother and child have washed thoroughly and had a blessing ceremony in the *ǰéṣṭak
han* (lineage altar house), they can return home. But some places (Chet Guru is one) are
still considered too *onjesta* (indicated with diagonal lines). When a woman from Chet
Guru has left the *bashali* after the birth of her child, she usually stays at Khoshia Aya's
house (the lowest house on the map) and does not return to the other houses in the
settlement until after her baby has had the *dhak bónyak* ceremony (at about one month,
babies are swaddled loosely around their backs and given their first taste of bread and
butter). Although they stay at her house, these women are careful not to walk on
Khoshia Aya's roof. They also avoid areas considered extremely *pragata* (indicated with
crosshatching).

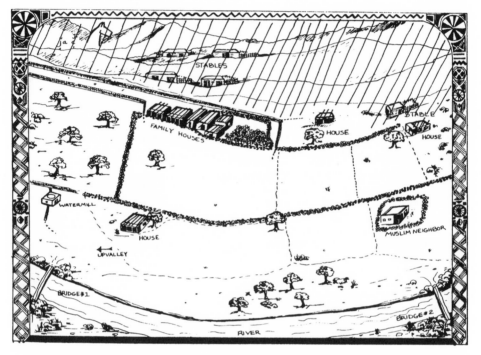

Fig. 5. After the ḍhak bónyak ceremony but before the gul parík ceremony. After the ḍak bónyak ceremony, women from houses in Chet Guru can return to their homes. They do not walk on the roofs of their houses, and they do not cross over the water channel that runs between the houses and the goat stables above. At about three months, baby and mother have their gul parík (going with the flowers) ceremony. Babies and mothers are blessed with bread and smoke. Mothers wear their special kupás headdresses. After the ceremony, women are freed of their association with the pragata of childbirth and return to the relatively unstructured onjesta/pragata landscape of nonmenstruating women.

How Menstruating Women Navigate the *Onjesta/Pragata* Landscape

Local spaces become more complicated when women are menstruating. Spaces considered *onjesta* and *pragata* change depending on whether one is menstruating or not and whether one chooses to go to the *bashali* during one's menstrual period or remain at home.

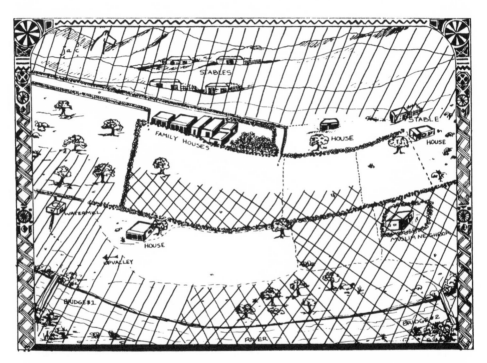

Fig. 6. Menstruating women staying at Chet Guru rather than living in the *bashali*. Women who remain at home in Chet Guru while they are menstruating are careful to avoid crossing the invisible boundaries into areas that are extremely *onjesta* (indicated with diagonal lines). They do not cross the water channel to the hillside above their houses or walk into the boulder field near the water mill (this area is vulnerable to landslides and is treated as *onjesta* as a way of protecting it), and they also take care not to walk on the roofs of their houses. They also avoid spaces thought to be extremely *pragata* (indicated with crosshatching) such as the fields beneath and down-valley from their houses and the houses of their Muslim neighbors. They move freely through unmarked areas.

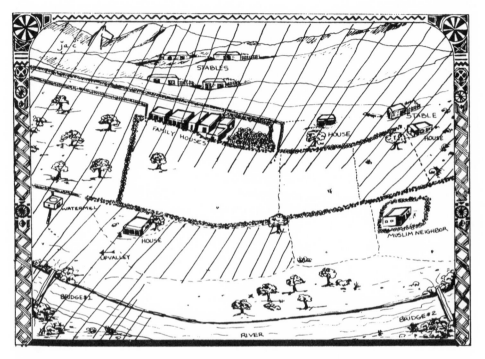

Fig. 7. Menstruating women living in the *bashali*. The *onjesta/pragata* landscape is different for women who choose to go to the *bashali* when they are menstruating (as most women do). Women staying in the *bashali* can visit or work in the unmarked fields. To get there, they walk down to the lower bridge near the mosque and near Muslim neighbor's houses (since the bridge upstream would lead into *onjesta* space and bashali women stay in *pragata* areas). The strip of field above Khoshia Aya's house and beneath the other houses in Chet Guru is disputed territory. Some women treat it as *onjesta*; others do not. For *bashali* women, the houses and fields marked with diagonal lines are relatively *onjesta* and they won't cross into this area until their period is finished and they have washed and left the *bashali*.

women reassess their relationships and responsibilities, especially as they review their desires to assert traditional Kalashaness (which is associated with careful attention to *onjesta/pragata* divisions) over the pull to "modernize."9

When women decide not to follow a certain custom, they often say simply *may čit* (my choice). The freedom women claim in other areas of their lives—in particular the right to disregard a custom or disobey an authority—is also respected here (albeit often grudgingly and with a lot of gossip). This doesn't mean that women are constantly making up the world—the broad outlines of the invisible landscape are respected by everyone, men and women alike—but it does give each woman a certain latitude in deciding for herself how far she is willing to go along with accepted norms. Rules about where one can and cannot go are not ultimately enforced by men or other women, although I can imagine extreme cases in which they probably would be. Moreover, most women say that to the extent that they do embrace customs they are "choosing" to do so.

Complicating this is the fact that the customs pertaining to *onjesta/pragata* spaces are considered the most meaningful aspect of Kalasha religion and therefore central to Kalasha identity. There is widely shared sentiment that keeping these customs well is the key to remaining Kalasha, a topic of constant concern. Kalasha men therefore find themselves in the vulnerable position of depending on women to maintain customs that are thought to keep the valleys safe and uphold Kalasha ethnicity. Men's agency involves the right to command women to keep customs, but they do not have the authority to enforce their mandates for long, nor the ability to oversee women in the first place.

The gendering of space in the whole valley is reproduced in miniature in every Kalasha household. Every house has a simple altar dedicated to Jestak, the goddess of home and family life, on the mantel on the far back wall of the house behind the fireplace. This space is called the *ónjesṭa wão*, the "pure place."10 The *ónjesṭa wão* is adorned with juniper or holly oak and sprinkled with the blood of a sacrificed goat. This same blessing is performed annually and again whenever there is a family crisis. Women never sit on or cross over the space just in front of the mantel11 because, they say, laughing, "You don't want to offend the old woman!" (By "old woman," they are referring to the goddess Jestak, although this is a play on words since it could also

refer to mothers-in-law, who tend—with a few notable exceptions—
to take these things much more seriously than do members of the
younger generation.) This means that, while Kalasha houses, which
are single rooms with a fireplace or stove in the center, are circular in
shape for men and children, they are U-shaped for women, who must
walk around the fireplace to reach a cooking pot or salt just on the
other side. (This is very convenient for naughty children, who taunt-
ingly skip across the line to evade an angry mother, who then has to
go all the way around to catch the little beast.)

Kalasha people's relationship to the spaces in which they live
seems strikingly different from Bourdieu's description of the unreflective *habitus* of a Kabyle house. Like the Kabyle house, a Kalasha house
is rich with gendered oppositions and "principles which organize
practices and representations" and point toward "procedures to follow, paths to take" (Bourdieu 1990:53). But, perhaps because the
Kalasha are constantly reminded of how different they are from everyone else in the world, their customs do not appear to them as "necessary, even natural." They are quite aware of the constructedness of
the space they live in and continually ask questions about how other
people do things, say, in India, Germany, or America. There is a
constant running conversation about how things should be done,
how they used to be done, and how they are changing. A person
dedicated to performing Kalasha customs well, like someone who
works hard and plans for the future, is called *kušuší*, a "try-er."
Houses are considered to be more or less *onjesta* depending on the
degree to which women respect the *ónjesṭa wão*, and this differs from
household to household. The effect is that customs do not become
absorbed into an unreflected habitus but are a meaningful set of traditions that must be *mindfully* practiced and therefore are conscious
statements about an individual's identity in relation to the group.

In fact, most women I talked to are inclined to agree that ironically the most *onjesta* household in the whole valley is run by a
Kalasha *šek* (Kalasha who have converted to Islam are called *šek*) called
Engineera Aya—a woman who converted to Islam over fifteen years
ago. "For me, it doesn't matter," she says, "I am Muslim, and I follow
my new religion faithfully, praying often and wearing my *dupatta*.
But my grandchildren and children are Kalasha, and they must do
their religion fully as well, or what is the point?" Engineera Aya's four
Kalasha daughters-in-law join with her in taking pride in the purity of

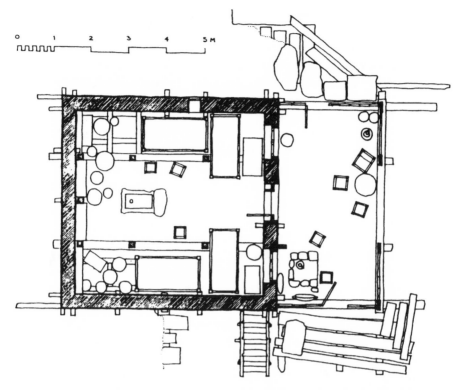

Fig. 8. Floor plan of a Kalasha house. (Drawing by John Harrison, 1995.) A typical Kalasha house. In the center of the room is a fire pit or wood-burning stove. The *ónǰeṣṭa wāo* is an invisible line connecting the stove to the back wall of the house, where there is always a shelf. Women can reach across this invisible line, but they never step across it. Small stools (*hányak*) are placed around the stove, and beds line the walls of the house. A door opens from the main house onto an open porch, where most family living takes place except in the heart of winter. There is also a fire pit on the porch, where meals are cooked in spring, summer, and fall.

their household, although they complain about it sometimes as well. The household in which the *ónǰeṣṭa wāo* is least attended to probably belongs to a Japanese woman who is married to a Kalasha man. "These old traditions," she told me many times, "are oppressive and difficult for women." She had her husband build their house with the fireplace against the far wall so that there would be no *ónǰeṣṭa wāo*. Both extremes are tolerated, "What can we do? It's her own choice," is a phrase heard over and over again.

Women are quite explicit in their assertion that *onjesta* places are not forbidden to them. "We just *don't* go there," Kalasha women insist, always using active verbs.[12] The very fact that women choose to what extent to follow Kalasha *dastúr,* or "custom," means that these practices become meaningful expressions of their identity as Kalasha women, providing a moral framework and a source of pride.

How Pragata *Spaces Feel and Change*

Understanding the affective associations women have for the place they live in, and their responsibility for it, goes a long way toward explaining why space changes when it does. *Onjesta* and *pragata* are not abstract "structuring principles" but deeply felt.

Many of the customs are quite onerous for women. Women go far away from villages and summer houses to wash their bodies or clothes or braid their hair because these are *pragata* activities and the villages are relatively *onjesta* places. In the winter, outside by the river, your hands freeze during the hour or so it takes to plait the five long braids every Kalasha woman wears. In summertime, many women have to walk miles from their summer houses and fields just to wash their faces, sticky from working in the hot sun. Once one of my older friends refused to clean out a festering wound on her foot because she was unable to walk to an appropriate location for washing. Women in the throes of childbirth walk over steep trails to get to a distant menstrual house, even in the dead of night. Women recognize that these customs are difficult and commented all the time to me about what a hard culture they have, how easy things are for me and *pátua* (their word for surrounding Muslim populations). Yet, one of my most touching memories is of watching my "aunt" wash after helping one of her daughters-in-law deliver a baby in the menstrual house. There had been a storm in the night, and a fierce wind was whipping up spirals of fallen snow. Under the circumstances, a quick splash would have sufficed. But Saras Gula Aya sat barefoot on the icy edge of a water channel, slowly and prayerfully washing every part of herself. It is hard to resist the conclusion that the very difficulty of Kalasha traditions is one thing that makes them intensely meaningful.

And yet I don't want to paint too perfect a picture. Once, when I was lamenting the demise of especially exotic *bashali* customs, my friend Gulabia Aya stopped my romanticizing. "Look, Wynne, if you like all that so much, after you have a baby, you sit naked on a rock waiting for a bird to chirp before you go outside to pee, and I'll go back to America with your husband and ride around in your car." Even though everyone would readily agree that keeping *onjesta* and *pragata* clearly separated is good (*pruṣṭ*) and indeed necessary (*zarúri*), not everyone is valiantly community-minded all the time. The fact is that these customs *are* difficult and often seem old-fashioned and impractical. When women decide not to follow them anymore, they'll often assert inconvenience as the first reason or simply say they felt too lazy (*may khalí del*). Their decisions have communitywide implications.

Because *onjesta* and *pragata* spaces are defined by what women do and where they go every day, as individual women change the way they act the way that spaces are used and marked by others changes also. This creates tension between men and women because men also have a stake in the purity of the valley but have little control over the details of women's behavior, especially regarding menstruation and childbirth. Men struggle with their desire to have more control over women, and older men especially complain bitterly, blaming every storm on women's carelessness. At the same time, most men say that they are proud of the cultural value of the freedom with which Kalasha women move in comparison with their Muslim neighbors. There is constant pushing, pulling, and reexamining, and the landscape changes accordingly.

Often, women simply change their minds about where they can and can't go, and as soon as one person breaks with convention others are quick to follow. Yasinga Aya, for example, an impish, animated woman of about fifty, decided in the winter of 1994 that it was too much trouble to move from her summer house up-valley to her winter house in the village—even though the upper part of the valley is made *onjesta* late in the fall and so should be avoided by women. Everyone was angry with her, but she held her ground. "What can we do, it's her choice" (*khē kárik, ása čit*), they all said. The next winter, four other households (among them people who had been fiercely critical of Yasing's mother) were planning to stay up-valley over the winter also, so a once-*onjesta* place would become *pragata*.

Even individual women don't cling to a particular position in the relationship with *onjesta/pragata* customs. Mayram is one of my favorite people. Her wide, easy smile makes everyone feel at ease, and her beauty is striking; she thinks so, too, and goes to great lengths to

braid her hair and wash often. After her grandfather died, she ig-
nored the instructions of older family members to wait until the next
day to braid her hair. "That's crazy (goṭ)," she said defiantly, "there's
no reason why women should have to be dirty." She took off for the
river, with four or five other women trailing behind her, shrugging
their shoulders and saying, "Well, if Mayram's doing it . . ." Mayram
often stayed home instead of going to the *bashali*, saying that it was
too difficult, too far away. But that very winter Mayram's infant
daughter died, and Mayram herself was sick continually. A few
months later, I saw her in the *bashali*. She said that before she hadn't
believed in these "old-fashioned" (ṣumber-áu) things, but after she had
endured so much loss and illness, she began to listen to her uncle—a
person she used to think was too zealous to be taken seriously. He
convinced her that she was becoming weak because she wasn't following Kalasha traditions. And it was true, she insisted. As soon as she
started going to the *bashali*, she felt much better. Now she was committed to it, she said.

When women do adhere strongly to their traditions, they are
usually motivated either by intensely felt embarrassment for things
out of place or the undeniable pride they take in protecting the landscape and people. The separation of *onjesta* from *pragata* spaces also
generates a separation between men's and women's knowledge. Men
are to know nothing whatsoever about women's reproductive cycles
or the process of giving birth. It is not that these things are "shameful" or "dirty." As long as they are kept in proper *pragata* places, they
are topics of lively conversations and joking and speculation among
women. But for a man to hear about, or, heaven forbid, see, menstrual blood or childbirth is cause for excruciating embarrassment for
things out of place, not done correctly—for the puncture in the separation between men's and women's worlds.

I was with my friend Taraki Bibia Aya when she went into labor
with her sixth child. I was very excited. Not only was it the first
Kalasha birth I would get to see, but it was the first birth I had ever
seen. Thinking it would surely be a girl (and thus slower to be born),
Taraki Bibia Aya waited until after her mother-in-law got the children
organized in the morning before telling anyone it was time to go to
the *bashali*. By then, it was too late. To her mortification, she had the
baby on the path near the village, still in an *onjesta* place and, worse, a
place where men might see. I didn't, in fact, get to see much of the

birth at all, as I was sharply posted as a lookout to warn away stray men who might chance to wander by. As she walked through the village and everyone knew that she had had a baby out of place, her embarrassment was intense, seemingly more dramatic than the pain of childbirth. When we got to the *bashali*, the first question that all women asked, even before inquiring about the health of mother and baby, was whether or not any men might have seen.

But it is not only embarrassment that compels women to embrace difficult traditions involving space. Most women also take great pride in the important role they play in protecting the purity of their land-scape. *Onjesta* places are vulnerable places, needing special care by men, who make offerings and prayers there, but also by women, who must go out of their way to do everything less casually than they otherwise might. Besides ritual altars, other locations are often discovered to be *onjesta* because they are particularly vulnerable to natural disasters and therefore in need of special protection. About five years ago, Khoshia Aya (Khoshi's mother) chose a large, convenient tree in the *daro* (a boulder-covered hillside that was the site of a long-ago flood) to urinate under when she was menstruating. Other women in the neighborhood followed her lead. But in the next storm a huge boulder rolled down the mountain, past this place and landed precariously on her rooftop. The whole family realized that the place must be *onjesta* and therefore in need of special attention. So Khoshia Dada (Khoshi's father) sacrificed a small goat and purified the area with juniper smoke. Not only did the women have to find another "pee plot," but the places where they could walk when menstruating or after childbirth changed dramatically.

Farms on steep hillsides with fragile soil, land near the river liable to be destroyed by floods, or settlements located in delicate alluvial plains vulnerable to the frequent landslides are all made pure and livable by the occasional blessings of men and the continual consideration of women. Women who live in these *onjesta* places take pride in the role they play in protecting their landscape, even vying with one another over whose land is the most *onjesta* and therefore whose lives are the most difficult. Sher Wali Khan's mother told me, "Our Dundulat (a summer settlement located in a flood plain and adjacent to a haunted forest known for scary monsters) is very *onjesta*. It is no place to be careless. My daughters-in-law and I must do everything right. If we weren't so conscientious, our summer houses, our fields,

How *Onjesta* and *Pragata* Spaces Change over Time

In 1985, menstruating women who chose to stay in Chet Guru while menstruating rather than moving into the *bashali* routinely urinated in the boulder field above Khoshia Aya's house. When a terrible landslide revealed this space to be *onjesta*, Khoshia Dada ritually purified the area with a goat sacrifice and juniper smoke. The *onjesta/pragata* landscape changed dramatically.

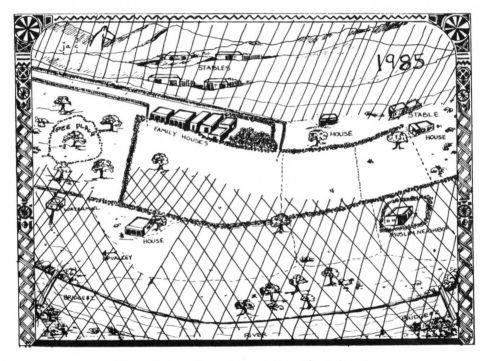

Fig. 9. Menstruating women staying at home in 1985

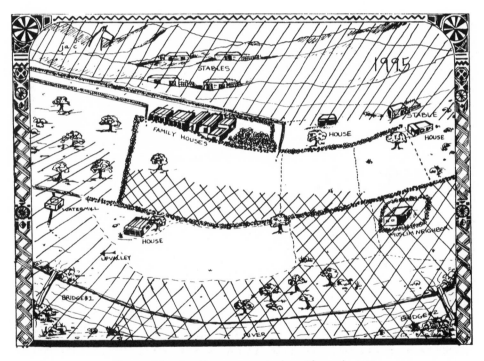

Fig. 10. Menstruating women staying at home in 1995

everything would be destroyed." "You think that is something," replied Mayer's mother, "you should see all we must do at our *onjesta* Damika [their summer home]."

So the reconfiguration of the landscape is not at present a one-way process of women giving up traditions and becoming less and less concerned with their role in maintaining the separation between *onjesta* and *pragata*. It is rather a constant ebb and flow between relaxing and reinforcing these standards.

Internal Boundaries

About twelve years ago, the United Nations International Children's Emergency Fund (UNICEF) built a new (unsolicited) *bashali* for the women of Rumbur, with a fancy metal roof and a toilet. Although there was nothing about the structure of the new building that necessitated changes in women's ritual culture, some women took this opportunity to rethink *bashali* practices. The most significant change was that women stopped thinking that they were obligated to go to the *bashali* every time they menstruated and instead began to "stay the night" (*bas hik*) in their own homes at times when leaving their children and work seemed inconvenient.

According to Sher Wazira Aya, one of several women who claimed to be the first to "throw off customs" (*dastúr hístik*),[13] the new *bashali* marked Kalasha women's entrance into a new, more modern (*onjáaw*) world. The changes were not uncontested. There was friction between men and women, according to Wasiara Aya, and also between more traditional women and the women who wanted to throw off customs, a struggle that continues today. "Some women must have started staying in the villages, and then other women followed," Wasiara Aya explained. "Men complained that women were causing floods and giving them toothaches and headaches. Men didn't say, 'now you don't have to go if you don't want to,' they said (and still say) '*dastúr kári!* (Do the customs!). But *istríža hóma dastúr púra ne kárik* (we women don't do our customs fully). Sometimes our customs are very hard on women—if she is sick, or if her child is sick, or if there is a lot of work to do and there are no other women in her house who can help her, or if she has her period for a long time, or very often, it is much easier if she can stay in her house! *khē kárik* (what can we do)?"

In fact, almost all the women I surveyed say they like staying in the menstrual house, the most *pragata* part of the Kalasha landscape (see chapter 5). Most women still choose to stay in the *bashali* during most of their periods, although they no longer have to do so. It is convenient and relaxing, because menstrual blood spilled out of place is intensely embarrassing, so staying at home requires constant vigilance and great care with menstrual rags. But it is more than just a place to deal with the *pragata*. The *bashali* is also the focus of intense female community, a chance to get away from home responsibilities for a few days, to visit friends and relatives, rest, drink tea, tell your side of the story. Still, staying home is an option many women value.

Older women say that when they were young they left immediately for the menstrual house, even in the middle of the night, at the first sign that their periods had started. The option of "staying the night" at home represents a radical departure from previous customs. Though dramatic, this change did not signify women's rejection of their responsibility for the *pragata*, only a rearticulation of it. New compensatory rules, far more complicated, popped up—not walking on the roof, for example, or eating meat from birds or animals from the high pastures and urinating in special places. These and other new customs illustrate an increasingly nuanced understanding and observance of *onjesta* and *pragata* space.

Had I been doing research before this change, perhaps I would have thought that women themselves were considered "impure" and thus, as "conveyors of impurity," had to stay in impure spaces, especially during menstruation, an "impure time." The new rules women established for themselves that allow them to stay in the village indicate quite clearly that what they are concerned with is keeping the world in balance by avoiding the transgression of *boundaries* between differently valenced spaces. The emphasis is on the invisible lines that divide *onjesta* from *pragata* spaces, rather than on the spaces themselves. As long as a menstruating woman is in the village and stays entirely within the boundaries of *onjesta* spaces, she is *onjesta*—though not as *onjesta* as nonmenstruating women (who remember, are still *pragata* in comparison with men). A menstruating woman, therefore, occupies a sort of middle ground and takes care to stay within the boundaries of places that are neither very *onjesta* nor very *pragata*.

She continues to touch other people, cook for them, and take care of her children and fieldwork. In fact, by following a series of complex paths it is possible to go most places in the valley. She avoids more *onjesta* spaces—such as the areas near goat stables or altars or, like Khoshia Aya's "pee plot" in the earlier example, places that have been proven especially vulnerable. She is even more vigilant in avoiding the boundaries that mark off *pragata* spaces. In this case, *pragata* space is explicitly defined as those places where women who *are* staying in the *bashali* *are* allowed to go. If a menstruating woman crosses one of these boundaries, she immediately becomes *pragata* and must go straight to the *bashali* instead of home. Muslim neighbors and their houses are also off limits to menstruating women who are "staying the night" at home. *Bashali* women, on the other hand, freely visit Muslim neighbors and relatives who live in accessible parts of the valley.

When a menstruating woman staying the night at home has finished her period, she crosses the boundary to the *pragata* and heads to the river, or to the menstrual house, to wash—just as women do who are staying in the *bashali*. As soon as she crosses the line, she is *pragata* and no longer touches children or other people who are still *onjesta*. She'll wash her body thoroughly, braid her hair, and wash all her clothes. She'll either wait for her clothes to dry or put on clean clothes that someone else has brought down to her (she can't touch them until she has washed or they'll become *pragata*). She is still *pragata* (and can hang out with women in the *bashali*, talking and eating) until she either crosses the boundary into more *onjesta* territory or touches someone who is not in the *bashali*. Then she returns to a landscape in which she has to be far less careful. The only places that she will avoid are the *bashali* grounds themselves, ritual altars, and goat stables.

Because the lines dividing *onjesta* and *pragata* space are so complicated, and so local, and because they change depending on whether women choose to respect them or not, these boundaries are the subject of almost daily discussion. Saras Gula Aya ranted on and on about the irresponsibility of our neighbor, who allowed her new daughter-in-law (who didn't yet know the intricate spatial patterns of our summer lands) to pass from *onjesta* to *pragata* to *onjesta* to *pragata* space on her way to the *bashali*. Surely the unseasonable rain was evidence of her reckless behavior.

Yet much of the concern over boundaries is more lighthearted than this. A favorite joke played by almost everyone is what I came to think of as the "pushing the boundaries" game. The *bashali* in Rumbur is located right in the center of the valley, on the only road, directly across from the Exlant Hotel. Boys, men, and nonmenstruating women are continually passing by and looking in to see who is there. *Bashali* women dare them to cross over, and other people make lots of playful, hesitant starts in that direction. *Bashali* women are constantly calling out to people on the road, "Come on down and drink tea with us, we've saved some for you" or "Here, have some cheese?" Often *bashali* women tease passersby by threatening to touch them (which would mean that they would become *pragata*, like the unfortunate English woman who wandered in at the beginning of this chapter, and they would have to take a bath before going up-valley again). Men often tease toddlers who are staying at the *bashali* with their mothers by calling to them and then stepping quickly away before the child can reach them.

There is, then, a running conversation about boundaries in the Kalasha valleys, sometimes serious, sometimes in fun. The constant joking about crossing boundaries marks them off as volitional—which means that the power of these imaginary, shifting lines is not only as a "rule" that has to be respected but as an option with real consequences. What makes boundaries here so powerful is not that crossing them is utterly unthinkable but that it is so completely possible.

Cultural Survival and External Boundaries

I think the attention to internal boundaries between *onjesta* and *pragata* space is in large part motivated by deeply felt concern over societal boundaries between the Kalasha and their Muslim neighbors. As I described more fully in chapter 1, the Kalasha are perhaps the most ethnically marginal people in northern Pakistan. The Islamic world has threatened to pour into the Kalasha valleys for the last five hundred years, so each conversion is magnified by a long history of fear of cultural annihilation. Today, as a tiny ethnic and religious minority in a sea of Islamic peoples who, despite their own deep divisions and differences, celebrate a common faith in Islam, the Kalasha are everybody's Other. The problem of how to secure their community from further encroachment is part of everyday discussions.

There are two reasons why ethnic boundaries are such a problem for the Kalasha. First, the edges of their culture are so near, so always visible. The Kalasha don't blend subtly into surrounding populations. You either are Kalasha, or you have said the *kalima* and you are Muslim, and there is nothing in the middle.[14] Second, ethnic boundaries are brittle, or rather they are permeable in only one direction. Conversion is a one-way street. You can leave the group and convert to Islam, but you can never return (because you would be killed by Muslim neighbors), and no Islamic person could ever convert to Kalasha (although I recently read a newspaper article claiming that a Spanish photographer has "become Kalasha"). Every conversion is thought to make Kalashadesh a little less *onjesta*.

Muslims occupy a telling structural position in Kalasha cosmology, being unambiguously *pragata*. Muslims are said to be *pragata* specifically because Muslim women don't take proper care during menstruation and also have their babies in their houses instead of going to the menstrual house.[15] As far back as anyone can remember, Muslim houses could be used as a substitute *bashali* if a woman were sick or if deep winter snow made walking impractical. *Onjesta* and *pragata* spaces are therefore defined around Muslim settlements within the valley, with the central bazaar and far lower part of the valley, where more Muslims live, being more *pragata* as well as the uppermost part of the valley where the Nuristani village is located. In preparation for the coming of Balumain during the winter solstice festival, Chaumos, men purify the whole valley with juniper and hold purification ceremonies for themselves (*istóŋgas*) and women (*siṣ áu sučék*). Kalasha *šek* (Kalasha who have converted to Islam and their descendants) are asked to leave the villages. If you touch a Muslim or a Muslim dwelling or a mosque during this time, or leave the valley, you become *amátok,* forbidden to participate in the festival.[16]

Given the position Muslims are assigned in Kalasha cosmology, I had long suspected that ethnic tension between Muslim and Kalasha lent emotional force to the understanding of the world as divided between the *onjesta* and the *pragata*. Like other things that are *pragata* (menstrual blood, birth, death), Muslims introduce insecurity and disorder into the Kalasha world; but because Muslims are not motivated to control the *pragata* or strive for an *onjesta* landscape it is a *pragata* that is doubly dangerous. Kalasha women then take on symbolic responsibility for all impurity, managing their own bodies because they care about Kalasha culture, and so the unpredictability of the *pragata* is reined in, brought in line. Maintaining an *onjesta* Kalashadesh becomes a way of maintaining Kalashaness itself. However much women may resist the considerable burden of "doing Kalasha custom," it becomes meaningful and worth doing when ethnic boundaries are threatened.

When I returned to Rumbur in the summer of 1995, my friend Wasiara Aya told me that she was really angry. There had been a small rush of four or five conversions from Kalasha to Islam over the winter. Moreover, the goats in the valley had been producing very little milk. Everyone was concerned, and the men who were *kazí* (Kalasha historians and ritual experts), who are rarely motivated to collective action, had been stirred to hold meetings and issue a bevy of proclamations in order to save their culture from extinction. The *kazí*s declared that the reason why things were going so horribly wrong was that people, especially women, were no longer keeping the old traditions: the valleys were becoming *pragata.* They decreed that this should stop. Women would go to the menstrual house every time they had their periods; women would stay twenty full days in the menstrual house after having a baby (they had been staying only twelve or thirteen days); women would not go up-valley or to the other Kalasha valleys without wearing their special *kupás* headdresses; and people would stop keeping chickens (which are associated with Muslims and traditionally avoided by Kalasha, though recently many women had begun keeping chickens to sell, so this was another decree that was directed only at them). Wasiara Aya was annoyed that she would have to start going to the menstrual house again, because she is a *kawalíak istríža,* the only woman in her house, and so has no one to take up the slack for her when she is away. And she was angry that she had to give up her chickens, an important source of income for her. "So you don't think it's all a good idea?" I asked her. Wasiara Aya, who always thinks both ways about everything, replied, "Of course it is. If we don't keep our Kalasha customs, we'll be lost. It's necessary." It wasn't so much the sacrifices she minded, she said, but rather the fact that all the responsibility fell on women's heads. "Oh well," she told me later, "things won't stay this way for long."

Doreen Massey has cleanly described space as "social relations 'stretched out'" (1994:2), a phrase that reminds me of the constantly shifting goat paths in the Kalasha valleys, which lace their way up the steep scree slopes to the holly oak forests above. Kalasha people's paths, too, are cut in scree, not in granite, and people know that they have shifted and will shift again. In large part, the invisible landscape here is volatile because of the shifting relations of power between men and women and the different gendered agencies exercised by each group. Men act on the landscape by issuing proclamations and performing rituals. Women act on the landscape by means of their physical movement through it, by the care (or lack of care) they give it. But, as this example—and indeed every other example in this chapter— illustrates, both men's and women's agencies, are, as Ivan Karp has written, "composed of elements that are contradictory, paradoxical and often conflicting" (1995). Men may make the world *onjesta* with their words and prayers, but they depend on women to maintain this *onjestaness,* and men know they have little control over women's behavior—indeed, their cultural commitment to women's freedom explicitly involves a lack of absolute control of women's behavior. Women, even as they claim the right to make individual choices, know that they never act solely for themselves because each woman's freedom (in this case her right to make choices about her commitment to "doing custom") has a tangible and lasting effect on the physical as well as the social and religious worlds of Kalashadesh.

In the next chapter, I will argue that this freedom is supported by women's valuable contributions to subsistence and the necessary freedom of movement required to get their work done.

Chapter 3

Women's Work

In the spring, after the winter snow separating the Kalasha villages from the Nuristani village up-valley has begun to melt, Nuristani women trek down to sell the *khawá* baskets they have made over the winter. These large conical baskets, made of sturdy wooden frames interwoven with alternating stripes of white and black goat hair, are used every day by every Kalasha woman, a remnant of the time when exchanges between these communities were more central to their economies. Kronza Aya bought one for me, saying that she thought I looked incomplete and if I wore my new *khawá* instead of my green nylon backpack tourists wouldn't recognize me since I would be "completely Kalasha" (*saw kaļáśa*). I felt silly and a bit conspicuous as I left to make my rounds that first day, but I was greeted everywhere with compliments on how lovely I now looked, how I now looked like a true woman (*sahí istríža*). A woman wearing a *khawá* is on her way somewhere, perhaps somewhere far away, usually either going to work in her fields or returning home with the bounty of her labor. Tucked in the basket are who knows what wonderful things, perhaps some walnut bread or pears, peaches, apples, or tomatoes. Besides being functional, comfortable, and graceful, *khawá* are thus evocative of the most celebrated qualities of Kalasha womanhood—freedom of movement, hard work, and the productivity that results from both.

Kalasha men and women do very different kinds of work, work that takes them in different directions, requires different skills, and encourages different sorts of sociality. In turn, what Kalasha women (and men, too, of course) are thought to be *able* to do is in large part understood through what they *do* do. This chapter makes one simple but fundamental point, a point symbolized for me (and also for

Kalasha themselves) by the *khawá*. The agricultural work Kalasha women do—the responsibilities they undertake in terms of production and distribution, their movement through and creative shaping of the landscape they live in, and, importantly, the value their work is accorded in the community and their own understanding of themselves as valuable, productive people—underpins (and limits) the agency women claim in other arenas of their lives.

Making a Living

Kalasha people, like most peoples carving out their lives in narrow valleys throughout the Hindukush, practice a mixed economy that combines transhumant pastoralism with small-scale agriculture. By creatively utilizing the range of resources available in their vertical landscape (cf. Brush 1977), the Kalasha are able to craft a living in an otherwise difficult environment. Livelihood practices encourage cooperation and interdependence between men and women but also a necessary division of spheres of influence. One of the first phrases I was taught in Kalasha was, *a may krom jhónim, may berú tása krom jhoníu* (I know my work, my husband knows his work). Men are almost entirely responsible for the care of livestock and for the resulting dairy production, while women do the majority of the agricultural work. As I discussed in the previous chapter, this division of labor echoes throughout Kalasha cosmology, so that ritual separation of things and places conceptually associated with men and women is one of the primary tenets of Kalasha religious life.

What Men Do

Pastoralism is prestigious because goats have social, ritual, and economic importance. The size of the family herd[1] (primarily goats, but Kalasha also keep a few sheep and cattle) is an important marker of wealth and status, and merit feasting continues to be one of the primary avenues through which men compete with one another for status within the community (Darling 1979). Goats are offered in sacrifice on important ritual occasions or during purification ceremonies, and the sacrifice of many goats is necessary for the proper funerals of both men and women. Finally, the many types of goat cheese that men produce are a source of culinary delight and the staple protein food.

Men's role as primary pastoralists leads them on a seasonal transhumant migration that begins in June when they take their herds from winter stables near the villages to spring pastures at about 9,000 feet. The high pastures, or *son,* are located above the upper tributaries of the river that runs through each valley. The pastures are the collective property of each community, with rights at particular grazing sites inherited through male lineages (Parkes 1990b:643). Women and girls accompany men on the first day of the yearly trek to help coax and carry the young animals. All women thus have some experience of the high pastures and so can join men in waxing poetic about the beauty and freshness of the mountains. Men remain in the high pastures all summer, making cheese and butter (and eating a whole lot). They graze their flocks in still higher pastures as the summer sun uncovers tender alpine meadows at 12,000 feet, returning in autumn to lower pastures as these recover late in the season. Finally, as winter edges near, snow urges them back to the villages where the animals will be fed on fodder (collected and dried by women the previous summer) and taken to graze in the nearby holly oak forests until the next spring.

In addition to their pastoral responsibilities, men make sporadic, but intense and significant, contributions to agriculture. Men are responsible for building and maintaining the elaborate system of stone water channels and wooden aqueducts that trace across the valley from the central river, bringing the water that transforms the dry hillsides into productive farmland. Corresponding with this intensive agricultural commitment, men also invest a great deal of labor in constructing new fields by clearing boulders and creating terraces. Men carry load after load of goat and cattle manure to the fields, or spread the chemical fertilizer that has recently also become common. Men plow the fields using oxen and seed the crops. Men frequently also help with the harvest and are responsible for the final separation of wheat or barley from chaff and for removing kernels of corn from the cob. Men also keep bees and harvest the honey and harvest grapes to make wine.

Pastoral and agricultural responsibilities don't involve all Kalasha men all the time. Brothers and herding partners take turns, and some men don't like the herding life and rarely participate. There are a couple of men who are master house and stable builders. One man is a full-time jeep driver, and several own small stores in the tiny bazaar in the center of the valley. There are two Kalasha schoolteachers. A few Kalasha men own hotels (though most hotels are owned by Pakistanis from outside the valley). The last twenty years have seen an increase in Kalasha boys who opt for formal education instead of contributing to herding or farm work, although there are few opportunities for educated Kalasha men either within or beyond the valleys (except as anthropological informants). Unlike Muslim neighbors, very few Kalasha men migrate out of the valleys to work. Within the last ten years, wage labor, readily available on the seemingly endless government and nongovernmental organization (NGO) development schemes, has become another important male activity, and most Kalasha men are involved in wage work periodically.

What Women Do

Men's pastoral work takes them away from the community during the summer for months at a time. When I conducted my pilot study in the valley, I was amazed at what seemed to me to be villages made up almost entirely of women. Kalasha women perform three types of productive labor: housework, childcare, and fieldwork. While much of everyday life revolves around the first two, it is fieldwork—the logistics of it, the skill involved, their acknowledged control over this domain, and the generally recognized value of their labor—that is most intimately tied to the concept of women's freedom.

Housework, or *dúray krom,* is almost entirely women's responsibility. Every one to three days, women take grain from the family stores and grind it into fresh flour at the mills that run, even in winter, on the water channels. Women do almost all of the cooking, baking *tasíli,* the staple pancakelike bread made of wheat or corn flour, three times each day. Interest in learning to efficiently and evenly spread the thin batter with the back of her hand onto a hot, convex griddle is one signal that a young girl is beginning to leave childhood behind. Women also organize some sort of side dish—usually beans, cheese, or greens—to accompany the bread. Women sweep the house, air out the bedding, do the dishes, make the tea. Women do all the laundry. Doing one's husband's laundry is one of the only domestic tasks that *wives* are expected to do (i.e., laundry is *wives'* work, not simply *women's* work). One young man in the community consistently asked his sisters-in-law to wash his clothes, and this was taken as a sure sign that the marriage was in trouble. Women also card and spin wool, weave headdresses and belts and special ceremonial clothing for men, and sew dresses for themselves and their daughters. Men's everyday clothing is made by professional tailors in Chitral.

While most Kalasha fathers are attentive and loving parents, it is the rare man who would wipe snot from a kid's nose. The minute-to-minute needs of children—for food, warmth, clothing, and washing—are taken care of by women. Child care is so taken for granted, such a constant aspect of women's lives, that I couldn't find a general Kalasha word for it. In extended families, the care of children is shared by the women of each patrilineal, patrilocal household, although each mother devotes more energy to her own children than to nieces and nephews. Grandmothers tend to be especially devoted caregivers—even allowing their categorical grandchildren to nurse at their breasts—but all the women in the house take turns watching the children so that others will be free to do fieldwork or housework. New mothers (who live in extended households) are excused from almost all other domestic or agricultural responsibilities so that they can focus their attention on their infants.

In the summer months, when the goat stables are *pragata*, women take care of the family milk cows (during the *onjesta* months of winter, men take care of the cattle). Cows are milked each morning, and the milk is boiled, then used in tea or allowed to turn to yogurt. Surplus milk is churned (in a goatskin bag by women or old men) into buttermilk, which is an important part of the diet in the summer before fruits and vegetables have ripened. In 1995, 28 percent of Kalasha families owned no cattle, but most families with no milk cows receive some buttermilk from friends and relatives.

Women have little access to cash, although money is increasingly important to the Kalasha household economy. Some women sell part of their bean or walnut crops. Some make a few bottles of wine to sell. A few older women work as traditional healers and are compensated, sometimes in cash, sometimes with food, for their services. Some women keep chickens (although they are *pragata* in Rumbur and Birir and so were banned from villages recently [see chapter 2]). As of 1997, most women still believed that the time and energy they put into their crafts were quite valuable, and so they were not willing to sell their handiwork for the bargain prices tourists find elsewhere in the country. As a result, there was only limited opportunity for women to market their textile work as souvenirs for tourists. One of my friends runs a small guesthouse, and one woman cleans the valley dispensary. One young woman, who completed her high school education in the valleys, now receives a monthly stipend from an NGO to be a women's community organizer. Any cash women earn is their own to keep and spend as they see fit, although it is a rare woman who earns as much as she needs. Men's far easier access to cash through wage labor, and the fact that money has not been incorporated into the shared household economy, is beginning to tip the balanced division of labor. Women (as well as "traditional" men who work as shepherds [*wal moč*]) are not *entitled* to a share of men's wages, as they are to the fruits of men's pastoral and agricultural work. Women increasingly find themselves dependent on the generosity of men for "gifts" of cash, and as money becomes ever more necessary I fear this dependence may increase, eroding somewhat the power and prestige women earn through their agricultural work.

At present, however, the Kalasha economy is still primarily subsistence based and women's significant contributions to the household economy are recognized as essential. Women are entirely responsible for the daily maintenance of their households' cereal crops, primarily corn and wheat but also barley and millet. Winter wheat is followed by a summer corn (or barley) crop that will be harvested late in the fall. The next year that field will be allowed to lie fallow until late spring, when it will be planted with a single crop of corn. Corn is intercropped with beans and squash. Each field must be irrigated every four to six days. Women release the water from the channel above and guide it down each row. Each cornfield is carefully thinned so that the strongest plants remain and are evenly spaced. Women frequently weed each field, and both weeds and thinnings are dried for fodder. Women take pride in this work, claiming that carefully tended fields produce much higher yields. Women keep small vegetable gardens of onions, tomatoes, carrots, and potatoes and sometimes radishes, broccoli, and okra. Women and men both participate in harvesting cereal crops. Women harvest beans and squash and walnuts. They also pick fruit as it ripens and dry apricots, pears, and mulberries for the coming winter. Fieldwork (*čet krom*) takes precedence over all other labor (except, as I noted, the care of infants). It also took precedence over my own fieldwork, which I was expected to put aside when there was *real* fieldwork to be done.

I wouldn't argue that Kalasha women's housework is "invisible" (Moore 1985:43) since it is clearly thought of as necessary "work." But (with the exception of weaving and designing clothing) most housework is simply something women do, not something they think much about or invest much of their identity in. (In contrast, Chitrali women I know take great pride in keeping their houses immaculate and cook far more elaborate meals than Kalasha women do). Women's agricultural work, on the other hand, and the fact that their responsibilities are greater than those assumed by neighboring Muslim women, is a source of personal pride for most. The intelligence and skill necessary to balance the many tasks that make for bountiful harvests, their clearly essential contribution to the subsistence of their families, the power they claim to distribute food, and the fact that they feel physically and emotionally invested in the landscape in which they live are all directly linked to the idea that Kalasha women are free. Women's agricultural work is therefore both a model of and a foundation for women's agency.

I want to describe for you one of the days I spent with the girls in my family because as I was with them I realized that even as children—a time in their lives when the line between work and play is blurred— Kalasha girls begin learning to value their freedom to move about the valley, to think of themselves as autonomous decision makers, to take pride in their work, and to see that their significant economic contributions are valued by others. (I also want to show you the pleasure they take in their lives and their obvious appreciation of the natural beauty of Rumbur's landscape. For most Kalasha people, this, too, carries over into adulthood.)

Following the girls as they took the family's sheep out to graze on the intensely new green world that follows the muddy winter did not seem like field "work" but rather pure delight. Lilizar, at twelve, was lithe, quick, and agile and not quite aware of how beautiful she was becoming. As the oldest girl in her family, she was responsible for the sheep in the spring and fall, between the seasons when they are in the high pastures with her father and uncles and the cold winter when they are kept in the winter stables and fed dried grass.[2] A pack of little sisters and cousins trailed behind her. She was clearly in charge and

ordered the younger girls around ruthlessly. For the most part, they
did what she said, just for the privilege of getting to go along. Lilizar
told me that the sheep are wholly her responsibility. She said that she
herself knows what to do with them and where to take them, scouting
out which fields have good grass and alternating routes so that no one
pasture will become too depleted. As we walked along, she repeated
every few minutes that neither her father nor her grandmother tells
her what to do with them. The sheep know the paths, and the girls
skipped along behind them, hopping up hillsides and over rocks,
shouting, "pppphhhuusshht," which the sheep know means to move
along (there is a different vocabulary of sounds for each species of
animal).

The girls seemed really happy, and happy, too, that I was with
them, so that they could point out all the potential treasures we
would find. "kutsí, kutsí, gok may mo pasháy!" they called back and
forth to one another, which means, "Morel, morel [a type of mush-
room available in the United States in gourmet food shops], don't
show me a snake." Bibi Han said that if you say these words you
won't see any snakes. Lilizar said that is stupid, since they are just
words. "You still might see a snake," she explained, but she repeated
the words over and over anyway. I was reminded of the snake penises
that Lilizar drew a few nights earlier when she was drawing pictures
in the privacy of my room. At their age, when being asked for and
given as a wife is a real and terrifying possibility, the girls certainly
don't want to see any "snakes." On the other hand, there are poison-
ous snakes around, and I was just as glad not to see any either.

The girls sang a lot. They take great pleasure in knowing this
landscape intimately. All the fields they passed belong to someone
they know, and they told me little stories about what happened here
or there, where mushrooms grow, and where you can find the angár-
bat (quartz crystals) that they speculated I could take back to America
and sell. Lilizar sharply posted the little girls at each corner of the
field, with orders to keep the sheep out of the freshly sprouted winter
wheat. She and Bibi Han took me to dig wild carrots on the riverbank.
The girls had set up lots of traps and triumphantly killed a pretty little
songbird (so much for Man the Hunter). The kids cooed over how
bright its yellow feathers were. Lilizar instructed me to put it in my
dress to take back to her baby sister.

As they hopped along, I thought about how joyful they seemed to feel, with spring newly sprung and themselves old enough to have earned the freedom that comes with responsibility. The next summer, during Eid, Lilizar's Muslim uncle specially saved one of the legs of the sheep he had sacrificed and presented it to her—a great honor for such a young girl. "It's for all her trouble taking care of our sheep," he said, and smiled at her.

Freedom of Movement

The freedom to move is integral to Kalasha women's identity. The traveling about that Lilizar and her sisters do as children will gradually expand as they grow up and take on adult responsibilities, until their range extends the length of valley and for some women into the two adjacent Kalasha valleys. For Kalasha women, kinship, marriage, and inheritance patterns are all structured so that as their circles of association widen with adulthood their agricultural responsibilities become increasingly dispersed throughout the valleys. Much of women's work involves moving from one field to the next, from your own fields to the fields of your natal family to summer fields, from the site of one harvest to the next. Of course, there is a high degree of variation among women. Some travel about daily, some very rarely. But however much any individual woman *actually* moves about, Kalasha women *think* of themselves as mobile.

It is in direct comparison with their Muslim neighbors that Kalasha women assert that they are free, *azát*. In surrounding Muslim communities, girls also act as messengers and shepherds when they are young, but the circles through which they move as children are gradually tightened as they approach puberty. Eventually, Chitrali Muslim women spend most of their time near the family house, work only fields adjacent to their houses, and leave the property only when they are escorted by a male relative and covered with a large white *piték* (the type of veil commonly worn in Chitral, a square of cloth large enough to cover a woman's head and much of her body as well).[3] Actually, the Chitrali women I know spend more time than most of my Kalasha friends visiting relatives in distant places, but the focus is on "being there" rather than "getting there." The actual journey involves a great (and exciting) effort to maintain purdah, bundling down narrow back passageways and hurrying into jeeps so as not to be seen and therefore thought shameless (*bešárum*). No matter how much Chitrali women travel, they represent themselves as people who stay put.

And yet I want to be careful not to give the impression that Kalasha women wander about aimlessly, for this would be considered very bad behavior. While for young Kalasha men "wandering" (*kásik day*) is considered appropriate and expected (although often annoying to parents and wives), Kalasha women's freedom of movement is always directly tied to *krom*—work or, more specifically, necessary activity. Visiting a friend who has recently had a baby in the menstrual house is *krom*, as is watering a distant field, helping with a friend or relative's harvest, grazing the family cows, and attending funerals and festivals. Women with "work" to do, walk openly from place to place and stop briefly to chat with both men and women they meet on the path.

Marriage expands the scope of women's *krom*, and the range and frequency of their travels extends accordingly. The complicated details and many variations of the Kalasha marriage system are expanded upon in chapter 6. Many girls are "given" in marriage when they are children. Girls marry outside of their natal patriline and eventually live in their husband's household. Most girls therefore marry into a family that lives in an unfamiliar place, often another village or valley. Leaving home is always a tearful and traumatic part of growing up. But Kalasha girls don't move into their in-laws' house once and for all. Rather, becoming established in your marital house is a long process that involves many years of moving back and forth between your natal home and your marital home. During adolescence, Kalasha girls have equal responsibilities to both families and are frequently called back to help with fieldwork or harvests at home (often the work seemed to be just a pretense to call home a much missed daughter, but, as I said earlier, movement is thought most appropriate when it is tied to work) until they are sought again by their in-laws. After girls start menstruating, their lives become even less settled, as they begin spending a week out of every month in the *bashali* (menstrual house—see chapter 4) and splitting the remaining time between their natal and marital homes.

Women retain lifelong ties to their natal families and are always considered members of their natal lineage. Female patrilineage members, *jamíli,* are notified first in case of the death of a family member and come streaming in from distant valleys and villages to mourn and help with the extensive funeral preparations. Married daughters and sisters are asked to come home to help with harvests and very often choose to spend festival times with their natal families. Bread is baked for and carried to all outmarrying daughters on feast days.

Some Kalasha women have had the opportunity to travel outside of the valleys. Many women have been to the hospital in Ayun or Chitral. Several groups of women have been down-valley to Peshawar and Islamabad and Lahore to sing and dance in cultural festivals. Recently, one girl is said to have gone to England. But most women stay closer to home.

As women grow older, their sense of personal responsibility to the household into which they married, and their children who are a part of that household, increases. Women eventually come to think of their husband's house as their house and their husband's lands as their lands. Barzangia Aya told me once, "When you are first living with your in-laws, it feels as though you are living in their house, working in their fields. But later the house becomes your own house, the fields your fields. I sometimes long for my father's house, but it is no longer his; now it belongs to my sisters-in-law, and I am a guest there." As women become increasingly tied down by obligations to care for their own children and fields, and later for their grandchildren and daughters-in-law, they have less time and opportunity to visit relatives and friends in other places. Yet, while actual time spent moving through the valleys decreases, most women still express their freedom of independent movement as an essential cultural value, both in everyday discussion and in song.

Many lullabies begin with phrase, "Don't cry my daughter [or son], I'm not going anywhere (or I'll take you with me when I go)." Even caring for children, which inevitably limits women's opportunities to move about, is thought of as a choice—women feel that they *could* go, if they wanted to, but they don't. Freedom, then, lies not so much in actuality as in possibility, in choice. Women feel that they *choose* to be wives and mothers, choose whether to stay with their husbands and families or go. Most choose, of course, to stay, but the fact that this choice is theirs to make is an essential ethnic marker, something they feel differentiates them from other cultural groups.

Women's Freedom of Movement and Agricultural Productivity

In Kalashadesh, the way in which irrigated, prepared fields are owned and inherited, and the fact that there is no tradition of hiring wage laborers to work excess land, means that women *must* be able to travel in order to tend their fields, which may be scattered throughout the valley. While tracts of uncultivated land may be held as undivided "corporate" estates of descent groups, fields that have been cleared of rocks and trees and above which irrigation canals have been built are the personal property of individual households. Sharing a house, and particularly sharing meals around one hearth (and the sharing of food resources this implies), define the Kalasha *kušún* (household) (Parkes 1997). "Ideally," Kalasha live in large, joint, patrilocal families. Only two Kalasha men in Rumbur Valley had two wives. For some time after adult children marry, all the sons and their wives and children live in the same house or adjoining houses. Daughters-in-law share fieldwork, cooking, and household tasks and help one another with child care. The zany, constant chaos (*alagúl*) of such a large family is often idealized in songs and in their image of a vibrant household as a "beehive." But the reality is that as families grow older sons and daughters-in-law become grown men and women with diverse opinions about how things should be done. Few households remain undivided after all the brothers have children or after the father dies (ibid.). Of 104 Kalasha households in Rumbur in 1995, 54 were joint families—but of those, only 11 families remained together after the adult brothers' father died. Many Kalasha households (41) therefore consist of a married couple and their young children. (In most of these families, then, there is only one woman to do housework, field-work, and child care, a point I'll come back to shortly.) Nine Kalasha households did not fit easily into these categories.[4]

Once a household is "divided" (*dur pážik*), the land, animals, and trees the family owns are also divided. Only men inherit land, and there is tremendous pressure on fathers to see that each son and his family receive an equal share of the estate. Not all land is equal, however, as irrigation, sun, soil quality, elevation, slope, and distance all mean that some parcels are more productive than others. So as not to show favoritism, land is usually split into smaller sections, so that each brother receives a share of better land and a share of more marginal land. An important aspect of women's labor then becomes traveling to and balancing responsibilities among distant fields, each of which needs to be weeded and irrigated to be productive in the harsh, dry climate of the Hindukush.

And Kalasha agriculture is enormously productive. Peter Parkes has demonstrated that Kalasha households hold on average only 0.6 hectares, less than a fifth of the average arable land reported elsewhere in the North West Frontier Province, yet they are compensated by grain harvests three or four times the yield elsewhere (1983:75–82). It is in large part the sexual division of labor in which women tend fields while men tend goats that enables Kalasha agriculture to be so productive. Animal manure greatly increases crop yield. Men transport manure in large baskets on their backs from stables and plow it into the soil before planting. Parkes has shown that Kalasha families that own large herds of goats will harvest twice or even three times as much grain as those without livestock (75). My own data show that this is still the case, even though chemical fertilizer is now commonly available. Kalasha households with herds larger than fifty goats harvest nearly three times the grain grown by families with no goats— even though these households have not quite twice as many members as households with no livestock.

Kalasha women's freedom to travel far from the home to manage disparate fields means that the allocation of household labor, and therefore the effectiveness of food production, is less constrained than in neighboring communities where women's labor (and therefore men's labor as well) is limited by their commitment to purdah. Allan has demonstrated that in Hunza, a similarly mountainous area that lies east of Chitral,

> Women cannot travel far beyond the immediate confines of the steading to work in the tiny parcels of land farther from home.

TABLE 1. Goat Ownership and Agricultural Productivity

	N	Avg. Man of Grain[a]	Household Size[b]	Adult Men	Adult Women
No goats	24	15.95	5.63	1.79	1.38
Less than 50 goats	47	24.7	6.52	2.21	1.65
More than 50 goats	30	43.85	10.53	3.5	2.47

[a]One man of grain = 37.4 kg (Parkes 1983).
[b]Including children and the elderly.

The net effect is low labor productivity, not only for women but also for children who perform minor tasks. It should be pointed out that in Hunza, under the strictures of Ismaili Muslims, women have much more freedom than they do elsewhere in South Asia, but the social constraint on movement nevertheless remains. (1990:404)

The fact that Kalasha women *can* travel beyond the immediate confines of the steading to work in the tiny parcels of land farther from home means that men are free to perform other tasks—such as herding and canal building.

Kalasha recognize that women's labor, rather than land, is the limiting variable in agricultural production. An essential part of the material basis for women's empowerment in Kalashadesh is the fact that there is commonly no use of wage labor for agriculture, so if men are going to get ahead they need women to do so. A family that holds more land than its women can work can lend land to another family (in exchange for part of the harvest), but each family depends on the labor of its own women for most of its staple foods. When coupled with the fact that, at least in Rumbur Valley, women are demographically advantaged in comparison with men (excluding children and elderly, in 1995 there were 256 adult Kalasha men and only 188 adult Kalasha women),[5] it becomes easier to understand why women are perceived—and perceive themselves—as quite valuable.

Women often commented that the yields they receive correlate directly with the amount of attention a woman can give her fields. They say the hardest lives belong to "alone women" (*kawalíak istríža*), those who are the only women in their households. Alone women have no one with whom to share the work, no one to watch the children or cook the meals while they work in the fields. Their fields suffer for this, and my friends would shake their heads with pity when we passed Khana Aya's corn, which was noticeably stunted compared to theirs. It is not only sexism that makes both women and men yearn for sons, for sons mean daughters-in-law, daughters-in-law mean more women in the house, and this means prosperity. I wish that I had thought to test this empirically, for measuring the yields between the fields worked by a woman alone and fields in which the responsibility was shared would have been straightforward—and interesting to the Kalasha as well as to me. However, a comprehensive economic survey of all Kalasha households in Rumbur Valley[6] showed that households that produced enough grain to meet their consumption needs had an average of 2.24 adult women (defined as a woman who has begun menstruating), while households that bought grain had an average of 1.71 women.

Women themselves recognize that it is women's industry and self-motivation that allow a family to have a comfortable, even a beautiful, life. Women who can't work well, like Zar Begima Aya, who has been sick and weak for years, continually apologize for themselves and express sadness at not being able to work as hard as they would like. "Ah, sister," she would sigh every time I visited her, "You should have seen me before I was always ill. Oh how I would work! Up at dawn every day. My corn—how tall it grew! Now, look, my daughters have to do everything." Of course, not all women like to work, although those who don't come in for sharp criticism by other women (and men as well). Hard work isn't the only way Kalasha women gain respect in the community, but it is directly connected to women's identity.

I remember asking Saras Gula Aya about Bibizara Aya, a quiet and serious older woman who had been brought in as a second wife to Takat Jana Dada after his children were grown. It was rumored that Takat Jana Dada and Bibizara Aya were in love when they were young. She married another man, but only had one child, a daughter. After her husband died, she came to live with Takat Jan's family. I wondered if Takat Jana Aya, a woman with a notorious temper, was jealous of her cowife. "Why should she be jealous (*kháča jhoniú*)?" I was told. "Bibizara Aya does so much work for them. Takat Jana Aya knows lots of words [she is a renowned composer and has an equally

TABLE 2. **Number of Adult Women per Household and Agricultural Productivity**

	Households	Avg. Number of Women per Household
Purchased grain[a]	67	1.71
Did not purchase grain	33	2.24
All Kalasha households	100	1.9

[a]Of 104 Kalasha households, 3 consisted of single men who did not buy grain but lent their fields to relatives and received a portion of the crop. One woman lives alone and receives all her sustenance through begging from friends and neighbors. These 4 households are not included here. Also not included are households of converted Kalasha, 9 out of 10 of which purchase grain.

renowned sharp tongue], but Bibizara Aya only knows how to work [meaning that she can't defend herself verbally against her cowife, but she doesn't need to because she works so hard]." She said that before Bibizara Aya came to live with the family they had nothing. Now, thanks to her hard work, the family has every good thing— "fruit, corn, wheat, tomatoes, pumpkins, every good thing comes to this family now, and all because of her hard work." Saras Gula Aya recalled that one year Bibizara Aya didn't come to her husband's house, choosing instead to stay in Bumboret with her daughter. That year again there was nothing. Takat Jana Dada was angry and blamed his first wife for chasing her off. The next year they talked her into coming back. Indeed, Bibizara Aya spends the summers alone on the family's summer lands, far from Takat Jan's main house, and does all the work herself, even the harvesting. Over the course of the two years I lived in Rumbur, four different women told me her story, always adding that her work had brought prosperity to a struggling family.

It is not simply the fact of working hard and being productive that is important to Kalasha women but that women's work involves considerable skill and judgment. Just as Lilizar asserts over and over that no one is telling her how to shepherd her little flock, so do adult women prize their autonomy in food production and distribution. Despite the fact that land is inherited only by men and held in the name of the father, in the Kalasha families with which I am most familiar it is the women who orchestrate the complex dance of producing and storing food over the summer and stretching their stores over the long winter.

In the summer, Saras Gula Aya worked twelve hours a day, rising an hour before dawn so she could avoid the heat of the sun at midday. She would water or weed for three or four hours before one of her grandchildren brought her breakfast of salted milk tea and cornbread to eat in the field. Only when the sun was directly overhead would she return to the house, where she would invariably find some other work to do. Her daughters-in-law complain that she works even when everyone else sleeps. Saras Gula Aya is far-sighted in her approach to farm management, thinking in the spring about the summer and fall, and in summer about the winter, and launching such projects as a tree nursery, which will take years to bear fruit. She does more than her share of the unpleasant work rather than assigning those tasks to someone else (although she surely has the authority to do so). "How can I sit still and do nothing?" she always asks, "I have so many things to take care of—here are my tomatoes, there my corn, here the cows, there the trees. If I don't remember, no one else will."

On one particularly long day, Nizara Aya and I were pulling grass from beneath a forest of tall corn plants. We'd carry it to the roof of the stable, where it would be dried for the cows to eat in winter. I looked despairingly at the small patch we had cleared, and the endless sea before us, and lamented, "We'll never be able to finish all this. Look how much there is!" "I know," Nizara Aya sympathized, "My sisters [husband's wives] and I thought that, too. 'Let's wait until after the harvest when this will be much easier,' we told *isprés* [her mother-in-law]. But she said that Mohammed Aya [their Muslim neighbor] would get all excited seeing so much grass and come out here and pull it up herself to feed to her own cows." Anyway, "what could we do?" she sighed, since the work in the fields was organized and directed by her mother-in-law, who would do it all herself if they balked. She told me that she and the other daughters-in-law know how to do some things themselves and often make suggestions or take responsibility for smaller projects—Bayda Aya, for example, always plants the vegetable garden. But her mother-in-law has final authority, and no one ever contradicts her, including the men. She also directs their work in the fields, telling them when it's time to harvest and plow and plant. "What do our men know about the fields?" Nizara Aya asks, adding, "They always look to their mother also."

Distribution

Gulsambar is one of my favorite Kalasha children, as difficult as she is delightful, and I learned a lot by watching her grow up. When I first came to the valleys, she was about four years old and prone to the most outrageous temper tantrums. She would cajole and whine, *"may de, may de"* (give it to me, give it to me), and then start crying and screaming to get whatever she wanted—walnuts or fruits or bread or sugar, especially sugar. And she wasn't satisfied with her "share"—she wanted *all* of *everything*. Tired of listening to her, her mother would give in and hand it over. Gulsambar would sniff, wipe her tears on the sleeve of her dress, and break into a wide grin. Then she'd cheerfully redistribute her hard-won loot, saving only the littlest bit for herself. I realized that already Gulsambar had learned the power of distribution, an important responsibility of adult Kalasha women.

Linked to the beaded necklaces that are so symbolic of Kalasha womanhood (chapter 3), women carry enough keys to make any janitor jealous. In addition to the keys to the family house, women carry keys to the *pastí* (wooden sheds for storing food), the *gonj* (storeroom) in each house, and numerous trunks. Although staple foods are shared by the whole "house," the woman of each nuclear family has her own private, locked space where she keeps special foods: pears, apples, dried apricots, wine, gifts from friends or natal family. Young wives have small trunks that are usually given to them by their natal family when they first marry. Husbands (never anyone else) build wooden storehouses for their wives after they have a couple of children. Having your own shed is an important symbol that a marriage has stabilized, that the young couple has begun to think of themselves as a unit in some ways separate from the larger family.

Each woman decides what will be eaten when and what will be given away, doling out treats to husbands and children and calculating which foods will be needed for special events—the birth of a child, festivals, visitors—as well as saving something for unforeseeable crises such as funerals. Men borrow and return keys to the storehouses, but they rarely carry them themselves. Allocating resources is a difficult job. Fall is a time of seemingly unlimited abundance. Wine flows, pears, apples, apricots, and walnuts drop from the trees, and children beg continually for *čičílak* (roasted corn). But the fall harvest has to be stretched over the rest of the year to avoid a hungry springtime. In addition, relationships between women and between families are continually shored up by the flow of gifts of food. The Kalasha pride themselves on being generous, and it is important never to appear stingy. Yet the line between giving all you can and saving what you must is pencil thin.

When I was recording the contents of Lilizara Aya's storehouse in late winter (one pear, three bottles of wine, a small sack of walnuts and a bunch of empty baskets), she told me some folklore that she said originally came from the Nuristani village at the end of the valley. Because the Nuristani village is at a higher elevation, colder winters mean that the water canals, and thus the mills that they power, freeze, so Nuristani women calculate and grind the flour they'll need for winter in the fall. One young woman could never seem to make her flour stretch until spring. Every year she tried to be more careful, and every year she would fall short and her family would be hungry for several weeks. A wise old woman offered to watch what she was doing and tell her how she could improve. After observing her work for several days, the old woman noted that the younger woman would taste a small pinch of flour to see if it were rancid before she made it into bread for her family. This small amount, stretched over the year, accounted for the shortage every spring. While surely mythic, the story captures the seriousness with which women take their responsibility to ration food for their families over the long winter.

Control over food distribution requires skill and discipline and is an important area of autonomy that women claim for themselves. Mizoka Aya told me that when she fought with her husband it was inevitably because he thought she was too generous with their produce. She would never agree with him, she said. She knew how much they need and how much she could share. It was her "choice" to whom and how much she would give.

As Friedl points out (1975), and as four-year-old Gulsambar had already discovered, control over the distribution of food is an important power base. Like Gulsambar, Kalasha men also realize that control over the distribution of food is a powerful position. Men usurp this responsibility (along with the cooking) on prestigious ritual occasions.

Women's Work and Their Connection to the Landscape

Women's work and responsibilities tie them emotionally as well as physically to the land into which they pour their creativity and dedication. Women feel deeply connected to the landscape and see themselves as crafting it through the generations. That only men inherit land is a technicality—something taken for granted and not worth talking about. Women see fields and houses as their own. At first, a young wife talks of her "husband's" house and lands, but years of labor and deepening social connections transform it into her own. These are "my" fields, "my" cows, "my" house, "my" grassy spot, women assert. Bayda Aya's husband is a jeep driver, a prestigious occupation that means that he is rarely home. He suggested that they sell their land in Rumbur and move to Bumboret to live near her natal family since he spends almost all of his time in the larger Kalasha valley. (It would be an unprecedented thing to do.) Bayda Aya refused. Later she commented to me, "It's strange. Since I first came here ten years ago, I've been so homesick and dreamed always of going back to Bumboret. But now I think that my place is here, my children's place is here. This place is in my body."

The stories women tell about places involve chains of women who worked the land and the changes each made. One of the most beautiful places in all of Rumbur is Sanduriga, a small, high, side valley with lush summer fields and a commanding view of Palar Mountain. After I returned from a visit, I told Saras Gula Aya about what and whom I had seen there. She said that she hadn't been there herself in thirty years. Her father used to have a tiny piece of land there. They would plant corn, and she would go back and forth to weed and water and harvest. At that time, there were very few summer houses, and women walked the steep five-mile trek every day. ("How soft women's lives are now!" she commented.) She began describing the land to me—where the pastures were and the grassy places for sitting and where the tall cedar trees were and who had how much land. As she talked, she named the women who were there then and remarked on what contributions each had made. Many of the women are dead now. She remembered what a hard worker Gillian's grandmother's mother-in-law had been and how Gillian's grandmother had taken over for her and made improvements also. She remembered how Nurshadin's mother's place was nothing but cedar trees and a little scrubby corn. There was no house and no stable. Nurshadin's mother herself had planted all those fruit trees to make a fine orchard and a beautiful little grassy spot (*bronzíkik*) where you can lie back and see all the mountains. For Saras Gula Aya, even though the land is passed patrilineally from father to son, the changes in the landscape call back memories of the chain of women who lived there, molding the land as they made a living for their families.

Chet Guru, our family's summer land, changed remarkably even in the short time I lived there. One day Saras Gula Aya and I were sitting on a stone wall, watching her sons break up a huge rock with dynamite. It was backbreaking labor. The rocks were carried to the edge of the field where the master builder was constructing a wall. Later they would fill the wall with dirt, level it, and make a flower garden—a concession the younger generation has finally won from their mother/mother-in-law, who says, "Since you can't eat flowers, why plant them?" I said to Saras Gula Aya, who is about sixty years old, that it was amazing to think that only forty years ago Chet Guru had looked so different. This pleased her. She told story after story about how in her in-laws' time there had been nothing—just some fields that were not very productive because you had to plant around so many rocks. There were no walls, no houses, no fruit trees and only two walnut trees. She pointed to each of the walls and remembered which field had been cleared to build them. She showed me the tree under which her husband's mother used to cook. She showed me where there had been a little hut where she would stay the night with her children in the summer when there was too much work to walk all the way back to Kalashagrom in the evening. With a little ingenuity and patience, they had made this place beautiful and productive. She walked me around from tree to tree, telling me who had planted each one. The oldest ones were planted by her father-in-law but the others by her or by her sons on her instructions. She said that she missed her father-in-law. "He gave this land in my children's father's name," she said, "but I feel that he gave it to me in spirit."

As Marx has argued, in any division of labor human potential is carved up as each individual assumes identities and capacities associated exclusively with his or her particular sphere of activity (1965:45, quoted in Giddens 1971:63). Kalasha women's agricultural work demands the capacity to assume near total responsibility for day to day maintenance of the farm. The capacities and identities associated with Kalasha women's work—the decision-making ability required by their work and the freedom of movement demanded by their disparate obligations, autonomy, foresight, and creativity—form a template for agency in other arenas of their lives. The following chapter deals with the way in which Kalasha commitment to women's freedom and choice (and the tacit comparison to women from neighboring Muslim communities such an identity implies) is made manifest through Kalasha women's fashion.

Chapter 4

Fashion

Most Pakistanis as well as foreign tourists in Pakistan easily recognize Kalasha women's dress, although they are likely to know little else about Kalasha culture. The Pakistan Tourism Development Corporation plasters airports, travel agencies, and hotels with pictures of dancing Kalasha women. Everywhere in the country you can buy poor quality postcards showing Kalasha women and even poorer quality imitations of their headdresses. A popular Pakistani pop band recently made a rock video featuring women dressed in Kalasha outfits. The Kalasha themselves recognize that their dresses are strikingly beautiful and original—possibly the most beautiful way of dressing in the world, women often add. I was often told that I should wear my dress in America and charge for pictures. "Don't just wear it," Iran once added, "Make a film and charge money if people want to see it. Then later you can make another film and charge them again." "Don't be silly," her mother responded, "everyone would fall in love with her. Think how much trouble that would be."

The last decade has seen a resurgence of interest in the anthropology of cloth and clothing (cf. March 1983; Schneider 1980; Weiner and Schneider 1989; Schevill et al. 1991; Heath 1992; Tarlo 1996). Within South Asia, the importance of clothes is by no means unique to the Kalasha. Indeed, clothes play such an essential role in South Asian identity politics that Gandhi placed the issue of what to wear at the center of the struggle for Indian independence (cf. Bayly 1986; Bean 1989; Tarlo 1996). Yet outside of museum literature there has been surprisingly little regional academic attention given to the problem of what people wear and why they wear it. In her wonderful book *Clothing Matters* (1996), Emma Tarlo redresses this gap in the literature. She suggests that the birth of fieldwork coincided with the marginalization of dress in Indian anthropology "because at the precise moment when anthropologists developed close personal contact with the people they studied, they ceased to pay attention to their clothes" (4). Further, she argues that it is partly because clothes are so *obviously* important as markers of social and personal identity in India that they have been so little discussed. Since the 1970s, as more women anthropologists have gone to the field, clothes have begun to reappear in ethnographic accounts of South Asian life.[1]

Throughout this chapter, I have chosen not to use the word *costume* because it carries implications of exotic otherness, of "dressing up" (for Halloween or a play, for example) and of fixed, unchanging, tradition-bound forms (Joyce Flueckiger, personal communication). None of these connotations is appropriate for Kalasha women's clothing, which is a dynamic and personal expression of both individual and collective identity. Instead, I think that the word *fashion* (with its connotations of fashioning or making, its associations with self-expression) better captures Kalasha women's sense of personal investment in the clothes they create and wear.

Susan Bordo has offered a powerful critique of what she has called the "general tyranny of fashion" in the lives of Western women—"perpetual, elusive, and instructing the female body in a pedagogy of personal inadequacy and lack" (1993:254). Kalasha women do not seem to suffer from the sort of body image tyranny that Bordo describes. They are not marketed to, so inspired changes in women's clothing really do represent a form of "self-fashioning." Also, one wonderful thing about Kalasha women is that their standards are not impossibly high, so they are relieved of the perpetual inadequacy many Western women feel. Kalasha fashion therefore offers more room for play, for "fashion" in the sense of process, of crafting.

However much fun, the game of Kalasha fashion is also serious. Women's elaborate clothing and jewelry are central markers of Kalasha ethnicity, both within and beyond the community. While many other aspects of their traditional culture—rules about marriage (see chapter 6), merit feasting (Darling 1979), religious rituals (chapter 2), and so on—seem to be relaxing, women's dresses are becoming ever more elaborate and central to the Kalasha identity as a unique people. While her clothes may all look the same to outsiders, in fact each woman's dress is both an important expression of her individual identity and a manifestation of important cultural values. Her choice of colors, combinations, and patterns, the amount of decoration, and careful attention to detail allow for her creative expression of self. Yet the result is a constellation of features that is also an evocative symbol of the identity of the Kalasha collective. Through their continual attention to and elaboration of their dress, Kalasha women are not simply "wearing" ethnicity but are actively involved in making culture.

Heaven Is in Our Braids: Women's Clothing and Kalasha Identity

The process of identifying "Kalashaness" with Kalasha women's clothing begins at birth. Kalasha babies spend the first three months of their lives firmly swaddled because, their mothers say, babies scare themselves with otherwise spontaneous flailing of unorganized arms and legs. Infants are held and talked to continuously and nursed whenever they pucker their tiny mouths into little Os, a sign that they are looking for the breast. Babies' faces are often decorated with a black paste made of burnt goat's horn, which protects them from cold in the winter and sun in the summer and is thought beautiful. Cradled in the ample black folds of their mother's dress, they must see her face, and the faces of the women and children nearest her, their beads and headdress making familiar bold patterns in the flickering firelight against the blackness of the soot-covered ceiling above. As they get a little older, they are released from their swaddling and begin, with both hands and feet, to grasp Mom's beads while they nurse. A crying baby is distracted by the subtle clicking of the glass beads and jangling jingle bells of a woman's headdress. A fussy toddler will be given a hank of beads to play with. Kalasha babies were usually happy to let me hold them when I was dressed as a Kalasha woman, yet would cry when confronted with the strangeness of my Western T-shirt or the *shalwar kamiz* (the long shirt and baggy trousers that are the national dress of Pakistan) I sometimes wore. From the earliest memories of every Kalasha person, beads, headdresses, and black dresses are associated with mother, with women in general, and also perhaps with self and safety and comfort.

During the *gostník* ceremony that takes place during the winter solstice festival, boys and girls aged two to three years are dressed for the first time in traditional Kalasha clothing by their mothers' brothers. It is an important moment in which children are recognized for the first time as members of the Kalasha community.[2] The clothing is provided by the mother's brothers' (*móa*'s) family, and the children are supposed to be dressed by a man in that category (although in many cases the toddlers refuse and are dressed by a female relative instead). Most Kalasha children enjoy lifelong relations of reciprocity and warmth with their mother's natal family and think of this as a special place where they are loved and supported, given lots of gifts, and disciplined very little. Girls receive beads from aunts, grandmothers, and friends of their parents and wear their headdresses for the first time. Girls are thereafter dressed every day as little replicas of grown Kalasha women. Boys and men, however, are indistinguishable from non-Kalasha men of surrounding communities. Within the last forty years, men have discarded their own distinctive dress (except for special occasions and burials) and now wear *shalwar kamiz* and Chitrali caps, the regional mens' dress of northern Pakistan. Men therefore move easily from the valleys into the surrounding world, while women carry all the distinguishing physical markers of Kalasha ethnicity.[3]

When I first came to the valleys, I tried as best I could to explain to the family I lived with what it was that I was doing. "So much has been written about Kalasha men," I started, "but I want to write about what Kalasha women do, what they think about." "Ha," laughed Lilizar's father, "I can save you a lot of trouble. Beads. Kalasha women think about beads." Men love to insist that beads are worthless and women's desire for them is purely frivolous. Everyone, including Lilizar's father, laughed as Lilizar's mother retorted, "Don't listen to him, sister. Kalasha men like beads, too. Any old average woman, who can do nothing special but manages to string a few beads together, looks really beautiful to men."

In fact, every Kalasha woman does far more than string a few beads together. Twenty years ago, women wore heavy woolen dresses that they made from the wool of black sheep, carded and spun over the long winters. Older women marvel that while more and more basic materials are bought with cash rather than made by hand the work of making women's clothing seems to take as much time as ever—it just gets more complicated and elaborate. Currently, women's dresses are made with eight to ten yards of black cotton cloth, heavily embroidered with interlocking designs (done with a hand-turned sew-ing machine) around the neck, sleeves, and bottom with skeins of yarn—neon orange, yellow, pink and blue are the latest rage. The dresses cover women modestly from wrist to ankle, and are drawn up with a thick woolen or yarn belt that wraps three or four times around the woman's waist. The belt is handwoven and brightly decorated, with long fringes that accentuate the neat pleats of the dress. The excess material from the dress is bunched over the top of the belt, forming a large pouch (*wéi*) in which all manner of good and useful things can be carried and hidden.

Around their necks women wear as many as fifty hanks of color-ful glass beads, each hank consisting of four to eight strands. A woman's bead collection may weigh as much as fifteen pounds, and she wears it every day. For special occasions, even longer and more elaborate sets of beads may be added. Red is the classic color, but yellow, orange, and white are currently popular also.

Each woman has two headdresses. The small one, called a *susútr*, is a woven circle of black sheep's wool, which balances on the back of the head, and has a long strip of material that runs down the length of the back. It is heavily beaded with rows of glass beads, buttons, and bells. Circling the crown are two rows of fine cowrie shells divided by small chains and accentuated by beads. The *susútr* is worn all the time, except when a woman is sleeping at night. Women feel naked without their *susútr* and even reach for it when they sit up at night to nurse their babies or stoke the fire. Each *susútr* has a distinctive jingle, and after a short time I could guess who was walking by my window by the sound of the jangling gait.

The larger headdress, called a *kupás*, balances on top of the *susútr*. It is made of a wider strip of wool, again, the blackest possible, and decorated with five hundred or more cowrie shells, as well as beads, buttons, bells, and medallions. It is topped off with a large pom-pom, which is usually red or, more recently, neon orange. The *kupás* is worn for special occasions such as festivals and trips to the other valleys. It is also worn when visiting an especially "pure" place, when one is in mourning, or simply to keep the sun off when working in the fields on a hot day.

Every Kalasha woman wears five carefully plaited braids—two in the back, two on each side, and one on her forehead that she tucks into her *susútr* or behind her right ear. Girls start growing a forehead braid when they are about two years old, add braids in the back at around seven, and begin letting all of their hair grow as they near adolescence (leaving them with a couple of years of unruly hair that sticks up every which way, despite the constant attention inspired by these teenagers' budding self-consciousness). Beautiful, thick, long braids are much admired, but neatness is the most essential quality. Braids should be precisely divided, tightly plaited, with no hair out of place. Women replait their hair every four or five days in the summer (braids start to get "fuzzy" after several days), spending a relaxing hour at the river washing and stiffening their braids with the resin from Russian olive trees (a precious resource, usually collected by children as gifts for mothers or aunts or grandmothers). In the winter, the whole process waits much longer—even my own vanity waned at the thought of washing in the icy river in February.

A Kalasha woman who converts to Islam immediately cuts her hair and adopts Muslim dress. Guliara Aya's sister was madly in love with a young *šek* (his father had converted to Islam, so he had been born Muslim). Against the wishes of her family, she converted so that she could marry her lover. Guliara Aya told me that her sister stoically resisted attempts by her family and friends to change her mind and proudly recited the *kalimah* ("There is no God but Allah, and Mohammed is his prophet"). But she sobbed as she gave her beads and headdresses to her sisters and friends. Holding the hank of beads her converted sister had given her ten years ago, Guliara Aya said, "When I think about these beads, *may neasálak híu* (I have no desire to "be"—a phrase that refers to an empty, indefinable state of longing). She said she knew as soon as her sister took them off that she had really become Muslim and that while she only lives a fifteen-minute walk down-valley they would no longer dance together at festivals, travel together to funerals in other valleys, or walk to their father's summer land to harvest pears.

Women's dress does more than mark *women* as either Muslim or Kalasha. There are continual reminders that women's attire is an important way—perhaps even the most important way—in which the entire Kalasha community marks itself off from surrounding populations (cf. March 1983; Smith 1995). One young woman scandalized the community by posing for photographs in a *shalwar kamiz* for her Punjabi suitor. Last spring several *kazí* (religious leaders) tried to forbid women to wear shawls that cover their dresses and headdresses,

Fig. 11. A Kalasha *ṣuṣútr*. (Drawing by Ken Hall.) Each
woman wears her *ṣuṣútr* all the time, hanging it on her
bedpost while she sleeps so that she can put it on if she
needs to get up in the night.

Fig. 12. A Kalasha *kupás*. (Drawing by Ken Hall.) The *kupás* is
worn on top of the *ṣuṣútr*.

though a shawl is a practical and popular accessory in the cold winter. "We are not Muslim," explained one ritual elder, "and our women should not cover themselves." Another striking example happened one day when I stumbled onto a conversation between my neighbors and a local Muslim man who claimed to have talked two Kalasha girls from Bumboret into converting. The subject of conversion led inevitably into a conversation about heaven, since in the view of most of the more fundamentalist Muslims in the vicinity the Kalasha will go straight to hell unless they embrace Islam. "Heaven," declared an older Kalasha woman, "is in our braids! If it weren't, why would you all fight over them?" I confessed my confusion, and they explained that local Muslims think that the possession of a converted Kalasha woman's forehead braid (which is cut when she converts to Islam) guarantees that one will "see heaven."

Fashion and Agency

It's easy to fall into the assumption that women's clothing is a conservative holdover from an exotic past, to see Kalasha men as cultural innovators while women plug the dike against the potential flood of modernity. But you don't have to live in the Kalasha valleys long to see that this is wrong. Far from being a static, conservative form, women's dresses are continually evolving—changing so fast, in fact, that my own dress was rather embarrassingly old-fashioned after only two years in the field. Through their continual attention to and elaboration of their dress, Kalasha women are not simply "wearing ethnicity," not just representing it, but are actively involved in making culture (cf. Douglas and Isherwood 1996; Tarlo 1996). As Janet Berlo suggests for Maya women of highland Guatemala and Chiapas, Mexico,

> In many regions, textile work is central to being female. It is the arena where a woman's individual creativity and technical expertise join to express cultural norms. . . . Cloth makes manifest deeply held cultural values that may otherwise be imperceptible. In fact, it may be women's very crucial job to translate these ephemeral values into material objects. (1991:440)

Through the ongoing practice of crafting dresses, Kalasha women make manifest three cultural values, each of which marks them off as distinct from their neighbors. Women construct their clothes in such a way as to heighten their visibility, thus effectively proclaiming their right to be seen in a region where most women embrace the symbolic invisibility of maintaining purdah. Second, the combination of individual women's creativity and the continual drawing in and reworking of ideas and objects from outside the valleys makes women's fashion a continuously evolving form, reflecting the dynamic flexibility of Kalasha culture generally. Finally, each woman's clothes are made of materials and labor given by friends and relatives and so are more than an expression of her identity as Kalasha but also a physical representation of her intimate social world.

But before we get too serious it's important to remember that most women find the making and wearing of their dresses fun (which is not to say that it is not also a lot of work). Lilizar's father is right that techniques and strategies for acquiring the necessary beads and shells and cloth are among women's most passionate topics of conversation. I think many Kalasha women would agree with Elizabeth Wilson that "we consistently search for crevices in culture that open to us moments of freedom. Precisely because fashion is at one level a game . . . it can be played for pleasure (1985:244). Kalasha people love to laugh, dance, and drink wine. Women's dresses are characterized by this same sort of relaxed exuberance. Women put enormous amounts of creative energy, time, and resources into crafting their clothes. Very little about women's dress is sensible—it is too heavy, and getting ever heavier, too expensive, and growing more costly every year. They like to take fashion risks, trying out new patterns and colors. Old women as well as young take immense pleasure in being beautiful—not just for festivals but every day.

Visibility

During my fieldwork, I won the Louis Dupree Prize for promising fieldwork in Central Asia. In an effort to share the reward with the members of my family, my husband and I rented a jeep and took five of my Kalasha sisters, two brothers, Lilizar, and a collection of toddlers to a nearby valley that was renowned for its hot springs. I was surprised at my impulse to hustle my friends into a private hotel to avoid what Doris Lessing has called "that long, hard, dark stare" of local Pakistani men (1987). But the women didn't seem to mind at all.

They marched boldly into the bazaar, joking with and demanding price reductions from the merchants and stopping along the way to scamper up trees looking for Russian olive tree resin, while their husbands and I trailed sheepishly behind them. A crowd of perhaps fifty men gathered to watch, but the women would not be persuaded to turn back. They found a cool spot under some trees and sat down, in the midst of their entourage of onlookers, to eat plums. "Look, sister," they laughed, "see how surprised all those men are? They must never have seen anything like us! Maybe they think we come from the moon!"

Textile work is also an important medium of expression for neighboring Chitrali women, but Chitralis tend to put their energy into decorating their houses with beautiful embroidered tablecloths and cushions. I often thought that perhaps Chitrali women's sense of self is projected into the family compounds in which they spend so much of their time. Kalasha houses, by contrast, are quite simple, and Kalasha women seem to direct all their creative efforts into decorating their bodies. Through this attention to dress, they emphasize the visibility of women, their insistence that women can—even should—be *seen*. Kalasha women stand out. Black dresses form the ideal backdrop to show off a stunning display of color and design that can be easily spotted from clear across the valley. Subtlety isn't much valued, but boldness is. Whereas Muslim women hide from strangers, turning their backs and veiling at the threat of a passing jeep, Kalasha women stand up and look to see who it is.

Dynamism

Having read much of the existing work about Kalasha, I came to the valleys half expecting to find a world frozen in time, the "Land of the Lost" of my childhood cartoon days. While much has been written about the distinctiveness of Kalasha culture, most of the existing literature was written with the purpose of bringing "to light many aspects of the pre-Islamic culture" of the region (Aug. Cacopardo 1991:311). For many researchers, the Kalasha are most interesting for what their "archaic" religious practices can tell us about the larger cultural region of Nuristan, whose inhabitants are now all converted (and thus no longer interesting?). Jettmar, for example, states that "the fact is that [the Kalasha] can still be studied as a traditional pagan or non-Islamic community" and thus contribute to our understanding of pre-Islamic culture (1986:8; see also 1961). And Parkes laments that the "intriguing 'lost world' of the Kafirs was tragically destroyed before it could be further documented." As the Kalasha have escaped this fate, Parkes sees in the study of Kalasha culture an opportunity to study "a 'pastoral religion' that appears to have been characteristic of many other herding societies in the Hindu Kush prior to the arrival of Islam" (1990b:639). I myself came to the valleys looking for holdovers from an exotic past in my particular determination to study menstrual houses. But such scholarship tends to treat Kalasha culture as frozen. Tourist literature feeds and elaborates on this fantasy, promising visitors glimpses of "exotic pagans," "primitive tribesmen" tenaciously clinging to the old while the rest of the world rushes ahead.

I was therefore unprepared for the cultural world into which I arrived, a dynamic, flexible world in which the new is easily embraced and the old sometimes carelessly discarded and sometimes reverently resurrected. At first, my own Western ethnocentrism led me to lament how quickly things seemed to be changing and worry that the Kalasha would be yet another example of a culture that had "survived" tremendous pressure for hundreds, even thousands, of years only to unravel after a few decades of exposure to "us." But the longer I was there the more I sensed that an important aspect of Kalasha resilience was to be found in their very flexibility, their delight in innovation, and their dynamic ethos, which allows them to continually make and remake culture while maintaining a sense that their community is distinct and their traditions valuable.[4]

Names are a delightful example. There is a baby Akiko, named after the Japanese woman who has married into the community. Princess Di's visit to Chitral (wearing a very short skirt by all reports) inspired a baby Diana. There is an Engineer, a Commander, and a Driver. There is Election Bibi and Pharansisi (France). Anthropologists Peter Parkes, Gillian Darling, and Vivian Lievre have left their legacy in children named Peter, Gillian, and Bibi Han. For a few weeks, there was a baby Wynne, but her continual crying demonstrated that she didn't like her name, and so it was changed. Borrowing from their Chitrali and Pathan neighbors, there are also lots of Mohammeds and Khans. After the Gulf War, three Kalasha babies received the name "Saddam Hussein." "Don't you realize," I said to one of the mothers, "that Saddam Hussein is a big Muslim hero?"

"Oh, well," she replied, "it's a nice name." There are also many traditional Kalasha names such as Mashar Beck, Buda, and Mushiki. With the names they give their children, Kalasha pull in the world around them and make it their own.

Even during the short time I was in the valleys, many traditional practices were resurrected. Last summer, Kalasha in Rumbur began keeping *den* again by selecting young men to patrol the length of the valley to see that fall grapes, corn, walnuts, pears, and pumpkins were not eaten until after the Uchau harvest festival at the end of August. This practice was once widespread in Nuristan (Jones 1974), and it has continued to be important in the Birir Valley, but it had not been practiced in Rumbur for some time. Gillian Darling documented a "cultural revival" that took place in 1975, when Katarsing offered a *biramór*, a huge merit feast the likes of which had not taken place in at least thirty years (Darling 1979). In this feast, and in a previous wedding feast (*sariék*) that Katarsing had offered for his oldest daughter a few years earlier, he revived many traditional practices but also proudly added innovative elements of his own, which were admired and later copied by others (see Klimburg 1995).

Seemingly timeless and remarkably uniform, Kalasha women's clothes appear at first glance to epitomize the fierce, conservative nature of a people who cling to tradition against the odds. Yet one doesn't have to be around long to realize that the world of Kalasha fashion embodies the dynamic ethos that pervades Kalasha culture generally.[5] One of the great joys of doing fieldwork in such a small community was being able to see "culture in the making," to trace patterns of change to the individuals who initiated them.

Guided by an embodied aesthetic sense, women understand which elements are essential, which color and form combinations are most beautiful: they know what works. But there is also enough latitude for choice that each woman's dress, headdress, and beads become powerful expressions of her self-identity. Her choice of colors, combinations, pattern, amount of decoration, careful attention to detail, or a more relaxed attitude are all ways of pronouncing who she is. Wasiara Aya's penchant for old-fashioned beads and her insistence that her *susútr* incorporate woven decoration instead of being entirely covered with beads (it's much lighter that way, but slightly geeky) marks her as someone who is practical, active, and not vain, while her meticulously pleated skirt attests to her careful nature. Because

Kalasha villages are built into the steep valley walls. One family's roof is another family's patio. Here people from all three Kalasha valleys gather for a funeral in Birir Valley.

Grom village in Rumbur Valley on a dark, quiet day in January

Kalasha women clean wheat so that they can make bread for a marriage celebration (*khaltabarí*)

A goatherd watches over his flock

A young man makes cheese in the high pastures

A woman makes *čạháka*, an unleavened morning bread, from corn flour

Fall is a time of abundance. A baby boy celebrates by eating grapes.

A Kalasha man

Women singing *lač ghọ̄*, lighthearted "embarrassing songs" on the "day of the beans" during the Chaumos winter solstice festival

A young girl learning to sew

Wives of Chitrali officials have come to observe a festival. They asked me to take a photograph of them with Kalasha women.

Female relatives from different villages catch up at a Chaumos gathering

A girl washes her *ṣuṣútr* headdress near the river

A woman in the *bashali* offers the first peek at her newborn baby after their *ačhámbi* ceremony

Three cousins from the same household begin their daily laughter and mischief

Wasiara Aya helped me to assemble my own dress, I ended up looking a lot like her and so discovered much later that I was making statements about myself that I had not intended. Taksina, on the other hand, wears the widest, heaviest *susútr* possible, the latest colors of beads (orange and yellow—strung in solids rather than patterns for the most striking effect), and the newest, most elaborately decorated dress. Her dress and jewelry testify to her youth, her cutting-edge sense of style, her skill as a craftswoman, and her ability to garner the necessary resources to put together such an expensive outfit. A few women, both old and young, reject entirely this evolutionary "peacock's tail" of design and material and hold fast to traditional woolen dresses with a minimum of decoration.

Women's clothes have probably always formed important connections to the world outside the valley.[6] Cowrie shells are an evocative example, linking Kalasha women to oceans and people they have never seen. Cowrie shells are the most essential decorative element in women's headdresses, the one item for which there is no appropriate substitute. Mark Kenoyer, a South Asian archaeologist with a special interest in beads, told me that cowrie shells are symbolic of powerful female sexuality, representing a "denticular vagina." My friends found this uproariously funny. The species used by the Kalasha, *Cypraea moneta,* is found only off the Maldives. These shells were once widely traded throughout South and Central Asia and used as small currency. They are currently in very short supply and terribly expensive (two rupees per shell), and women go to great lengths locate them for their young daughters' headdresses. (A thinner, more brittle species of cowrie is less expensive and used to make cheap replicas of Kalasha headdresses to sell to tourists.)

Beads and bells came to the valleys via trade routes from all over South and Central Asia and the Middle East. Kalasha women once wore small black beads around their throats, and this was thought to be both beautiful and a way of protecting oneself against goiters. "Before," explained Saras Gula Aya for my tape recorder, "we put black beads right around our necks, below that we put all kinds of beads."

There were white ones. There were red ones, yellow, blue, green. These different beads we put lower down. We also took these different kinds of beads and strung them into a *gaduláy,* and those we wore beneath the black beads. Women said if you put red beads right at your neck, you would get a goiter. Later, they stopped bringing black beads—sometimes, sometimes, somewhere they would bring them but not often, not all the time. There were no black beads, so women sometimes put red beads near their throat. Also white, yellow, those they use. Our throats don't swell up. You can see that that was just talk . . . just old-fashioned words. (June 28, 1994)

She explained how Kalasha women learned from pastoral Gujar women, who were beginning to settle in the region, to make *kapabán* chokers out of multiple strands of colorful beads and dividers carved from cow bones. "If this throat could be seen, we would die [of embarrassment]. It's not beautiful like this, look, look! Now, no, where do they bring the black beads? Or even now women would put them there."

Women's clothes reflect shifts in the global marketplace, so that in a very real sense women's dresses and jewelry can be partially read as a map of connections that reach far beyond the valleys themselves. Beads are brought into the valleys by traders, who try to guess at what will appeal to the quite discriminating women. Vivid orange and yellow glass beads from Czechoslovakia were an immediate hit, and light blue was slowly growing in popularity. Red oblong beads from Iran (and their more modern transformations into yellow, white, and orange) are always sought after. I saw a sad sack of pale green beads roundly rejected by everyone. Also highly popular are military coat buttons and airline pins (some women's *kupás*, the most conservative element of Kalasha women's clothes, now proudly proclaim, "Fly Delta").[7]

The most dramatic recent change in women's clothing came in the late 1970s when a group of young Kalasha women was taken to Karachi to dance in a folk festival. Wasiara Aya, then a young girl, was along on the trip. The girls claimed (perhaps with some exaggeration) that they nearly died of heatstroke in their heavy woolen dresses. So Wasiara Aya tells that they bought black cotton cloth and sewed replicas out of the lighter material. So much more comfortable were these newfangled dresses that upon their return they continued to wear them, holding fast against the gales of laughter and communitywide sentiment that the new cotton dresses were hideously ugly. Soon, though, everyone was making them. Presently, only two or three women in all of Kalashadesh, admired for "keeping up custom," continue to wear woolen dresses.

The most frequent changes in fashion, however, have little to do with culture contact but with the creativity of individual Kalasha women. My friend Huran and her sister-in-law, Dina Aya, both from the larger valley of Bumboret, have set themselves up on the cutting edge of Kalashadesh fashion. In 1993 at the spring festival, Joshi, the two claim to have been the first to decorate the hems of their dresses with a solid ten inches or so of *čoṭ* (decoration). Their new design requires first sewing a solid background color and then a geometric or floral design on top of the background. It takes a lot more yarn and so bears testimony to a woman's wealth as well as her skill and creativity. At first, says Huran, everyone said, "How strange, and how wasteful! Look how much thread it takes!" But by the winter solstice festival, only eight months later, "everyone" was sewing dresses like theirs, and by the next spring the fashion had penetrated Rumbur Valley as well. The next year, Huran thought of making a checkered *susútr.* She said that she had designed a similar wristband for her daughter, and this gave her the idea. She and Dina Aya rebeaded their *susútr* in orange and white checkerboards, again, just in time for Joshi. Initially, even I thought it looked silly, as I had been there long enough to adopt at least a little aesthetic sense. But, again, although the new design was originally thought strange, the idea was picked up and spread rapidly through the valleys until little girls everywhere were begging their mothers to rebead their headdresses and adult women began to make them for themselves as well. "Now everyone says 'the women of your house are so clever,' " proclaimed Dina Aya happily. The two told me they are already thinking about what they will do for Joshi next year. Meanwhile, the new beading technique seems to have sparked a little efflorescence of design possibilities, with arrows and triangles and zigzags springing up where formerly there were only solid bands of colored beads.

Having, Being, and Interbeing

As Georg Simmel noted, "Inasmuch as adornment is also an object of considerable value, it is a synthesis of the individual's having and being" (1950:340). Kalasha women's clothing is extraordinarily valuable.[8] Women go to great lengths to procure the money and materials necessary to dress themselves and their daughters, so each woman's clothes and jewelry bear testimony not only to her individual creativity but also her resourcefulness. Although Simmel goes on to say that this connection between having and being is not true of ordinary dress, in the case of the Kalasha the ordinary *is* extraordinary. The sheer expense and effort involved in fashioning women's clothing links what women have, what they wear every day, to who they are and by extension to who the whole Kalasha community is. Further, because beads and shells, bells and buttons, and skill and labor are recycled and continually exchanged, women's dresses come to represent more than having and being (wealth and social position) but also "interbeing"—a lifetime of affections and connections, a symbolic binding together of women's networks that are otherwise fragmented through time and space.

The French ethnographers Jean-Yves Loude and Vivian Lievre have written of Kalasha women's beads that "The prestige of a father or husband is judged, among other things, by the number of necklaces piled up on a woman's breast" (1988:42). I didn't notice this to be the case. Rather, women tend to see beads as a representation of the wealth of the woman herself—whether she procures it through her own labor or her social network. As Saras Gula Aya explains (again for the tape recorder),

> If there are only a few beads, they say *ga ačók* [bare-necked, an insult]. She wasn't able to buy beads. She doesn't have any money, they would say. Or she has lots of beads, lots of beads, she is wealthy (*paysadár*). She made lots of beads. Lots of money. Bought, bought, bought, bought beads, wears so many.

Saras Gula Aya, and indeed most Kalasha women, talk in terms of a woman's personal wealth and prestige, not that of her husband's or father's.[9] Women painstakingly squeeze juice out of grapes that drop to the ground to make a few precious bottles of wine to sell (at Rs 100 to 150 per bottle). Others keep chickens, selling the eggs and pullets to neighbors who are visited by unexpected company. More recently, women have begun making handicraft items to sell to tourists, although most have little opportunity to market their goods since they speak neither English nor Urdu. Other women sell excess beans or dried mulberries or apricots, and some sell off a goat or sheep every so often. The cash a woman makes from her enterprises is her own, kept under lock and key in her private box. Although I assume it must happen sometimes, I have never seen a woman beg her husband for bead money. Women sometimes send men to Chitral to buy beads, shells, or material, but more often they buy these things themselves from the traders who pass through, claiming that men aren't discriminating enough.

This is not to say that men don't contribute significantly to the outfitting of the women closest to them, only that they don't seem to *have* to—their contributions are seen as gifts rather than obligations, and these gifts testify to the *quality* of their relationship with wives and daughters rather than to the mere fact of it. Annette Weiner and Jane Schneider have noted that the tendency for clothing to be an emotive symbol of attachment is common across many diverse cultures. A characteristic of cloth, they write, "is how readily its appearance and that of its constituent fibers can evoke ideas of connectedness or tying" (1989:2). Each Kalasha woman's clothing can be read as a map of her significant relationships across the valleys and across her lifetime—material manifestations of enduring ties with friends, bonds with natal family, acceptance into the community of women in her marital home, and reminders of her courtship with her husband and other lovers (cf. Cohn 1989; Werbner 1990; Tarlo 1996).

At their *gostník* ceremony, when mother's brothers hold children on their laps and dress them for the first time in traditional Kalasha clothing, three-year-old girls receive gifts of beads from aunts, grandmothers, and their mother's special friends. Girls are taught to remember which necklaces came from whom. As she grows up, these beads form the foundation upon which newer necklaces will be piled. Although lots of beads are lost in the rough play of growing up, most women still have some special *gostníkani mãík*, *gostník* beads, which have been carefully restrung many times.

When women marry, they receive sets of beads from each of the women in the new marital family—husband's sisters and husband's brothers' wives, close cousins, and special beads from her new mother-in-law. Often women will take beads from their own necks to welcome the new bride. Again, she will remember which beads came from whom. If the marriage fails, her former in-laws may ask that the beads be returned, but usually they don't, and the beads remain a reminder of this important event in the girl's life. When May Gul left Hyatt after three years of living with his family, his mother told me that she was so angry she asked for all the beads back. May Gul cried and cried, begging that she be allowed to keep the necklaces. She had come to the family with nothing, explained Hyatt's mother. "If I had taken her beads, she would have been *gai achok*. She'd worn those beads for three years, how could I take them from her? I decided to let them be," she concluded.

Beads and bracelets are also exchanged between women as a peace offering to right wrongs. If a woman finds that another woman has been having an affair with her husband, the offending woman, at her own initiative, will offer *rumíš* to her lover's wife, a gift of jewelry meant as both apology and compensation. Pilin Gul still wears the brass bracelet given to her by Siaphat some thirty-five years ago, when Siaphat, then eight months pregnant with Pilin Gul's husband's child, came into the family as a second wife (see chapter 6 for a detailed account of Pilin Gul's marital history). I imagine that the bracelet, prominently worn all these years, was an everyday reminder to both women of the hard-won truce that allowed them to live together, sharing household and husband.

Besides these more formal occasions for the giving of jewelry, there is a constant exchange of small gifts of beads and special buttons, bracelets, rings, and cloth between friends and relatives. Most women carry with them small bags or tins of stray beads, which they freely give out to anyone needing a particular color or type to finish a design. Lovers often slip small gifts to their beloveds, which are cherished but usually not worn openly. Husbands and fathers, brothers and uncles and grandfathers bring cloth, yarn, shoes, socks, and jewelry to the women closest to them. Many men earn enough money to outfit their entire family with a new spring wardrobe by selling the morel mushrooms they find in the mountains.

In addition to the continual exchange of materials, there is also a constant flow of work and skill between friends and relatives who live in distant villages and valleys. Among the first questions women ask one another when they haven't been in touch for a while is, "Who made that belt for you? Who sewed your dress? Who put the beads on your *susútr?*" Women take special care of their mothers and grandmothers, remaking and updating their headdresses and dresses. Friends often offer to sew or weave for women who have new babies or a lot of fieldwork or simply as a favor. Nieces sew for aunts, and vice versa, sisters for sisters, and childhood friends for their girl-friends who have long since moved far away from their natal homes. The recipient will send the unfinished yarn or cloth to her friend, tucking a small gift inside—a few handfuls of walnuts, some fruit, or some precious resin for her hair. Although Lader Bibi hadn't been home to her natal village in Bumboret Valley for three years, she saw her favorite sister's daughter at a funeral. Her niece offered to sew dresses for all four of Lader Bibi's daughters. Every day the girls would watch for passing jeeps hoping that one of the men from Bumboret might bring their dresses. It was very exciting, since the dresses could be delivered by almost anyone. And of course along with the dresses came greetings and updates from Lader Bibi's entire family in Bumboret. Men live in one place their whole lives, but women's networks span valleys and decades. The constant give and take of labor and materials allows women a way of maintaining physical connections with loved ones over long distances. A woman's dress and beads are therefore more than expressions of her individual identity, more than a symbol of her "Kalashaness." In a very real way, women wear their hearts on their sleeves, their intimate social networks woven into the very fabric of the clothes they wear everyday.

Fashion and the Limits of Women's Agency

Yet while Kalasha women create and wear clothing as active interpretations of collective and personal values, there is a disjuncture between the meaning of women's clothes within the Kalasha community and the way women's dress is "read" by outsiders—both Pakistani and foreigners. This problem of miscommunication through dress is, of course, by no means unique to the Kalasha (cf. Tarlo 1996; Lurie [1981] 1992; Hoffman 1984). But among Kalasha the schism between their own understanding of their dress and the way it is read by others could hardly be wider. The very code that for Kalasha people symbolizes their personal freedom and visibility, their connectedness to community and to the larger world, is received as proof that they are backward, exotic, and sexually available. Perhaps because their clothing is so radically different from anything worn in the region Kalasha become a blank slate onto which outsiders can project all sorts of fantasies about them.

One fantasy, which is complicated because it does merge into the edges of rhetoric to which the Kalasha themselves cling, is the idea that women's clothing—especially the fact that they do not veil—is evidence of "women's liberation." It is true that in the rest of north-western Pakistan Western women (and perhaps Western men, too) experience tension that is generated by the constant vigilance necessary to keep the sexes separated. Most female tourists feel a bit harassed by the time they arrive in Kalashadesh. Constantly being stared at and misjudged for what you are wearing is tiring and after a while extremely annoying. Westerners entering the Kalasha valleys sense immediately that things are different. Foreigners are as ready to embrace Kalasha women as kindred spirits as the Kalasha are ready to identify with Westerners. Given that many Westerners misunderstand Islam and are predisposed to identify this cultural form as oppressive to women, they jump on the notion that the Kalasha are our feminist "ancestors," autochthonous people who live in a "natural" way, and that the rest of the region is in the grip of some hegemonic perversion against which the Kalasha have held out.

Once, for example, a photographer came to Rumbur. She had a copy of a *Time* magazine article about "Women and Purdah." There were pictures of women in all sorts of different *burkas* and veils. She wanted to photograph Wasiara Aya (who, because she and her husband have worked with many anthropologists, is probably the most photographed of all Kalasha women) looking at the magazine with a horrified expression on her face. She said that she would try to sell the picture back to the magazine, along with a short story about how Kalasha women were holding out against the oppressive institution of veiling throughout the rest of the region. The photographer told Wasiara Aya's husband that she would pay him if he would let her photograph his wife and would send more money to him later if *Time* bought the piece. (It never ceases to amaze me that Westerners can so easily treat Kalasha women as symbols of original liberated women and at the same time unthinkingly assume that they are the property of their husbands.) Wasiara Aya was slightly annoyed and proclaimed that if the woman wanted her photograph she should pay her, not her husband. The photographer tried to show Wasiara Aya how to sit and hold the magazine, so that the light cut through the door to her veranda in an artistic way and demonstrated how she should screw up her face in an expression of shock. Wasiara Aya looked at the magazine. She said that she thought the pictures were interesting.

She said that she hadn't known there were so many different kinds of *burkas,* and she asked where each type was worn. She thought that the silky material of one in particular would make a nice dress. But she didn't think they were horrifying. The photographer asked me to pose, to show Wasiara Aya what to do. She took several pictures of me, an American dressed up like a Kalasha woman, pretending to be outraged by pictures of Muslim women. Wasiara Aya kept making me laugh. Wasiara Aya posed too, but she never really succeeded in generating the appropriate expression of indignation about women in purdah. The woman never sent the money, and so far neither of us has turned up in *Time.*

Certainly both Kalasha men and women make a point of asserting that their women do not practice purdah. Their clothes and their actions are meaningful precisely because they are a way of defining themselves as "not Muslim." But for the Kalasha I think this is simply an assertion of difference and an assertion of their *right to remain* different. It shouldn't be read it as a statement of moral and cultural superiority.

Women's clothing is also read by outsiders, both foreign and Pakistani, as evidence that Kalasha women are sexually available, despite the fact that Kalasha women think of themselves as people who are extremely modest. During the summer, when the valleys are flowing with tourists, Kalasha women suffer from frequent harassment and unwanted propositions from outsiders. One of the most common questions people asked of me—the Punjabi wives of Chitrali officials, Pakistani men who work for aid organizations in Chitral, male and female Pakistani tourists, and foreigners from several different countries—was "What do they wear under their dresses?" I never heard anyone wonder what Muslim women wear under their *shalwar kamiz.* Yet women's dresses could hardly be more concealing, wrapped head to toe as they are in some eight yards of thick black cloth. Their dresses are meant to cover them thoroughly, and thin material that allows light to shine through in the sunshine is thought to be terribly inappropriate and embarrassing. There is even a whole minigenre of stories about what happens when there is an earthquake, and women, in their fear, run outside "naked"—which means that they are wearing the long underwear and sweater they wear to bed.

Finally, women's elaborate "costumes" are read as proof of their exotic otherness and evidence that they are unchanged primitive ancestors of us all. Greek tour groups, for example, come to the Kalasha valleys in large caravans searching for their cultural heritage and passing out little vials of perfume in bottles decorated like Greek vases and coins sporting Alexander the Great's head.

So while Kalasha women's clothes do serve as a material metaphor for women's agency—an active, embodied manifestation of changing cultural and personal values and ideas—women's dress also marks the limits of that agency. Fashion is a powerful, creative vehicle for expressing identity. Yet women's clothes also limit the very freedom and dynamism they represent because Kalasha women's clothing is so marked that it is impossible to escape the boundaries of their small cultural world—at least without discarding the dress that is so important to them. As well as being misread by people from the outside, women's dresses prevent them from traveling freely throughout their nation. As we saw in the last chapter, an essential component of the idea of women's "freedom" involves the ability to travel openly. As more and more tourists come to the Kalasha valleys, and as better roads and more traffic have made travel to Chitral and beyond relatively simple, many women say they long to see and learn about the world beyond the valley walls. Bayda Aya, echoing a remark Wasiara Aya had made earlier, told me she had never been jealous of anything before, but when she sees *anglís* women she feels jealousy in her heart, thinking, "If only I could walk about the world as they do!" I told her she should go or that I would take her and we would go together. "How can I go?" she asked, gesturing at her dress and pulling on her braids. "What do you mean?" I said, "You are beautiful! Go just as you are." "No, sister," she shook her head, "Here I am beautiful. There, I am only strange." While some Kalasha women have visited Peshawar, Karachi, and Islamabad, when they do they adopt Muslim dress and are dependent on male escorts. Bayda Aya said she wanted to walk about as I do, she didn't want to stay in a hotel room all day, hide beneath a *burka,* or stick with fear to her husband's side. As on the women's march detailed in the preface, the effectiveness of Kalasha women's agency screeches to a halt at the borders of their community, as the very vehicle that empowers them *within* Kalashadesh also stigmatizes them *without,* marking them as forever outside the larger Pakistani society.

Chapter 5

The Kalasha Bashali

The existing anthropological literature about the Kalasha menstrual house assumes that the *bashali* (*bašáli*) is a place where women are restricted, confined, exiled (Schomberg 1938; Siiger 1956; Graziosi 1961; Palwal 1972; see also Robertson 1896). The Italian anthropologist Paolo Graziosi (1961), for example, writes about the *bashali* in this way:

> It was said that an image of the goddess Dezalik was kept in the bashali, or women's house; Siiger had heard of it, but it had not been possible for him, or for any of his colleagues who had visited the Kalash valley, to penetrate that building, where women are relegated when they are in a state of impurity . . .
>
> One day during the month of September, 1960, a fortunate circumstance occurred, allowing me to enter a bashali. . . . It was about midday and all its inmates were at work in the fields. We pushed the door of the small building and it gave at once, so we entered the dark room where, upon an altar in a corner we saw the wooden statue of the divinity who protects childbirth. I was thus able to photograph, sketch and measure the statue, draw up a plan of the room, and sketch its scanty furniture . . . (149)
>
> The segregation of women during the menstrual period and at childbirth is of course practiced among many different peoples. The horror felt for their state, considered impure, leads primitive communities to take all the necessary precautions to avoid dangerous contacts between impure women and all other members of the group. (150)

It isn't hard to imagine what a violation Graziosi committed when he trespassed into the *bashali*, knowing that men should never set foot on *bashali* grounds. But putting aside the potentially devastating cosmological implications of his act (and the sheer rudeness of it as well), Graziosi's account illustrates a naive attitude toward women and "menstrual pollution" that is typical of much of the literature about menstrual houses cross-culturally: women are not cast as agents, participants in the creation of cultural traditions, but as prisoners to rules made by and for men (though indeed the men themselves are seen as irrational "primitives"). Women are actually referred to as "inmates" who are "relegated" to this small "dark room" with "scanty furniture" due to the "horror felt for their state." The male anthropologist *penetrates* (it's hard to believe he really used this all too appropriate word) this exclusively female space not with the aim of understanding the meanings associated with this institution but in order to photograph and measure it. The physical structure is deemed important and worthy of study, not the women themselves.[1] Sentences referring to women's activities are always constructed using passive verbs; women are spoken of as passive objects at the disposal of others. Finally, the horror of menstruation is taken to be so obvious that Graziosi did not find it necessary to back up this statement with supportive ethnographic material.

Kalasha women and men don't talk about their *bashali* in ways that support the implied claims of these early ethnographers. Women are active participants in the creation and maintenance of this institution. Menstruation and childbirth inspire neither horror nor disgust. The *pragata* blood associated with reproduction is entirely women's business, never spoken of in front of men, who are said not to understand anything about it (though women realize that this is a fiction). Women deal with menstruation and childbirth rather matter-of-factly, assuming personal responsibility for the welfare of the entire community by maintaining the separation of *onjesta* and *pragata*—the core principle of Kalasha religion. The menstrual house, as the most *pragata* space and the place where the *pragata* is managed through women's own active agency, is one of the most important Kalasha institutions. Remember the myth from the first chapter in which Nanga Dehar founded Rumbur by shooting two arrows that established the *bashali*, the most *pragata* place, and the altar at Sajigor, the most *onjesta* place? Indeed, on a number of occasions young Kalasha men who had been exposed to Christianity and Islam explained, in English, that their *bashali* was "holy"—as good, if as one-sided, a translation as "defiled" or "polluting" I suppose (see Keesing 1985 for a discussion of the difficulties in cross-cultural translation). "It is the most holy place for women," exclaimed Din Mahmat earnestly upon one of my earlier inquiries, "and very important to their lives."

The importance of the *bashali* in Kalasha women's lives goes beyond its ritual significance in Kalasha cosmology. Far from being a prison in which women are separated from the rest of Kalasha society and made powerless, the menstrual house is an important center for female culture and community and it enhances women's agency, both personally and collectively.[2] Further, what happens in the *bashali* has consequences that emanate beyond the *bashali* ground itself.

For example, in the following beloved myth a young woman's bravery and courage saves the community of *bashali* women, and thus all of Kalasha society, from sure destruction. This woman also founds a lineage to which people still trace their descent (told by Saras Gula Aya):[3]

A long time ago, a man had only one daughter—no son, only one daughter. The girl's name was Shuragali. He wouldn't give that one daughter as a bride, saying, "I have only one daughter. How can I give her away?" So he didn't give Shuragali as a bride, and a hawk came and sat on a rock. The girl saw that there was a hawk sitting over there, and she went to see and found that there were wheat seeds on the rock, so she picked them up and ate them. She ate them, and she became pregnant. She became more and more pregnant until her time was near. Her mother and father noticed and said, "What has happened to you? Who has done this to you?" "I ate some wheat," Shuragali said, "Some wheat that the hawk left over there on the rock. Nothing else."

Her parents were distraught because during that time women were being eaten, eaten by a dragon (*tiriwéri*), and no one who went to the *bashali* to have a baby was left." When "*zánti*" women, women whose time had come, went in the evening to the *bashali* to have their babies, the dragon would stand in the doorway and call, "Should you come here so I can eat you, or should I come in and eat you?" Then the women would say, "Eat me wherever you like. If I go there you'll eat me, if you come here you'll eat me. It's all the same." Then the dragon would come in and eat the women and the new babies, too. He'd eat them and leave. It happened like that over and over, until there were almost no women left. So, when Shuragali was ready to leave for the *bashali,* her mother and father were crying, "He'll eat my daughter, my one little daughter, the dragon will eat her. He ate the women all up, and now he'll eat her, too."

But Shuragali said to her father, "Why are you crying, Dada? Bring seven loads of juniper, seven loads of straw, and seven loads of wood. Why are you crying?" So the father went to bring the seven loads of wood from the floodplain, seven loads of straw, and seven loads of juniper. Shuragali's time had come. Her time had come, and she went to the *bashali,* although her mother was crying, "the dragon ate all the other women, and now he'll eat my daughter, too!"

So Shuragali took the wood, brought loads of it, and made a huge fire. Then she took the coals and she dug, dug, dug, dug, dug, dug a huge hole by the door and put the coals in it and covered the hole up with the straw. Then she had her baby, and took him and sat by the fireplace inside the *bashali.* The dragon came to the door, and said, "Shall I come in there or will you come out here?" Shuragali replied, "Before you ate everyone, [so] come on in here. Why should I bother going to you?" So the dragon stepped into the *bashali* and fell into the pit. Scraping and clawing he tried to get out, and he died like that. Shuragali killed the dragon, and then she sat and waited, holding her son.

The next morning, *really* early—at the time the Muslims have their first call to prayer—the girl's mother and father were crying. "Oh my little daughter, the dragon ate her." Suddenly, the daughter was at their door, and she said, "Oh, don't cry, I am alive. For the community of *bashali* women (*jamilishĭr*) has been rescued. I killed the dragon. Now the community of women can rest easily. Why are you crying?" Then her parents were really happy. They wished her congratulations on the birth of her son, and she left.

Because of Shuragali, the *bashali* dragon was killed and now women can go to the *bashali.* And from that one daughter a whole lineage was born in Bumboret. Nojoge were born from the son of Shuragali. Shuragali's son's name, now what was it? I don't remember . . .

Of course, women don't ordinarily have much call to slay dragons. Still, the Kalasha *bashali* is a place where women do things that would be surprising or inappropriate in other contexts. It is a place where women feel free to behave in ways they ordinarily don't. Here they conduct their own purification ceremonies, make their own ritual offerings. They are more open about sexuality and reproduction and talk more candidly about husbands and mothers-in-law. They are more playful and physically rough. Here they can smoke cigarettes, sleep late, take naps, drink endless cups of tea, flirt with passersby, sing and dance simply for the joy of it. When young women elope, the *bashali* is a most common springing off point. It is a place where individual women can escape, at least partially and intermittently, the intensity of social life in a small valley. It is a place, as my friend Asmara Aya so elegantly put it, where *wã šíaw*—where there is "space." In this chapter, I want to show you the ways in which the *bashali*, far from being a place where women are "confined," provides women with space from which to act—to be creative and religious; to be part of the *jamilishír*, the larger community of women from which they are usually divided by family, village, and household; and to make personal decisions about reproduction and marriage away from the intense social pressure of village life.

And yet the *bashali* is also very much a focus of community-wide interest. Far from being separate from the rest of valley life, it is central to it—both culturally and physically. The *bashali* reminds me of a pool that forms behind sheltering rocks in the river, a small, calm spot in the rushing of life. The water streams around it, making it seem separate from the river, but in the same breath it *is* the river—made of the same water and continually circulating. There is a constant flow of people and things into and out of the *bashali*, as everything and everyone—food, firewood, bedding, cooking utensils, goddess figurines, women, Shuragali's seven loads of straw, wood, and juniper—come in from the outside. And of course everyone, men and women alike, is born there and thus brought out from the inside.[4]

Building the *Bashali*

Testifying to the fact that the *bashali* is of intense local—and international—interest, the *bashali* in Rumbur has been torn down and reconstructed three times in the last thirty years (in comparison, a well-built house in the region could easily last much more than a hundred years). The first menstrual house anyone remembers was built during the time when the oldest people in the valley were children, probably sixty-five years ago. It was set back further from the main path through the valley, and women claimed that this old menstrual house was haunted by a spirit who would frighten them at night. Old women say that it was small but very warm. "It was nothing fancy," Mushiki recalls, "just a little *kutúyak* [a small shelter], but we liked it. In the summer we young girls slept outside. We played and played. We sang songs and told stories. There were no beds, they weren't allowed—but we didn't need beds. We stripped off our dresses and slept on top of them."

When Katarsing, perhaps the most influential man in Rumbur, gave his great *biramór* (the most prestigious merit feast) in 1977, he made a promise to reconstruct this *bashali*, which had fallen into some disrepair (Darling 1979:142), and offered to build it closer to the main path so the women would no longer be frightened and hidden so deep in the woods. "Women are not allowed to eat the meat of male goats," he told me, "so I wanted to give something to them, too." As Darling notes, Katarsing had found the ideal opportunity to ensure that his name would go down in the annals of Kalasha oral history. "Not only was he performing the largest *ónjesta biramór* in more than fifty years, but during this major accomplishment in the sacred realm, was promising to refurbish the most central symbol of the impure domain, the women's menstrual hut. Both the plan and the timing of its announcement are indicative of Kata Sing's adroitness and ambition" (142–43). Women wax poetic remembering this bashali, loved for its new front porch and thick walls.

During her first visit to the Kalasha valleys in 1983, Birgitte Sperber, a Danish geographer who has since come many times to the valleys and has developed deep friendships with many people there, describes being invited to visit a *bashali* in Bumboret. Overcome with "pity" that the poor women had to be secluded during menstruation and delivery, she wanted to "help" by finding a donor to provide money for metal beds for the menstrual houses in all three valleys. Traditional wooden Kalasha beds are considered *onjesta*, and therefore are not allowed in the *bashali*, but metal beds from outside were deemed acceptable. UNICEF agreed to donate the money, but upon her return the next year Sperber found (to her horror) that the entire menstrual house (as well as menstrual houses in Birir and Bumboret) had been rebuilt—complete with a metal roof, a toilet, and fireplaces instead of a central fire pit (1992a). The money had been given to a Chitrali contractor, who had demonstrated little concern either for the suitability of the design or the quality of the construction. The walls were poorly made, and the wind whistled through them. The fireplaces did not warm the large building, so women built a fire in the center of the room, causing a ceiling fire that left a gaping hole in the roof. Traditional flat roofs could be repaired by the women themselves (men are not allowed on *bashali* grounds), but this tin roof required special skills and materials. Sperber comments that she was embarrassed and has learned not to interfere.

In 1994, the Rumbur *bashali* was rebuilt again, using money donated by Renata Hansmeyer, a wealthy Swiss woman with good intentions but little understanding of the political or social implications of her actions. She visited the *bashali* and proclaimed that the conditions under which the women were living were appalling. "We tried to tell her that we're fine, but she acted disgusted," Zarina, who was there during her visit, told me. "It was embarrassing." The new *bashali* was built by a young Kalasha man, using Nuristani laborers. Its construction fed the factional political divisions within the community and led to widespread disagreements about religious issues and bitter accusations of misappropriation of funds. It has two rooms (Hansmeyer insisted on a separate room for labor and delivery, not understanding that women like to be together, supporting one another through labor and helping to care for the infant after it is born). It has a washroom and a kitchen (something no other Kalasha houses have) as well as a separate toilet (which the women stopped up with paper so that no one would use it, claiming it was too far to the river to haul water). Three separate fires must now be built, rather than one central fire, meaning that three times as much wood is needed, far more than is usually available. It also has a metal roof, and the walls are covered with already chipping concrete. There is a wide front porch. It is painted white with bright blue trim, which women say they think is beautiful, since it looks modern, "like a guesthouse." Hansmeyer instructed that there be a wall separating the *bashali* from the road so the women would have privacy. Some women like this, while others say it was better when they could chat freely with passersby.

I was worried, at first, that the construction of this new *bashali* would initiate the further erosion of *bashali* culture. I worried that having separate rooms would divide the community, that the cement floor would make it difficult to clean up after childbirth, and that having a tiny kitchen instead of a central fire would mean the social time spent cooking together would become a chore assigned to one or two individuals. But I realize now that I had stumbled into the same blindspot that Graziosi did in 1960—equating the building itself with the institution. Women's practice of going to the menstrual house, and the community they have built there, are still vital and growing. This new building, for all its flaws, is better than the one that preceded it. Still, I am troubled by all this intense intervention.

The *bashali* is more than a focal point of women's community; it is an essential part of the entire community. Giving money to build or repair religious structures does nothing to ensure the survival of Kalasha religion. Indeed, it robs the community of an opportunity to come together, as Takat Jan explained quite clearly: "We Kalasha are getting lazy and selfish and spoiled waiting for handouts from *anglís* [Westerners, including Japanese]." He says you can hardly blame them, since if someone is going to give you money why would you do it yourself? "For example, what if Wynne here gave me a bunch of money to build a new Manhandeo (an altar above Grom village)? I'd eat part of the money and do a half-assed job because it really isn't my money. Then in about ten years, when it started to crumble because it wasn't built well in the first place, instead of rebuilding it ourselves, we'd just wait around for another Wynne to come along and give us more money. It didn't used to be like that," he went on, "before, we were truly poor. Then we built our own Jestak Hans, our own Mahandeos, our own *bashalis*. Building our own *bashali* is not a burden— one goat per family or a couple of kilos of cheese—it is a pleasure." He continued that building and maintaining their own institutions builds cohesion in the community, as people would get together and discuss every detail. The result was a community building in which people took pride. Individuals who donated money (like Katarsing when he built the previous *bashali*) accrued prestige as well. "But now look at us. Soon Westerners will be showing up offering to give us money to bury our dead. Then, when my family member dies, I'll wait for the money to come through instead of holding my own funeral rites, and maybe later I'll have to bury him with a spoon."[5]

A Day in the *Bashali*

It's important to emphasize at the outset that *bashali* life isn't idyllic. Not everyone likes it all the time. After I had been in the valleys long enough to ask permission from many women and understood enough Kalasha that I could be sure to do things properly, I went to the *bashali* during my own menstrual periods. It was a case in which participant observation really worked because I think that in the two years that I lived in Rumbur I came to feel about the *bashali* pretty much the way most women do. Sometimes I had to go at inconvenient times, when I had other things I'd rather do, or when there was an important ceremony or a fun festival I would have liked to attend. In the winter, it was really cold, and the thorough ritual washing before departure was almost unbearable. There were times when I was hungry, and no one brought food. Sometimes the fleas and lice were so thick that none of us could sleep. Sometimes it was crowded and smoky and hot and boring. Nights were long, and I wished the babies would stop squalling. I missed my husband, and other women said they missed their families, too. As the months of my fieldwork flew by, it seemed as if I was always in the *bashali*.

But usually I looked forward to going, looked forward to the break in my routine, looked forward to not being able to write field notes for a few days (since paper is one item that cannot be brought back out of the *bashali* once it is taken in). I came to love the companionship as well as the novelty of being around women I didn't get to see often otherwise, the warm welcome on arrival, the excitement of seeing who you would be living with for the next few days. I heard a lot of juicy gossip and learned about things women don't talk about in other contexts. I took naps in the middle of the day, ate a lot, drank lots of tea, and took leisurely walks. I enjoyed learning and telling stories and singing songs and dancing. I smoked a little hashish and a few cigarettes. I felt a special bond with the children I saw born. I went home bearing gossip and stories and greetings for my family members from the other *bashali* women.

I want to reconstruct my first visit to the menstrual house for you as a way of introducing the social life and physical experience of being in the *bashali*. This day was typical, but every day I spent there was different, depending on the season and more importantly the mix of personalities of the other women who were there at the same time. I have left out certain details of women's practices that seemed to me to be especially private, those that cannot be seen from the road or are strikingly different from rituals performed in other public contexts.[6] As elsewhere in this ethnography, I've used pseudonyms in order to protect privacy.

I was frightened the first time I went to the *bashali*, afraid that I would do something wrong or would be in the way. I was also excited. We had talked about my attending the *bashali*. I explained that it was necessary for my work and that I would write about what I learned there. I told them I wanted to go since everyone else seemed to like it so much. Every Kalasha person I talked to, men and women both, had agreed that I should go. I waited until I could speak Kalasha fairly well, until I had begun to wear Kalasha women's clothing, until I had joined the women in the annual purification ceremony (*sịs aú sučék*) at the Chaumos winter solstice festival. I waited through two months of amenorrhea, dismayed that my reliable body was failing me.

Finally, my period came and I went downstairs, careful not to annoy the goddess Jestak by walking on the roof above her head, and announced that I had begun menstruating and that I wanted to go to the *bashali* this time. The women in my family proclaimed that I was too *nazúk*, too delicate and pampered, to enjoy myself there as they did. They proclaimed that I would be cold and hungry and that they had no special food to send with me. They would be judged, they said, by the quality of the food they sent with me. Eventually they relented and agreed that I should go and spend just the last night of my menstrual period there, wash, and come home. I could take walnuts and dried mulberries with me this time, since I wouldn't be there long, and the other women would appreciate the treat. If I liked it, I could go whenever I wished thereafter.

Five days later, after breakfast, my aunt and sisters seemed almost giddy, explaining to me over and over all the *bashali* rules, telling stories of the first time they went there and all the silly things they did. The menstrual house is the most *pragata* place in the valley, and women take great care to separate themselves from the blood that is the source of the *pragata*. "You must never eat without first washing your hands," they explained, "or touch your feet or the bed or the floor without washing your hands afterward." Dishes of food are never set directly on the floor or the bed. Shoes that are taken into the *bashali* are not taken out again, and the same is true for rubber, paper, and ceramic dishes (though, as with every rule, pragmatic exceptions are readily made). Everything else that goes in is thoroughly washed before being brought out.

There is only one *bashali* in Rumbur, shaped by all the Kalasha women of the valley. Women come from as far as five miles away in the summer. In the winter, when families have returned from their summer lands, everyone lives within a one-mile radius of the *bashali*. Old women say that when they were girls—"Oh, Kalashadesh was soooo *onjesta* then"—they would leave for the *bashali* immediately upon discovering that they had begun menstruating, even if it meant walking by torchlight in the middle of the night. Now most women spend the day in the village, organizing food, knitting, or spinning to bring along, and wait quietly until evening to walk down, taking their nursing toddlers with them.

Lilizar walked with me to carry my shoes, which must be removed as soon as you cross into *pragata* space. Along the path people sang out, "Hey sister! Are you going to the *bashali?*" It was a February afternoon, and the barefoot walk through the snow was excruciating. My frozen feet made the welcome upon entry seem even warmer. I was rushed inside to thaw out, questioned eagerly by the women there about family members and friends who lived in my village of Kalashagrom, and quickly updated on the most exciting turns in Begim's recent elopement. Then Taksina and Lulu, the two youngest women there, grabbed my hands to take me on a tour of the grounds, passing me a pair of pink plastic slippers, *bashali* shoes that women donate when they get a new pair.

Located just across the river from Badtet village, fifteen feet from the only road, and directly across from the Exlant Hotel, the *bashali* sits in the geographical and social center of the valley. The *bashali* grounds are approximately one and a half acres and heavily wooded with large holly oak trees that have gone uncut for centuries. The grounds are bounded by the road in the front, a water channel in back near the river, and fields to either side. The area is littered with candy wrappers and old shoes and other trash that women don't bother to pick up, since it would mean touching the ground and since it can't be taken off grounds anyway. Near the water channel are large pots for boiling water to wash clothing, flat rocks that are ideal for scrubbing, and trees that provide privacy for bathing outdoors in summertime. Each woman hides her own comb and a bar of soap in a tree or under a rock. Women never share combs, saying that if your hair tangles with someone else's, the two of you will argue. "Is that true?" I would ask. "Who knows?" was the invariable reply, "probably not. But it's what we say." Deep in the holly oak forest is a section of woods that even *bashali* women don't enter readily, the graveyard for women who die in childbirth and infants who are stillborn or die before it is time for them to leave for home.

I was glad that Taksina was there with me, as her forceful personality and genuine good humor and brazenness are a good foil for my tendency to feel shy and withdrawn. She suggested that we wash my clothes so that they would have a chance to dry by the next morning. It was a cold day, but the sun had begun to shine through. We hunted up dry kindling to make a fire to heat water so our hands wouldn't freeze while we did laundry. I changed into a borrowed dress. While I washed my underwear, Taksina grabbed my dress and belt and scrubbed both in the cold canal water, chattering and laughing even as she shivered. Washing clothes in plastic sandals and a thin dress made the weather seem even colder. We made several trips back inside to warm up by the fire.

Later when I complained that Taksina had done all the work, the other women said, "Oh, she's young and has no children to look after, what else should she do?" It is true that compared to their responsibilities at home life in the *bashali* is not arduous. Women informally take turns cooking and washing up, collecting wood for cooking in the summertime, making fires, filling containers of drinking water at the river, and tending the new babies. Young women are expected to offer to do the most difficult chores (though nothing in the *bashali* is really all that strenuous), and when the girls balk older women complain about "girls these days" and remember how enthusiastic they were when they were *moráy*—nubile young women.

Besides the minimal chores that *bashali* women must do to feed themselves and keep warm, there is little work.[7] In fact, in a cross-cultural survey of existing literature on twenty-six menstrual houses throughout the world, the only consistent similarity amid a bewildering array of different customs and beliefs was that during their time in all of these varied menstrual houses women experienced a reprieve from their normal labors (Maggi 1992). In every case, women were relieved of the responsibility of cooking for family members, and, with the notable exception of the Dogon of Mali (Strassmann 1991:105), women were also freed of their responsibilities in food production. Both Alma Gottlieb and Emily Martin, commenting on the prevalent assumption that menstrual taboos are "oppressive," note that "prohibitions" against women working could as easily be seen as a boon to women as a form of male dominance (Buckley and Gottlieb 1988:14; Martin 1987, 1988).[8]

After we had finished washing, Taksina and the other teenage, childless girls and I went to sit in the field just above the *bashali*. On the high water canal across the river, fifteen or twenty of the young men from Balanguru village had gathered to play drums and dance in the sunshine. The high valley walls cast a shadow over Balanguru well before early afternoon, so the sunny spot is a favorite gathering place. But as there are lots of other sunny places that don't look down directly on the bashali I speculated, "Are those boys dancing for us?" "Whatever else?" Lulu giggled. Little girls, both Kalasha and Muslim, were playing tag all around us. Taksina kept yelling at them to watch what they were doing—if they touched one of us she'd have to throw them in the river. Slowly the shade crept over us, and we retreated inside to shell walnuts for the evening's porridge.

After all the fuss my family had made about food, I had expected dry bread and black tea. But because Silima had recently given birth the *bashali* literally flowed with all good things, brought by Silima's friends and relatives as a way of offering their congratulations. We begin with *išpónyak,* a thick porridge made from wheat flour and topped off with walnut oil. (Walnut oil is pressed by hand out of mashed walnuts. The walnut paste is kneaded, and water is added a drop at a time to extract the oil. It is a very "hot," rich food, especially good for new mothers.) Wazira Aya took charge of the whole operation, issuing food and commands. Kashkar teased that she was our "mother" and assured me that we would be well provided for. Fifteen minutes later we ate wheat bread with two kinds of cheese, which someone dropped off for Silima. We had just started eating the walnuts and dried mulberries I had brought when Iglas' Aya showed up with a big plate of cooked rice. She said she had made it for me, worried that I would be hungry! (I later learned that when there are no newly delivered babies food in the *bashali* is not so abundant. Everyone brings something with them when they come, and families drop off flour or bread during the week, but sometimes meals resembled a potluck in which everyone assumed everyone else would bring the main course. When there is little food, everyone eats less, including those who contributed what food there is.)

As dusk fell, speculation began about who would come that evening. Since groups of women tend to be on the same cycle each month, everyone knows who is expected and who is late. Zarina Aya should have been there yesterday or the day before, two women commented. Could she be pregnant again? They sang a favorite *bashali* song:

> khošmas ta wázi gála
> andáy kúra bata híu, bašáli
> kúra bata híu

> [Khoshmas has [is said to have] washed and gone
> Who will come here again, *bashali*
> Who will come again?]

Four other women arrived in quick succession around nightfall, Zarina Aya last of all. After the traditional kissing of hands, cheeks, and braids, each was rushed to the fire and offered bread and cheese while everyone checked up on all the people they shared in common. Altogether there were twelve women, four toddlers, and one newborn baby.

Life in the *bashali* reminded me of an ongoing slumber party. While they are there, women, even the most vain of young women, seem not to worry much about how they look. Belts are loosened or not worn at all. The *bashali* is the only place where women can take off their ṣuṣútr headdress, and often the heaviest of their beads, and relax—not worrying that their braids are "fuzzy." It is the only place where I saw women wander about aimlessly, sleep well past sunrise, or dance and sing purely for the fun of it.

Zarina Aya had brought a little hashish and one cigarette. We all shared it, and, though it didn't go very far split among twelve women, it set the tone for a relaxed (and slightly naughty) social evening. Zarina Aya does not walk the straight and narrow path of Kalasha morality. She smokes a lot, flirts a lot, and is widely rumored to have lovers. But Kalasha society seems to have a fairly high tolerance for individual variations in behavior. Although she is the subject of lots of juicy gossip, Zarina Aya is well liked. She is a gentle person, generous with her friends, and a loving and playful mother.

Hours of talking and storytelling commenced. They talked about husbands, and mothers-in-law, about recent elopements, about the political conflicts the people of Rumbur were having with the people of nearby Ayun. The best storytellers were pressed to tell their tales. I told "Jack and the Beanstalk," a story far more meaningful in this place where people can imagine the horror of having a son trade your only cow for a handful of beans. I crept into bed and drifted in and out of elaborate stories about king's sons, fairies, evil step-mothers, and cannibalism.

I closed my eyes for a second and woke to a rousing game of "show us your newly developed breasts." The younger women were all being coerced into revealing their budding breasts. Since Kalasha dresses are so modest, whose breasts were large and whose nonexistent was a surprise to everyone. Girls with small nipples were teased that they had been letting the boys pinch them. Taksina and Lulu began wrestling rambunctiously, trying to pinch one another. Then they grabbed up Zarina Aya's seven-month-old daughter and tried to see who could get the baby to nurse from them. This was slightly illicit. "Oh-bayyy-ohhh," gasped Silima in amused astonishment. Other women shook their heads at the silly antics, but no one put a stop to the game. A little later Taksina started getting out of hand, and she was sharply put down by one of the older women for saying things that were too embarrassing, gossip that was too pointed.

While the central part of the evening's social life was shared by everyone, there were clear differences in interest between the older women and girls who had not yet had children. The girls bolted outside whenever they heard someone on the road, and we could hear them out there giggling with passing boys. Everyone stayed up until well past 11:00, far later than the usual winter bedtime.

One by one, women began to turn in. There were only six beds, and Silima, because she had a new baby, slept in a bed by herself. The rest of us doubled up or tripled up in the narrow beds. A huge bonfire was built in the fire pit, and I was uncomfortably hot through the night. Kashkar wrapped herself around me, tenderly stroking my face. It was hard for me to sleep in the arms of an unfamiliar woman, but I appreciated the relaxed, physically intimate way in which women relate to one another here. Women woke up in shifts and added wood to the fires. The new baby cried, and Silima called out for Kashkar, "Sister, can you take him for a while?" Kashkar was sound asleep, her arms and legs twisted around me. Zarina Aya got up quietly, moved her own toddler to the center of the bed, and went to pick up Silima's baby. Silima said she hadn't been able to sleep all night and was too tired to care for him. Zarina Aya reswaddled him and rocked and sang softly to him until he fell asleep, then tucked him against his sleeping mother. Around 4:00, three other women got up and swaddled the baby again, talking quietly around the fire for a while. At 6:00, the women who had gone to bed earliest got up and made tea, while everyone else slept well into the morning.

While we waited for the winter sun to come out, we drank tea, ate yesterday's leftover bread and cheese, and talked. Finally, giving up on the sun, Kashkar, Lulu, Taksina, and I all went back to the water channel to finish washing so we could go home. Beads, headdresses, socks, menstrual cloths, dresses, belts, earrings, bracelets, and eventually hair and bodies are all thoroughly scrubbed. Wazira Aya came down and asked Lulu if she were "washing" today, a euphemism for asking if her period was finished so that she could wash and leave the *bashali*. Lulu said she was. "Show me," demanded Wazira Aya. Lulu looked at her in disgust and started to protest, but then she relented and offered proof that she was no longer bleeding—"You see, the *pragata* is finished," she said defiantly. Taksina was not so lucky. "Ohbayooo," Taksina said, disappointed. This was her eighth day in the *bashali,* and she was homesick. Wazira Aya turned to me and explained that young girls (she herself is only twenty-three or twenty-four) sometimes try to go home too soon, so they check one another. She didn't ask Kashkar or me for proof that our periods were finished.

Kashkar and Lulu and I continued, heating up big pots of water and pouring it for one another as we held our breath against the cold and washed under the overcast sky. The transformation complete, we hurried back to the *bashali.* Silima sent Lulu to scrub her feet again (they admittedly hadn't come very clean). "You need to scrape harder," Silima chastised. "People will think you didn't wash well." I remember thinking how beautiful Kashkar and Lulu looked and felt clean and new myself. Zarina Aya teased us that tonight would be our *amátak trómiš*—our evening of becoming impure, hinting that now that we were "*onjesta*" again tonight we would sleep with our husbands.

I was sent home with messages from *bashali* women for sisters, mothers, brothers, and friends in my village—some general greetings, and some more specific instructions such as, "Tell Bibi Nara Aya that I will come in two days, so she should finish my daughter's headdress." On the way out, a woman brought us water with which to wash our feet one more time. "Don't come back for nine months," the women called out as we left. Everyone I met on the way home asked politely, "Hey, sister, did you wash?"

A Quantitative Sketch of Women's Reproductive Lives

I want to pause for a brief quantitative sketch of Kalasha women's reproductive lives. Understanding women's reproductive life histories, including the variation between women, is important for understanding the role the *bashali* plays in women's lives and how the impact of this institution shifts over the course of the life cycle. In the West, most women so regulate their reproductive careers with birth control that it is easy to forget that menstruation is a relatively rare event in natural fertility populations such as the Kalasha. In such populations, menstruating one week out of every month, month after month, is typical only at the beginning and end of a woman's reproductive life.

Because menstruation is marked religiously, socially, and spatially by the fact that women go to the *bashali,* Kalasha women seem to have remarkable memories of their reproductive histories, and most were interested in recounting them for me. I conducted an extensive "marriage and fertility survey" in which I asked women to detail their reproductive life histories, recalling how long they menstruated before becoming pregnant for the first time, the outcome of each pregnancy, birth spacing, how long each child was breast-fed, the duration of lactational amenorrhea, and, if menopausal, how long after their last pregnancy they had ceased menstruating.

I interviewed eighty-three women and threw out only one interview that seemed unreliable. I talked with all women I was able to make contact with and made an effort to interview women from different villages, of different ages, and from different economic locations. Most women were interested in the questions and were happy to participate. The sample consists of twenty-three menopausal women, twenty-eight women who were currently menstruating, twenty women in lactational amenorrhea, and eleven pregnant women. There are likely more menstruating women in my sample than in the general population simply because, as I noted in earlier chapters, Kalasha women move around a lot, so the *bashali* was an easy place to locate women with time for an interview.

Table 3 describes the average reproductive career of the twenty-three menopausal women I interviewed. A hypothetical average woman's life in the *bashali* would be shaped like this:

During the first 3.5 years of her reproductive life—the time between her first menstruation and her first pregnancy—she would go to the *bashali* 41.6 times. Given that women report staying in the *bashali* 5 to 6 days each month (some say 5, some say 6, some

TABLE 3. **Average Reproductive Career of Menopausal Women**

	Average	Range	Comments
Number of years menstruating	22.8	16–28	
Number of pregnancies	8.4	1–16	
Number of years menstruating before first pregnancy	3.5	1–11	
Number of live births	7.3	1–11	All women in this sample had at least one child.
Number of stillbirths	0.3	0–2	17% report stillbirths.
Number of miscarriages (*khóda nás*)	0.9	0–6	48% of women had at least one miscarriage.
Number of children who died before one month	1.0	0–5	52% report at least one child died before one month.
Number of (additional) children who died before one year	0.6	0–2	57% report at least one child died between one month and one year.
Number of (additional) children who died before age five	0.7	0–3	47% report at least one child died between one and five years.
Number of surviving children	4.9	0–10	One woman had no surviving children.
Number of months breast-feeding each child	24.5	22.8–31	
Number of months in lactational amenorrhea	15.7	0–31.3	
Number of years between cessation of lactational amenorrhea following last pregnancy and onset of menopause	4.4	1 mo–12 yrs	

report going anywhere from 4 to 10 days), she would spend 229 days in the *bashali* before she became pregnant with her first child. Approximately 18 percent of her total time during this part of her life is spent living in the *bashali*.

During the next 14.9 years of her life, the time between her first pregnancy and the end of lactational amenorrhea after her last pregnancy, this hypothetical average woman will be pregnant for a total of 5.9 years (during her 7.5 completed pregnancies and .91 miscarriages) and will be in lactational amenorrhea for 7.3 years. (I did not record the time in postpartum amenorrhea following a miscarriage, stillbirth, or newborn death.) This leaves only 20.7 months in which she will be menstruating (out of a total possible 178.7 months), which means that she'll spend 114 days in the *bashali* as a menstruating woman. After the delivery of each of her 7.5 completed pregnancies, she will spend an average of 16 days in the bashali (the time women spend varies between 12 and 20 days), for a total of 120 days. During this period of her life, she'll spend 234 days in the *bashali*—approximately 4.3 percent of her time.

Our average woman menstruates for 4.4 years between the birth of her last child or pregnancy and the onset of menopause. Kalasha women noted that their cycles became extremely variable just before the onset of menopause (cf. Treloar et al. 1967), but if we assume that they go every month they would be in the *bashali* a total of 292 days, again, 18 percent of their time.

Kalasha women can expect to spend slightly more than two full years in the *bashali* over the course of their reproductive lives. Two-thirds of that time will take place before their first pregnancy and after their last.

I want, however, to compare this average woman with several real women whose lives had quite different reproductive trajectories. There is a lot of variation between women, and this variation has dramatic effect on the amount of time each woman spends in the *bashali* over the course of her life.

1. *Pilin Gul's Reproductive History.*
Pilin Gul says that her average menstrual cycle lasted 5 to 6 days. Over the course of her life, she spent a total of 1,133 days in the

bashali, 3.1 years. She never experienced lactational amenorrhea and says that going to the *bashali* was sometimes difficult because she had to bring her young nursing infants with her. In the winter, when her infants were very young, she would stay at her Muslim neighbor's house so she wouldn't have to carry the babies through snowstorms. Otherwise, she says she always went to the *bashali* and never chose to "stay the night" at her own house.

TABLE 4.   **Reproductive History of Pilin Gul (married, cowife, with five adult children; approximate age 53)**

Preg. No.	Child's Name	Menstrual Age[a]	Live/Mis./ Still	Months Pregnant	Months Lived	Months Breast-fed	Lact. Amen.	Months in Bashali[b]
		3						
1	W	0.75	l	9		1.5	0	36
2	D	2.5	l	9		2	0	21
3	S	2.25	l	9		2	0	18
4	R	2	l	9		2	0	15
5		2.5	s	10	0			20
6		0.75	m	3				6
7		0.75	m	3				6
8	G	0.75	l	9		2	0	0
9		2.75	l	9	3			24
	(Menopause)	5						60
Total months		276		70			0	206

[a]"Menstrual Age" refers to the length of time a woman has been menstruating. Most Kalasha women do not keep track of how "old" they are but found it quite easy to tell me how many years they menstruated before they became pregnant for the first time, how much time passed between the birth of the first child and the next pregnancy, and so on.

[b]"Months in Bashali" refers to the number of times a woman went to the *bashali* between pregnancies.

2.   *Khoshma Gul's Reproductive History.*

Like Pilin Gul, Khoshma Gul also raised five children to adulthood (and had one daughter who drowned at age twelve). She says that she, too, went to the *bashali* regularly and stayed there 5 to 6 days. Her reported menstrual career was almost 4 years shorter than Pilin Gul's, and she was in lactational amenorrhea an average of 1.3 years after the birth of each child. As a result, she spent only 450 days in the *bashali* over the course of her reproductive career, about 1.25 years.

TABLE 5. **Reproductive History of Khoshma Gul (married, with five adult children; approximate age 48)**

Preg. No.	Child's Name	Menstrual Age[a]	Live/Mis./Still	Months Pregnant	Months Lived	Months Breast-fed	Lact. Amen.	Months in Bashali[b]
		2						
1	G	0.75	l	9	12 yrs	2.5	12	24
2	G	3	l	9		2	20	15
3	WJ	2.4	l	9	1.5 yrs	1.5	15	0
4	K	2	l	9		1.5	12	0
5	S	2	l	9		2	0	3
6		1	m	3				9
7	S	0.92	l	9		2	22	2
8	K	3	l	9		4	24	5
(Menopause)		2						24
Total		229		66			105	82

[a]"Menstrual Age" refers to the length of time a woman has been menstruating. Most Kalasha women do not keep track of how "old" they are but found it quite easy to tell me how many years they menstruated before they became pregnant for the first time, how much time passed between the birth of the first child and the next pregnancy, and so on.

[b]"Months in Bashali" refers to the number of times a woman went to the *bashali* between pregnancies.

3. Sawarash's Reproductive History.

Sawarash's reproductive life history is a source of great sorrow to her. Both she and her sister were very "unfortunate," began menstruating well after their age mates, and had difficulty becoming pregnant. She also claims that she menstruated for 9 to 10 days each month, even when she was a young woman. Sawarash is a very careful, pious person and says she never thought about staying at her own house instead of going to the *bashali*. Nevertheless, staying in the *bashali* for so many days, month after month, was clearly a burden rather than a source of pleasure (although she said there were things she enjoyed as well). She cycled longer than most Kalasha women, never experienced lactational amenorrhea, and was pregnant only three times. Calculated at her reported length of stay of 9.5 days per month, she spent a total of 3,135 days in the *bashali*, or about 8 years, 7 months. Though I suspect that some of the figures she quoted me are exaggerated, they clearly reflect her feelings about the *bashali*. She said that she felt as if her work were constantly interrupted, and going to the bashali was a continual reminder that she was not pregnant—and she had desperately wished for more children. Sawarash told me, "If you go to the *bashali* a lot, your 'meat is finished' (*mos khul hiu*) and you get old fast."

TABLE 6.   Reproductive History of Sawarash (married, with one adult child; approximate age 58)

Preg. No.	Child's Name	Menstrual Age[a]	Live/Mis./ Still	Months Pregnant	Months Lived	Months Breast-fed	Lact. Amen.	Months in Bashali[b]
		10						
1		0.75	1	9	1		0	120
2		7	1	9	7		0	75
3	D	2	1	9		2	0	15
	(Menopause)	10						120
Total		357		27			0	330

[a]"Menstrual Age" refers to the length of time a woman has been menstruating. Most Kalasha women do not keep track of how "old" they are but found it quite easy to tell me how many years they menstruated before they became pregnant for the first time, how much time passed between the birth of the first child and the next pregnancy, and so on.

[b]"Months in Bashali" refers to the number of times a woman went to the *bashali* between pregnancies.

The Ritual World of the Bashali

In chapter 1, I demonstrated the ways in which Kalasha women actively participate in the creation and maintenance of the *onjesta* and *pragata* spaces through which their spiritual and physical world is organized. If you imagine *"pragataness"* as a storm that swirls across the landscape of Kalashadesh, the *bashali* is the eye of that storm, central to it and yet serene because it is there that the *pragata* is properly contained and rendered harmless. Going to the *bashali* is itself a religious act, a conscious effort on the part of each woman to do her part to maintain order in the world, ensuring fertility and productivity. It is also more than this. Women's religious expression is most vibrant in the *bashali*, for here women conduct their own rituals and make offerings to and ask for blessing from a goddess, Dezalik, who is all their own. In other words, in the *bashali* women speak with God directly,[9] rather than allowing men to speak to God on their behalf, as happens in most other contexts.

Very little has been written about the ritual or social life of Kalasha women in their *bashali*, although the very inaccessibility of this institution makes it an object of intense speculation for Kalasha men and male anthropologists, who both trivialize and eroticize *bashali* life. Parkes, writing of women's rituals in the *bashali*, comments, "Men know virtually nothing about this private cult (nor do I) except that it involves some seemingly bizarre forms of ritual lesbianism" (1983:196). Kalasha men, too, figuring that I didn't have sense enough not to answer embarrassing questions, often asked me "What do those women do in there? What do they talk about? Do they wear clothes?" In fact, women's rituals are no more (or less) bizarre or exotic or elaborate than men's. They don't overturn or invert the rest of Kalasha religion but refine and extend it by focusing attention on two essential components of Kalasha life: human reproduction and women's community.

Dezalik

At the heart of the *bashali* is the goddess Dezalik, who lives in the menstrual house and protects *bashali* women and their infants, especially during the difficult and dangerous process of childbirth. Although she lives in the *bashali*, the most *pragata* space in the valley, Dezalik is very *onjesta*: menstruating women take care not to touch her unless they have completed their cycle and washed thoroughly, thus becoming more *onjesta* and less pragata themselves. Presently she is represented by a wooden, eighteen-inch-tall triangular figure with an indented oval circle at the top and a diamond-shaped hole in the middle. She stands discreetly on a simple shelf against the back wall of the *bashali*, difficult to see because of the dim light, covered with black soot from the fires, her base strewn with the walnut shells of old offerings.[10] I asked Kimat Khana Aya, a jolly, spritely woman and a respected midwife (*súda uṣṭawáu*, lifter of children) what the circle and the hole represented. She leaned toward me and replied, conspiratorially, that the oval was her face, and the hole was her (whispering) *vagina*. This sent her young daughters-in-law rolling to the ground in gales of laughter, swearing that this was not true. "Well, whatever else could it be, crazy (*goṭ*)!" Kimat Khana Aya exclaimed in mock annoyance at their naïvete.

When a new *bashali* is built, a new figurine is usually also carved by a local Kalasha master woodworker. Old Dezalik figures are thrown beneath the branches of the largest holly oak tree, where they lie unceremoniously. Each one looks a little different—in fact, one resembled the horse heads that are found on the ritual altar of Mahandeo and in the Jestak Han (lineage houses). I didn't believe that this was a Dezalik figure since it was so strikingly different from the others. But older women like Mushiki swear that this was the Dezalik that was there when they were young girls, adding "the new ones look like nothing, not even a head, only a hole." "It doesn't matter what she looks like," Saras Gula Aya reminded me, "it's just wood anyway, not *really* Dezalik. We put the figure there to *remind* us of Dezalik." Dezalik, then, or at least the contemporary understanding of her, is an idea, not an idol.

Like other Kalasha gods and goddesses, Dezalik is (to anthropologists) disappointingly hypo-cognized (Levy 1984; see Parkes 1991 for a discussion of the nature of religious knowledge among the Kalasha). According to Georg Morgenstierne, who conducted extensive linguistic and cultural research in the Kalasha valleys in 1929 (as well as throughout the region during his lifetime), the Kalasha believed Dezalik to be the sister of Dezau, the god of creation (1951:165; see Palwal 1972 for a discussion of the associations between Kalasha divinities and their counterparts in what was greater Kafiristan). I tried this out with many women, saying, "I read in a book that Dezalik is the sister of Dezau. Is that right?" "Who knows, sister," would come the inevitable reply, "You're the one who can read. Perhaps it's right." "But have you heard this," I would press. No, they would say, they hadn't heard it, but that didn't mean it wasn't true. I could find no woman who claimed to know myths or stories about Dezalik, and she appears not to have a characterizable personality. "Dezalik is our *gaḍérak* [a respected "elder," a community leader]," the women explained simply on my first trip to the *bashali* and again whenever I asked. "She watches over us. She protects us." One woman added, "Men are afraid of her. She scares them. If they came in here, they would see her and run away frightened." Later, Saras Gula Aya elaborated for my tape recorder,

> When a new *bashali* is made, a new Dezalik is also made—made just like men make the *gaṇḍáw* [funeral statue] figures. Men make them, and then they are put in the *bashali* and we pray to her. She demands her share; she becomes Dezalik. We give her bread [food], right? We make offerings to her, that's her share, we call that her share. So the "one who eats her share" sits there; we throw bread to her, pray to her. When we pray to her, God [*khodáy*, the creator of God] sees. We just say we pray to her, and it is God who sees; it is a strange kind of praying. We just *say* Dezalik, we say Dezalik in God's name, forcefully and easily

[describing the degree of difficulty of each birth], this is God's work, grace (*méher*) comes from God. . . . It is there that we go to pray.

At family and community altars, men make offerings and sacrifices in which they pray for the health of the community, for God's help in protecting them from their enemies, for safety from landslides and floods, for the fertility of crops and livestock. In the *bashali,* women pray and make offerings solely about human reproduction, a domain that is their concern alone. *Bashali* rituals support young women, new mothers, and their infants socially and spiritually as they move through the exciting, frightening, and sometimes dangerous processes of becoming a woman, giving birth, and being born.

First Menstruation

One day, as I was walking up-valley past the *bashali,* I was surprised to see my young friend Geki. It was Geki's first time in the *bashali,* and she was the first of her age mates to go. She'd been there three days already, she said, and she liked it. She was eating watermelon with the other *bashali* women—watermelon, a special treat, had recently been brought to the bazaar, and Damsi Aya had bought two for the *bashali* women to share. Geki, Lulu, and Geki's cousin Shirin Shat walked off, giggling, their arms around one another's waists. I ran into Geki's mother and aunt later in the day and told them how happy Geki had seemed. "She may be happy now, but she about ate my head [drove me crazy] when she first went," Gekia Aya told me. Geki had cried and cried. She cried all night. She cried the next morning, refusing to get up out of her bed and drink tea. She cried all the way to the *bashali.* It was embarrassing to begin menstruating, they said, since everyone knows and makes comments. Although some girls are married quite young and shuttle back and forth between their natal home and their marital home for years, they are not expected to be sexually active with their husbands until they begin menstruating. Now Geki's husband would begin bothering her to have sex with him and would become increasingly jealous of her interaction with other boys.

The first time a girl goes to the *bashali,* she is ushered in enthusiastically by the other women there, who are of course surprised to see her. A woman who is almost finished with her period, and who characteristically stays in the menstrual house only five or six days (rather than someone with a history of long menstrual periods) makes an offering (ṭuṣulḗk) of three cracked walnuts, throwing them in Dezalik's face. "Make it finish quickly," the goddess is instructed. Walnuts are unambiguous symbols of fertility and sexuality, and walnuts themselves are loved by everyone, making everything from sauces to breads to dried fruits taste rich and sweet. Two or three days later, women from the girl's father's family will bring zánti aú, the same thick, wheat bread brought to honor a woman who has just given birth. The goddess will be offered her "share" of the bread, and again one of the women will request that she see that the girl will "finish quickly." After that, girls in her age group from all over the valley will come in turns to the edge of the menstrual house grounds to visit their friend, bringing with them gifts of food. For many of them, it is the first of many "grown-up" social calls they will pay to the bashali over the course of their lives as they are drawn into the communitywide responsibility women take for one another. On the sixth day, the new menstruator prepares to go home. This first time, she doesn't wash her own clothes or beads but is attended to by the other bashali women, who wash both her and her things before sending her home.

The average Kalasha girl will attend the bashali forty-two times (spending approximately 229 days there), until, as Saras Gula Aya says, "later, later, she will become pregnant, pregnant she will become zánti—her time to give birth will come."

Childbirth

The bashali is the only place where women talk openly about childbirth. Here young women can learn from watching others give birth, and laboring mothers can endure pain and intensity of childbirth in a place where they are supported physically, socially, and spiritually. While I was in the valleys, I attended three births. Two of these took place on the path en route to the bashali, so the emphasis was on rapid and discreet delivery rather than religious ceremony. The third birth I watched was a very easy delivery with no need to request help from the goddess. My descriptions of some rituals surrounding birth are therefore drawn from interviews rather than direct observation. Some details of rituals seemed especially private, so I haven't written about them here.

In my own culture, pregnancy and birth are public matters. I was pregnant when I began writing this chapter and was amazed daily that perfect strangers reached out to rub my belly and offer unsolicited advice, telling me stories about especially painful and long labors or miscarriages and birth defects. By contrast, Kalasha women's fear of the pain and many dangers of childbirth are private matters. Outside of the *bashali*, I rarely heard it discussed, except as the subject of rare whispered conversations between trusted friends. I remember my surprise at hearing Shaizara Aya, who had seemed to me to be supremely confident and relaxed, confide to her father-in-law's brother's wife that her fear of dying in childbirth had increased with every child. When she was younger, she hadn't realized that such terrible things could happen. In the *bashali*, however, conversations such as these are commonplace. Women who have just given birth are asked to tell and retell their birth stories to visiting women. Young girls (and young anthropologists) ask how much it hurts: "Less than having a tooth pulled without anesthetic," Bayda Aya once explained to me.

When Kalasha women realize they are in labor, they ideally wait quietly through the early contractions, notifying their family only when the pain becomes very intense. Mira Aya was so controlled that I didn't realize that she was in labor, though I had been having tea and talking with her and her family for hours. In retrospect, she did seem unusually quiet. She sat by her youngest son until he fell asleep and then announced to her husband that he'd better call the midwife and find someone to organize the necessary supplies—walnuts to offer to Dezalik, wheat and walnut oil for porridge, butter for the baby and to massage into the perineum. Mira Dada must have been taken off guard also because he scurried around frantically. He and I and the midwife (who in this case was Saras Gula Aya) had to run to catch up with his wife as she grabbed a torch and took off single-mindedly down the steep wooded slope to the river and then on up the road to the *bashali*.

Laboring women are usually accompanied to the *bashali* by one or two female relatives or friends. The women support the mother-to-be through the contractions, urge her to walk despite the pain, warn away men, and "catch" the baby if the urge to push becomes overwhelming. In the night, as Mira Dada did, men usually accompany their wives, lighting the way from a safe distance, so that they can neither see nor hear the laboring woman clearly. As I described in chapter 2, the presence of a man is intensely disconcerting and embarrassing to the women. For their part, Mira Dada and the other men I saw in his position all seemed concerned and unsettled by their helplessness, their lack of any role in this drama. Upon reaching the *bashali,* the women duck inside and the men go across the street to one of the hotels or to a friend's house to wait for word about the birth.

Inside the *bashali,* the women said that they had wondered if Mira Aya would come that evening. It was close to her time. As we came through the door, everyone got up to greet us with the traditional round of kisses to hands, cheeks, and braids. Kashkar arranged a bed for Mira Aya to lie on while Pirdausa Aya started a fire. Women took turns sitting on the bed with Mira Aya, stroking her face and telling her how good it was that she wasn't crying out. The other *bashali* women chatted and tended the fire. During the second, pushing stage, we all took turns supporting her by sitting and facing her as she squatted, stroking her face and hair and whispering encouragement. Saras Gula Aya checked her progress from behind, massaging her perineum with butter. God had blessed her with an easy labor, all the women commented, as a big baby boy slipped out after only fifteen minutes or so. There had been no need to pray for help. If the labor had been difficult, offerings would have been made to Dezalik, as Saras Gula Aya explained later:

> When *zánti* women [women whose time has come] go to the *bashali,* they bring some walnuts. Look, when we went with Taraki Bibia Aya we brought walnuts, but then she had the baby on the path—if she'd had it in the *bashali,* you would have seen it. If there is any difficulty, if the baby doesn't come quickly, at first they break one walnut—like this, they break one walnut and they pray like this—'Oh, my Dezalik of the *bashali,* make her deliver quickly, bring the new flower into her arms, don't make things difficult, your eating and drinking [for your sustenance].' We say that, breaking one walnut and throwing it to Dezalik. Then, if there is more difficulty, if she doesn't become *zánti* quickly, someone will call, "Oh, make an offering, make an offering, dear." Then one woman will go there and break three wal-

nuts, break three walnuts like this, and like this all the women together will say, "Oh, my Dezalik of the *bashali,* one has come under your care [?]. Bring health, set the flower in her arms, your eating and drinking." So we say, "bring health, bring health" we say, and then throw the three walnuts to her. Then if she doesn't quickly become *zánti,* again they call, "make an offering, dear." Again one woman goes there and breaks walnuts, breaks seven walnuts, and everyone, *everyone all together,* prays, "Oh, my Dezalik of the *bashali,* one has come under your care (?), bring health, set the flower in her arms, your eating and drinking." [If there is still more trouble, they begin again, first offering one walnut, then three, then seven.] They go on like that. Then she becomes *zánti.*

Saras Gula Aya explained that if the birth is unexpectedly difficult a hank of the laboring mother's beads will be placed around Dezalik. After the child is born, after the *ačhámbi* festival, the beads will be placed again on the mother's neck. If the baby is a girl, these beads will be given to her when she grows up. If it is a boy, they will be given to his wife.

The cord is tied off with a fringe broken from one of the women's belts and cut between pieces of sharp shale. Some *anglís* (probably UNICEF) donated scissors and other supplies for cutting the cord, Kashkar said, but they had disappeared very quickly. In the morning, the afterbirth is buried under the big holly oak tree. Immediately after the baby is born, the new mother will lie down and go directly to sleep while the other *bashali* women clean and swaddle the newborn. No matter what time it is, they also begin making the traditional thick wheat porridge topped with rich butter or walnut oil. This porridge is the original Kalasha comfort food—the first food introduced to babies and made when people are sick or simply feeling a little low. Before even tasting the porridge to see if it is salty enough, a bit of porridge is always offered to Dezalik. Then, hungry or not, the meal will be shared by everyone, and the new mother will be awakened and urged to eat. Later, the baby will be put to her breast, and the two will settle in for twelve to twenty days of resting (until the postpartum bleeding has stopped completely), during which they will be cared for continuously by the other *bashali* women.

Many of the customs that directly followed the birth of a baby were dropped twelve to fourteen years ago, as I discussed in more detail in chapter 2. I want to describe these former customs here because I can imagine them being of great interest to future Kalasha women and because older Kalasha women take great delight in recollecting them. The quotations are again from a taped interview with Saras Gula Aya, who vividly acted out her descriptions for me, to the amusement of her daughters-in-law and granddaughters, who fell off their stools and rolled on the floor in laughter.

> Before, in our time, we used to take rocks and cut the cord, cut it and tie it off with a string. And then, we call it [a secret word], the afterbirth that comes with the child. If it doesn't come out, if the afterbirth doesn't come out from the mother quickly, then we try all sorts of things—stick chicken feathers in her mouth, crush walnuts and put them like this on her head, we do this and then it comes out. Then we leave it until dawn. At dawn we go outside and look, women go out and look, look for men. "Men aren't walking around, come, come on," they say. So then a woman runs runs runs to the hollyoak tree, digs a hole, and buries it, buries the afterbirth under the ground.
>
> After she has the baby, she takes everything off, everything— beads, bracelets, earrings, even strings to tie her braids— eeevvvverything she undoes. These things are put far away. Then the next day, early, really early, they get up and look for birds. One woman, two women, go outside. The woman, she sits there naked, holding her baby, the *zánti* woman. That mother is naked—completelyyyyy naked. Then at dawn, they take one cloth for wrapping the baby (*boniátyak*) and cover the baby, and then she sits there like this, like this, crouching, crouching and holding her baby. Then the women go outside to look for birds. Soon they hear one: "tchcht, tchcht," it says. Then they go inside and call out, "The birds have sung, the birds have sung, put your dress on," they say. Then they sit there. Then she again runs runs runs, puts her dress far away, and runs to the place where they buried the afterbirth. She urinates there, urinates and then comes back to the *bashali*. There they put water in her hand—on the way out they put water in her hand, too. Three times, three times they put water in her hand, and she washes her hands like this. Like this, she washes her hands, and then she comes back through the

door and sits down. For six days they do this, our old custom, every dawn—the time Muslims say "arzan"—[and every evening] for six days. In our time, it was like this, like this my daughter. Now, no, now just a little.

The *zánti* woman didn't touch the menstruating women. They would give her water far away, holding it out for her like this and pouring it into her hands. They wouldn't touch her. If she were chewing tobacco, like this, they would drop it into her hand. If you touch her, you wash your hands. You wouldn't sit down— you would wash your hands right away. For six days, this is our custom. Before our custom was like this. The clothes that were used to swaddle the child for the first six days, these are called *pragáta bóniyak.* We tied them up with one of the belts used to tie the swaddling and hung them in the holly tree—you can still see some hanging there. We'd hold them out like this and tie them in the tree.

Before there were so many customs, many, many customs, now not anymore. Now they don't keep the customs—beads they leave around their neck, at dawn they don't go outside and look for birds, if they touch her they no longer wash their hands. Now nothing, nothing. They only do *ačhámbi.* "Third-day bread" they also do. In our time, there was so much culture, all these customs.

All of the discontinued customs were symbolic ways of creating space between the extremely *pragata* state just following childbirth (when the postpartum bleeding is at its heaviest) and the other women in the *bashali.* It is interesting to me that these old customs all involve personal inconvenience on the part of the new mother, so that when one woman asserted her right to "choose" not to follow them they very quickly fell out of fashion. The new jeep road brings cargo jeeps to and from Chitral, tourists, visitors from other valleys, and lots of foot traffic. Because the *bashali* lies next to the road, many of these customs, especially those that involve being naked, are hopelessly embarrassing for these very modest women. In fact, though, most women do observe the spirit of these customs, taking off most of their beads, leaving their dress unbelted, and staying inside for the first six days after the birth, going outside only in the early morning and late evening to urinate. These are days of complete rest for the new mother and baby. At the same time, all the elements that depend on communal effort—such as making porridge after a birth and performing the *ačhámbi* ceremony, are still very much intact.

The mother's husband's family brings *zánti aú* three times. The first morning after the baby is born the women in this family bake this bread, called "child's bread," and bring it to the *bashali* along with some especially good cheese that the family has hoarded to celebrate the birth of the child. The new mother won't go outside to greet her family, but the other *bashali* women will come out to receive the bread and visit about every detail of the birth and the health of mother and baby. A bit of bread is offered to Dezalik before the bread is shared by all the *bashali* women. A round of bread is also sent to the midwife on this first day. The child will have a special relationship with his or her mother's midwife the rest of his or her life, calling her *gáḍa āya* (big mother).

The family brings *zánti aú* again on the third day after the birth, this time called "third-day bread." Meanwhile, word of the new baby will have spread to relatives and friends across the valleys, who will have been flocking to the family's house to offer their congratulations: *bumbarák bo!* (Congratulations!) if the baby is a boy, *šaydár bo!* (You have something precious!) if she is a girl. Mira Dada had saved a big tin of his best cheese for the occasion. He dug it up it from beneath the water channel near his house where it had been safely hidden from the mice. The whole neighborhood was involved in cooking bread and making tea for the visitors.

Despite the safe birth and the celebration of the family, this story has a sad ending. Mira Aya left the *bashali* after only thirteen days, insisting that she had been there long enough, that her postpartum bleeding had stopped flowing, and that times had changed so that now it was unnecessary to stay such a long time. Although she was urged, scolded, and cajoled to stay longer, as the only woman of her house she felt she needed to get back to her fieldwork and her other children. The next week, she said that she had seen a red monster when she had gone to the boulder field near her house to urinate. A few days later her baby fell ill. I said it was pneumonia, but everyone agreed that we had to wait until his father came home to take him to the hospital in Chitral. I was holding him when he died. His sweet face haunts me still. A woman across the river divined (*istẹ̃ink kárik*— to divine using a bracelet dangled from a thread) that the child had died because his mother had left the *bashali* too soon, that the monster she had seen was evidence that she had still been in a *pragata* state. Mira Aya crumpled to the ground in despair and was sharply scolded by the usually kind women in my family. She was young and would have more children, they said. She needed to get up and take care of the ones she already had. The baby was gently swaddled in a white cloth and buried without a funeral in the graveyard. Friends and relatives returned to offer condolences.

ačhámbi

Finally, on the sixth morning, the family brings *ačhámbi aú* (*ačhámbi* bread) and prepares to perform the *ačhámbi* ceremony in which the new baby will be brought outside for the first time, washed, blessed, and introduced to the community. After the *bashali* women have made an offering to Dezalik, one of the *zánti aú* will be set aside. Later that day, two women accompany the new mother, and the three of them take this bread and perform a special ritual near the big holly oak tree. Then they go down to the water, where the new mother will wash for the first time since the birth of her baby. In the winter, all three women wash their feet and hands. In the summer, they'll take a much longed for bath. Then the women will wash their faces and return to the *bashali*.

The *ačhámbi* day tends to be exciting for everyone. The new mother is tired of staying inside in the dark *bashali*, husbands, friends and relatives look forward to seeing the baby for the first time, and little girls begin early getting wound up for their central role in this ritual. In the evening, one woman from the new father's family will round up all the female children who haven't yet begun to menstruate but are old enough to make the trek and head toward the *bashali*. Little girls from other settlements will stream in behind them. When we went to do *ačhámbi* for Gulabia Aya, the littlest girls were lined up and ready to go to the *bashali* at 10:00 A.M., though everyone told them it wouldn't happen for six or seven hours. They jumped about all day, pretending to purify one another and begging to be allowed to light fires. The girls bring new clothes and swaddling material for the baby, resin-soaked wood to make a fire, a cup to hold water, holly oak branches, and a big batch of bread and cheese.

When they reach the *bashali*, the girls will give the baby clothes and five or seven tasili breads to the *bashali* women, make a fire on the hill near the *bashali,* and sit down together to feast on the remaining bread and cheese. The *bashali* women take the bread and set it on the mantel for Dezalik—"It's *ačhámbi* bread," they tell her. Then one woman takes the baby and begins washing the child, swaddling it in the new, clean clothes. The new mother goes with another woman to the water channel, and again she washes her feet, hands, and face. If the baby is a girl, she collects five or seven little stones; for a boy, she gathers a piece of holly. Returning to the *bashali*, she asks, "Have you all washed my child?" "We've washed her," comes the response. The mother gathers her baby in her arms and hides it beneath a shawl, taking a large needle in one hand.

The new mother steps up to the boundary of the *bashali* territory, where the pack of little girls is waiting. Since the children are conducting the ritual, there is always a great deal of amusing confusion. One girl pours water into a second girl's hands. The second girl washes her hands, and then holds them out again. Her cupped palms are filled with water, which she then pours onto the outstretched hands of the new mother. The second girl takes a piece of holly, lights it, and circles it over her head before throwing it behind her. This should be repeated three times, although the kids often lose count, performing the blessing four or five times. When the ceremony is finished, the girls are the first in the community to get a peek at the new baby. Then they each grab a piece of resin-soaked wood, light it on fire, and charge up the mountain to the Jestak Han altar, where they pile up the wood and take turns jumping over the fire, shouting "*ačhámbi*-a-a-a-a" and shrieking with excitement at their own bravery. Now the new mother is free to come outside during the day to talk with visitors and sit in the sunshine. She can take a more thorough bath and braid her hair—a treat after six days.

I was often struck by the playful attitude women take toward their *bashali* rituals. While important and necessary, they are conducted with an air that is anything but somber. Once, for example, while waiting for Gazi Khana Aya to get ready for her *ačhámbi* ceremony, Nazibula Aya wrapped up her two year old and stepped up to the waiting girls. They acted out the whole ritual and were offered a glimpse of the new "baby"—who, spying her older cousin in the crowd, sprang up and squealed, "Hey, sister!" I never participated in male-only rituals at Sajigor or Mahandeo altars, but my husband tells me that, while often casual in their approach, men's rituals tend to be far more down to business.

Purification of the Bashali

Twice each spring the *bashali* itself is blessed and purified (*sučék*), once by the girls who live in the upper part of the valley and once by the girls who live down-valley. This, too, is a big event organized by the oldest girls who have not yet begun to menstruate. The girls go door to door the day before the blessing, asking that each household contribute wheat or corn to their cause. They sell the corn to buy things that the *bashali* women need—teapots or cups or plates or blankets. In the last fifteen years, Westerners and government officials and NGOs have been interested in donating beds, blankets, lanterns, and utensils for use in the *bashali*, "but when we were girls," explained Gazi Khana Aya, a serious woman of about forty, "it wasn't like that. We felt like the things we bought really mattered." The girls spend the morning grinding wheat at the water mill and have a party making baskets full of bread in several adjoining houses. The purification ceremony itself is exciting and funny because it involves having two girls run around the *bashali* naked, purifying it with burning holly oak branches. The day I saw them they argued and giggled the whole way about who would go in. One of the girls was Kosh Begim, a coy little nine year old who is the child bride of my friend Balaman. Balaman had just told me the day before that he would never allow his young wife to do this, but of course she never gave a thought to asking him. The group of about twenty girls ranged in age from about five to seventeen. They all proceeded to the *bashali*, where they discovered that they had forgotten the resin-soaked wood and were chastised for being so scatterbrained. It took them a good while to round some up. Then the two chosen girls undressed, one at a time, with lots of giggling as they attempted to get naked modestly behind the shawls the other girls held up to shield them (and occasionally lifted, revealing them to shrieks of laughter). All the men in the vicinity, including my husband, had been sharply chased away earlier. Finally naked, the two girls grabbed the burning wood and holly branches and streaked lightning fast into the *bashali* house, where they blessed it with the burning holly. They then peeked out the door and shouted that someone should throw them their underwear. Kosh Begim donned her pants, while the other girl wrapped up in a shawl, and they were sent running around the outside of the *bashali,* while everyone looked on laughing. Then the *bashali* women helped the girls onto the tin roof, where they giggled in embarrassment. They huddled together beneath the shawl and crept to each corner of the roof, shrieking each time they thought their "bottoms" might be "known." They were lowered off the roof and rushed back inside to warm up. The rest of the girls dispersed. The two girls would bathe and then be free to leave, not returning for five or six years when they would become menstruating women themselves.

The Social World of the Bashali

Although I knew better theoretically, having critiqued other anthropologists for the same thing in graduate seminars, I came to the valleys with this unexamined assumption tucked under my arm: I assumed that individual Kalasha women would see themselves as members of a community of women, defining itself against men and bound together by their shared experience of male dominance (for critiques, see hooks 1991; Mohanty 1985; John 1989; and Moore 1985). I tried in vain to encourage my friends to make generalizations about men and asked about men's work habits, sexuality, and how they treated their wives and children. "Some men were one way, and some another," was the inevitable reply—couldn't I see that for myself? Most men aren't interested in babies, but Sherdan even wipes the snot from their noses. Many men have affairs, but Khoshdina Dada never has. Some husbands are strict, some stingy, some indulgent. Gula Dada has loved to work since he was a toddler. His mother tells that when he was a child he liked to dig up little tree seedlings and replant them (he pretended to do this "for his wife"). Khan spends all his time drinking tea and playing cards in the bazaar. And the same was true of women—some were one way, some another. My friend and sometime assistant Wasiara Aya constantly made fun of my incessant survey taking (much to my annoyance, she often did this in front of other people). Not impressed with my explanation of sampling methods, she insisted that the differences between people were so great that I couldn't possibly learn anything by following the activities of only a few. My friends' reluctance to make comparisons that too simplistically swallow up the differences between individuals was a valuable lesson to me, one that I continually struggle to incorporate into my social science.

And yet there are times and places, set outside the context of the interdependence of everyday life, in which men and women set themselves in opposition and women *do* see themselves as women. The Chaumos winter solstice festival is one such time, a time when Rumbur Valley is at its most *onjesta,* a time when men and women achieve the idealized separation that is not possible in day to day life. The *bashali,* a place set outside of everyday places, as Chaumos is a time set outside of ordinary time, echoes this perfect separation of men and women. The *bashali* offers space for women to think of themselves as a community. Like all communities, *bashali* women are people of diverse opinions and positions, each with other allegiances and obligations. They are nonetheless bound together in this context by shared knowledge, work, space, and bodies. In this section, I want to delineate the ways in which the structure of the *bashali* contributes to the maintenance of *jamilishír,* the sisterhood of women, and comment on the ways in which this identity reinforces women's claims to freedom.

In societies that have "men's houses," separate buildings where only men congregate, ethnographers have inevitably been fascinated by the various ways in which these diverse institutions offer opportunities for social cohesion and socialization (Bateson 1958; Barth 1959; Mayberry-Lewis 1967; Hogbin 1970; Herdt 1987) and provide a dynamic repository for ritual knowledge in which cosmologies are not simply transmitted but "made" (Barth 1987). In *Gendered Spaces,* Daphne Spain argues that it is precisely the exclusive and secret nature of men's houses that make them so powerful (1992:67–79). As I noted earlier, "women's houses" have generally been thought of as places that mark the relative disempowerment of women. But in fact the Kalasha *bashali* offers an opportunity to women that is roughly analogous to what men's houses offer to men. The *bashali* is a space that is off limits to men, and knowledge about what goes on there is not discussed with them. As Georg Simmel noted, sometimes "secrecy is its own sociological purpose," that is, by the very act of sharing secrets "those who know form a community" (Wolff 1950:355). Women delight in the privacy afforded by their *bashali* and take it seriously, never discussing with Kalasha men the details of rituals, childbearing, or menstruation—to do so would be embarrassing, as these things are entirely "women's work."

It is not just that women's solidarity is created by the act of sharing knowledge. The structure of the institution organizes the way knowledge is transmitted, and this shapes the tenor of community life itself (cf. Barth 1987). Kalasha men's rituals always have a leader. Larger, more important rituals are directed by *kazis*, men who keep complex historical and ritual knowledge on behalf of the community. Smaller rituals are directed by elders in the family. But the membership of women in the *bashali* is constantly shifting, so that it is necessary that everyone understands *bashali* rules and be able to conduct *bashali* rituals. Women's community in the *bashali* (though not, of course, in everyday life, when women are acting as mothers-in-law and daughters-in-law and aunts and grandmothers) is therefore less hierarchical than men's.

Beyond shared understandings of rituals and reproduction, the *bashali* is a place where women's lives intersect physically and temporally, where women share property and purpose. Part of what Asmara Aya meant when she said that in the *bashali wã šíaw* is that there is space and time to get to know one another. Women often call the *bashali bašáli dur* or *bashali* house—*dur* in Kalasha connoting not only the physical structure but the people living there (*duráy moč*, or "house people," is another word for family). Inside the *bashali*, women interact as families do, sharing resources and work and responsibility for children. While men share ritual altars and high pastures and the little bazaar that has become the center of men's social life, the *bashali* is the only space in the valley that belongs in common to all women. I am reminded of a development project that provided land on which Kalasha women were encouraged to jointly grow vegetables for sale. The project failed utterly because in their daily lives women have their own families to take care of, their own work to do, and little incentive to act as a collective. But the *bashali* is a place where every woman comes, regardless of village or family or clan. Inside the *bashali*, women who otherwise have little in common work together, boiling and scrubbing the heavy cotton blankets, gathering wood for fires, cooking, and getting up at night to comfort an infant who is no relation. I noted earlier how girls jointly provision the *bashali* with the needed cups and pots and women donate worn-out shoes that are used by everyone.

I don't want to make the mistake of leading you to believe that women always achieve mystic solidarity simply by virtue of sharing time in the menstrual house. "It's terrible when none of your friends are there, *da ne kaṛiu* (it doesn't make one content)," complained teenaged Jalat Bibi, a sentiment I heard echoed many times. Yet one of the delightful things, for me at least, is that for a few days women whose paths otherwise rarely cross find things in common. I heard one dramatic example: Shah's mother and Geki's aunt had been angry with one another for years, and their feud came to a head when Shah wanted to marry Geki's younger sister and Geki's aunt refused to give her blessing. Although the marriage could have proceeded anyway, Geki's father said he wouldn't arrange the union unless his only sister could be persuaded. The two landed in the *bashali* at the same time. I was told that they didn't speak to one another for two days, but eventually the familiarity of eating together and sleeping in the same room thawed their mutual anger. Geki's aunt agreed to accept Shah's mother's apology along with some small gifts, and the marriage could go forward.

The privacy and free time afforded by staying in the *bashali* allow for an environment in which women behave differently than they do in the village.[11] It is of course a matter of degree, but inside the *bashali* grounds women related to one another more physically and playfully. Although Kalasha women tend to be affectionate to friends and relatives anyway, in everyday life touching is generally confined to greetings and goodbyes. In the *bashali,* women sleep wrapped around one another, stroll about arm in arm and hand in hand, and spend evenings huddled together around the fire. I noticed a lot more physical humor as well—pinching and slapping, for example—which otherwise was commonly only to young teenaged girls. Parcha Bibi once tackled me out of nowhere and wrestled me to the ground. Everyone but me seemed to find it particularly funny. I once stumbled across three women who were squatting in a circle in the woods behind the *bashali,* chatting and laughing about whose shit was the blackest—a result of eating charcoal, which women say is a "bad habit" but a very common one, especially in the *bashali.* This scene seemed especially funny since the four three-year old girls in my family had recently taken to holding hands and sitting in a circle for their morning pee. Perhaps the *bashali* is a place where women can recapture some of the unselfconsciousness of childhood. The *bashali* is the only place where women commonly sing and dance outside of a festival occasion. Almost every night the *bashali* is filled with song, and women encourage one another (and even coerce those who are shy) to dance in the center of a circle of clapping and laughter.

This extra physicality extends into an interest in sex, a subject I almost never heard women discuss seriously outside of this context. Given that the Kalasha are so sexualized by outsiders, and given my assumption that Kalasha women's claims to sexual freedom would correspond to an openness about discussions of sexuality, I came to the valleys expecting to find women willing to talk about sex. For the most part, they weren't. Before I learned better manners, I asked inappropriate and indiscreet questions that met with awkward, embarrassed silences. And so my first couple of times in the *bashali* I was surprised to receive a barrage of even more embarrassing and blunt questions about my own sex life and my husband's anatomy. Was it true that *aŋglís* had sex standing up? And how often did my husband like to have sex? Irak proclaimed that her husband could have sex five times in one night. I confessed that once or twice was enough for us. "Oh ho," cried Kashkar, "he must be very weak if he can only have sex one time in a night!" I was instructed to send him to the high pastures where he would grow more vital. Irak asked what Steve would bring me when he returned from Islamabad and could she share it? "Perhaps he'll bring her a big penis," suggested Gishen Bibi. "Would Irak like to share that?" I asked, as women fell off their stools and rolled on the ground laughing. Whenever firewood was low or the cookies or tea ran out, someone would comment that we should find a man and flirt with him so that he would bring more supplies. In addition, many women enjoyed homoerotic joking, a genre of humor I heard nowhere else. Women would comment that another woman was looking hard at her bottom ("Let her look, her husband has been up in the high pastures for such a long time, what else does she have to look at?"), joked about sleeping together like husband and wife ("I won't sleep in your bed, you'll make me pregnant!" "How would I make you pregnant, I don't have a penis"), and on and on. Erotic joking is an important part of the environment of intimacy and fun in the *bashali*. My questions about whether this same-sex erotic humor ever extended into physical, sexual relationships between women were received with blank incomprehension.[12]

Conversations also took more a more serious cast. In the privacy of the menstrual house, young women would discuss whether or not they had been sleeping with their husbands. I heard Matrik's mother-in-law (half) jokingly tell Matrik in front of other women that she should sleep with her son more. I heard other older women instruct young girls to wait to have sex until they were older, as pregnancy would trap them in marriage (see chapter 6). Young girls asked how much sex hurt. Women compared strategies for dealing with "pesky" husbands.

The openness about sexuality and the tendency toward more physical relationships with one another point to the most important, and perhaps most obvious, connection facilitating Kalasha women's community in the *bashali:* their shared embodiedness as female, as people who menstruate, miscarry, and give birth to children—some of whom live, and some of whom don't.[13] Indeed, the details of their reproductive lives are what bring them together as a community in the *bashali* in the first place. The *bashali* is a place of intense physical intimacy, where women share knowledge about their bodies that would be unthinkable in everyday life. Whereas birth for us is intensely personal, shared only with intimates and managed by medical professionals, every woman present at the *bashali* when someone comes to give birth is expected to participate, and the experience is private only to the extent that men are excluded. No Kalasha woman would think to be embarrassed about being seen by another woman—even someone she hardly knew—because the messiness, danger, and joy of birth is something women share with one another. Women compare the duration and amount of their menstrual flows and other details of their reproductive lives. The data I gathered about women's fertility histories were very interesting to my Kalasha friends. I found that women remembered accurately the details of other women's reproductive histories. The *bashali* is a place where none of the details of reproductive biology need be hidden—though I want to underscore that they are not romanticized either. One day Gulua, a woman in her early forties, came to the *bashali* for the first time in a couple of months. She went out back to the woods, complaining of a stomach ache. A while later she returned bearing a small, flat piece of slate. "Look what came out of me," she called, holding up a little piece of bloody tissue about the size of an index finger. A miscarriage, it was declared. One woman picked up a stick and began poking around, looking for the head. Standing in a circle, the women examined the aborted fetus, and then Gulua tossed it unceremoniously in the garbage pit next to the graveyard where women who die in childbirth are buried.

As these examples illustrate, Kalasha women have a fundamentally different relationship to reproduction, and to their reproductive bodies, than most contemporary American women. Emily Martin has shown how metaphors of failed production and alienation pervade American women's images of their bodies, how reproductive lives are given over to medical specialists and thus many experience the processes of menstruating and giving birth as frightening, disempowering, shameful, and fragmenting (1987). Kalasha women's experience of their reproductive selves is very different. It is certainly true, as I highlighted in the last chapter, that menstrual blood and the blood of parturition are explicitly *pragata* and that if not properly cared for this blood could have potentially disastrous effects. I had expected (hoped, even, I'll admit) that the cosmological significance of the blood that issues from women's bodies would be reversed in the menstrual house. But this isn't true either, at least not exactly. Rather, the menstrual house is a place where reproduction is demystified, approached with curiosity. In the *bashali,* menstrual blood and the blood of parturition are as normal as, say, a runny nose—a little inconvenient and messy, maybe, but certainly ordinary, even interesting. Of course, giving birth is still frightening and powerful, but each woman trusts that whoever is in the *bashali* when her "time" comes will know what to do and will take care of her. Each birth generates a community of memory and shared experience among the women present. Their association extends beyond the space and time of the birth in the *bashali.* They are connected by the children born into this community, who will call the midwife "great mother" (*gáḍa āya*); who may have nursed from another woman's breast, and thus will call her "milk mother" (*čhir āa*); and who will affectionately call other children born around the same time barabár (equal) or burubér (equal, affectionate). Because each woman stays in the *bashali* two to three weeks after the birth of a child, each child will have been held in its infancy by half to two-thirds of the menstruating women in the valley. This act of being enfolded and cherished within a circle of women will be reenacted again after death, when the deceased is encircled by mourning women who lovingly sing his or her praises.

The details of their reproductive lives form a body of knowledge and practice controlled entirely by women. While men may have something to say about almost everything else, in this arena they stand helplessly on the sidelines—looking on from a distance like Mira Dada or calling from the road to enquire politely about when this or that woman will wash. Men don't even have the words to ask directly about human reproduction since the names of women's reproductive organs and processes are the greatest secret of all.[14]

The Bashali Also Allows for Personal Space

The menstrual house offers women a space for an expanded social life, but it also serves as a place to briefly evade the thick tangle of social relations in the village and household. It was near Chaumos, a time when everyone in the valley is engaged in singing irreverent and pointed songs about everyone else. Begim and Zamin Khan had staged a botched elopement. Caught en route to their hiding place by her husband and uncles, she'd been dragged home struggling and crying, and Zamin Khan had been beaten by her husband's friends. The next morning, even before the valley burst into songs making fun of the whole affair, Begim took off for the *bashali*. I knew that she had been in the *bashali* just two weeks before, but when I asked if she were menstruating she snapped (uncharacteristically, for she is an unusually boisterous and jovial person), "Of course I am, why else would I be here?" Bayda Aya, who had come to the bazaar with me, pulled me close and whispered, "Why else would she be there? Of course, she's not menstruating again. She's embarrassed. She came here to wait for a few days until everyone thinks of something else to sing about." This was the first time I understood that the *bashali* is a place where women go not just because they *have* to but because they *can*. There were many examples. Retreating from the flurry of gossip and anger that follows an elopement (successful or not) was a common pattern.

And women would sometimes go to the *bashali* just to get away from home for a few days. One afternoon I passed Bronzik Gul, who was sitting near the river behind the *bashali*. She called out, asking why I hadn't come to the *bashali* the previous night. "There were so many women there, more than twenty." There weren't beds enough for everyone, so they built a fire outside and stayed up all night singing and telling stories. She said I should come just for one night. "Come even if it's not your 'time,'" she urged. "It's so much fun with

so many women around. Lots of women come even when they aren't
menstruating—Sumali is there right now, and she isn't menstruating." Later older women confirmed that it is common for young
women to go to the *bashali* when they aren't menstruating or to stay a
couple of extra days after their menstrual flow has stopped. One
mother-in-law, angry that her daughter-in-law had been at the *bashali*
eight days when she typically "washed" after five, sighed, "What can
I do? Only she knows if she is ready to wash or not."

Rumbur is a small world. It is a place where every relationship
has layers of history and multiple connections, a place where everyone knows what everyone else is doing. When I asked women questions about the strict purdah that is kept by their Muslim neighbors,
they always noted that they appreciated the "privacy" that walls and
doors and veils allow. In comparison, Kalasha social life is open.
Doors are never closed—or at least a closed door does not mean to
stay away. Kalasha build their villages up the sides of mountains,
where they can see and be seen, instead of nestled near river bottoms
as Chitralis prefer. Lives are lived outside. We'd sit on our front porch
and watch the people in the village across the river, commenting on
who was home, who was away and why, who had company, who
was beginning to cook dinner—and I'm sure they did the same.
When Asmara Aya said that the *bashali* is a place where *wã šíaw*, where
there is space, she meant this in particular: in the *bashali*, there are
fewer eyes on you. When you enter the *bashali* ground, you step into a
world where the people you interact with every day—husbands,
neighbors, in-laws, parents—can't influence you directly. They can't
talk to you unless you want them to, and they can't touch you at all.

This is important, especially for young women, because it means
that the *bashali* serves as a place where women can, and do, exercise the freedoms they claim for themselves. Their *bashali* provides a
space where women can go to make personal decisions about reproduction and marriage away from the social scrutiny and pressure of
village life.

In her two-and-a-half-year study of menstrual houses among the
Dogon of Mali, West Africa, Beverly Strassmann tested her hypothesis that menstrual taboos, and especially menstrual houses, evolved
as "anticuckoldry devices." By advertising female reproductive status, menstrual houses would help a man assess paternity, avoid marrying a pregnant woman, and avoid investing his resources in a child

not his own. She found menstrual house attendance to be singularly reliable evidence of menstruation. No woman gave birth to a child either early or later than nine months, and so Strassmann infers that no women in her study "faked" a menstrual period. Dogon men, she concludes, would be able to predict, as Strassmann herself could, when a woman had become pregnant and thus could avoid being cuckolded (Strassmann 1991). Among the Dogon, menstrual houses thus apparently limit women's ability to make reproductive decisions by making public what would otherwise be hidden (at least for a while). But the situation for the Kalasha seems to be quite different. It is true that a trip to the *bashali* does advertise female reproductive status but not reliably (although I must note that I did not replicate Strassmann's meticulous quantitative study, and so what I offer are qualitative observations that might inspire further inquiry).

Kalasha people, men as well as women, do pay attention to who goes to the *bashali* or observes the rules for staying in the house while menstruating. Women who are only three or four days late are barraged with suggestions that they are pregnant. A village elder once asked me if his factional rival's daughter had indeed gone to the *bashali* for the first time in three months and then shouted gleefully, "Ha, I knew it, she's miscarried a bastard child!" Women reported openly that if someone were to get pregnant by a lover while her husband was away, she would continue going to the *bashali* for a couple months until her husband returned (of course, each woman said that she wouldn't do that but knew others who had). Far from being an institution that helps Kalasha men assess their wives' reproductive status, the fact that women can and do go there when they are not menstruating means that it is further obscured.[15] And, while Kalasha women claim not to have knowledge of effective methods for inducing abortion (though they try eating lots of salt and jumping from high places), they report that women who are desperate sometimes do ask for medicine from nearby Gujar women. The ability to hide their pregnancy for a couple of months would give them time to make reproductive decisions without involving the entire household. (This, of course, is sheer speculation on my part, since no woman in my study admitted that she had done this—again, they knew others who knew others who had.)

When Kalasha people say that their women are free, they mean primarily that they do not live under the *ultimate* authority of their husbands: They are free to resist. But this isn't always easy, since along with this culturally acknowledged right is an equally strong sense that women *should* obey their husbands. In the *bashali*, this balance tips in favor of women. Parcha Bibi and I were nearly always in the *bashali* at the same time. She was young and wild, always flirting with pass-ersby. She had been given to her husband, Bandara, by her father when she was quite young. He was much older, and quite strange, and while he tended to grow on you after awhile he hadn't yet grown on Parcha Bibi (though my friends now write that they are quite happy together and expecting their first child). He would follow her around the valley, alternately cajoling her with promises of trips to exotic places and berating her for her unwifely behavior. But when she went to the *bashali* she could escape him totally. Each time he'd stand for a while on the edge of the *bashali* grounds, begging her to come and talk with him and bribing other women to talk her into coming out. And each time she would refuse, emerging only after he'd left in an exasper-ated huff.

Bibi Shan is one of only two Kalasha girls who have completed their high school education. (Now she is in Peshawar learning to be the first female Pakistani pilot—but that's another story.) While I was in the valleys, an English woman started a "guide program." Young Kalasha people who could speak a little bit of English would serve as guides for the tourists who come to the valleys in the summertime. Bibi Shan asked to be a guide and was chosen for the position. Her young husband forbade her to participate, saying that he didn't want her "running around" so much, associating with so many strangers. Bibi Shan left that evening for the *bashali*, slipping out the next morn-ing before he could prevent her from going to Chitral for training.

Women have apparently been using their *bashali* as a place to escape angry husbands for a long time. A. Raziq Palwal writes that he witnessed the following scene in the Kalasha valleys in 1970:

> A man came and yelled at his wife who was inside the Seclusion House. She came out, crossed the river water by jumping over it from rock to rock and reached her husband. They took positions of about one to two meters apart from one another. They talked but did not reach any agreement on their mutual problem. She finally walked away, but the man rushed in front of her and tried to stop her. As he was not allowed to hold, push or pull her, she

continued toward him. The man, probably instinctively, grabbed a stick and started brandishing it before her to keep her away. The woman continued walking toward him and forcing the man to retreat. Neither he nor his weapon was tabu-proof and the result of his endeavors was a failure. (1972:47)

Young women also use the *bashali* as a place where they can resist being coerced into marriages. When Taksina was seventeen or so, her family gave her as a wife to her dead sister's husband, Mirshadin. Her sister had died in childbirth, leaving an infant daughter and a grieving husband, so this match solved problems for everyone—everyone but Taksina. Because the entire community was in favor of this marriage, Taksina received little support, though she claimed Mirshadin hit her and constantly compared her to her dead sister. When she had exhausted other means of protest to this marriage—refusing to talk, running away to her natal family at every chance, flirting openly with other men—she finally retreated to the *bashali* for ten days. Mirshadin was beside himself. "I'll become Muslim," he told me, "I swear I will. At least my wife couldn't leave me." One night, Mirshadin, claiming that he saw Taksina flirting with the Pakhtun hotel manager (right across the street from the *bashali*), burst onto the *bashali* grounds and began hitting and shaking her. The other women finally persuaded him to leave. Mirshadin's act was shocking, and most women said they could remember no other case of a Kalasha man violating *bashali* boundaries. Later he would have to make expensive offerings at Sajigor in reparation. Taksina's father took her to Chitral, where X rays confirmed a cracked rib, and her father and mother finally agreed that the marriage should be dissolved. They would give Mirshadin's bridewealth back, and Taksina would be free. "What is one cracked rib," Taksina told me later, "I am free of him."

By far the most dramatic use of the *bashali* is as a stage from which elopements are launched. Chapter 6 will discuss elopement (*alaṣíŋ*) in more detail: going *alaṣíŋ* is the prototypical act symbolizing Kalasha women's freedom. The *bashali* is the place where these dangerous, complicated, romantic events are often organized and executed. Fredrik Barth told me that a woman eloped with her lover from the *bashali* while he was on a brief visit to Rumbur Valley in the 1950s. Of three successful elopements that took place during my fieldwork, two were initiated from the *bashali*. One of these women "fled" right from the bed I was sharing with her, while I, the intrepid anthropologist, slept through the whole thing.

Begim, the young woman who suffered the embarrassing failed elopement attempt described earlier, left before sunup with Zamin Khan. They'd spent the whole week planning her departure. Zamin Khan's friends came by again and again, hoping for the chance to talk to Begim alone. Finally, they all met by the river in back of the *bashali* grounds, and she agreed that they would try again that night. She seemed excited but not appreciably more giddy than usual, and I was surprised that she wasn't more nervous in the face of the life change she was about to undergo. She told me that they had come for her the night before, too, but she hadn't awakened. Begim's husband, Aktar Shah, and his friends were also circling around, having been tipped off that she was going to elope. Two nights in a row they stood on the road and threw rocks that clattered down on the metal roof of the *bashali* until Begim and her friends came out to yell at them. "Go ahead and go," Aktar Shah dared, "and we'll kill you and him and burn your house down." "Burn it already," retorted Begim. The next day, Begim announced that it was time for her to wash, and she washed all her clothes and braided her hair. Later in the afternoon, she came into the *bashali* house sighing that she had "started again" and would have to stay at least another night. That afternoon her mother showed up in a fury and attracted a crowd. She begged Begim not to elope, and instructed her to wash and come straight to her natal home, where they would work this out. Begim told me, and the other women in the *bashali,* that she would cancel her elopement plans since her mother was so upset—how could she disobey her own mother? We believed her. At least I did. And this was important to the success of her escape. While it is true that in the *bashali* there is less pressure and more room to maneuver, the *bashali* community is part of the larger one, and this necessarily divided their loyalties. Aktar Shah's mother's sister's daughter was there, as well as two other women who were relatives and friends. On Begim's side, Zar Gul (whose husband, Tarsing, is one of Zamin Khan's clan mates and the key organizer of the elopement) and Talimzar (who is Begim's father's brother's wife and one of her closest friends) provided her with cover and logistical and moral support.

That night the dogs started barking again. Talimzar went out to see what was going on. There was a pause, and then we heard her shout, "You boys stop teasing those dogs!" The next morning, the dogs barked again, and Talimzar went outside again. After she returned, Begim is said to have mumbled that she needed to urinate (I was sleeping at this point). Later Talimzar said that she had arranged everything, instructing Zamin Khan to come back at dawn, when no one would suspect anything, and throw a rock at the dog so that she would wake up and be able to rouse the notoriously sound sleeper, Begim. Begim had gone outside, put on her clean clothes, and sneaked up the back path to Balanguru with Zamin Khan, two of his friends, and her girlfriend, Lulu.

While the village raged with news of the elopement, the two lovers hid at Zamin Khan's mother's brother's house. When I visited them there, Begim told me that the *bashali* was the only place in the village where she was not being watched by her former husband and his friends. And it was the only place where she was not constantly lobbied by her natal family and her husband's family to stay or encouraged by her new husband's friends and relatives to go. She said that in the *bashali* she had decided for herself what she wanted.

A Space for Agency

> One goes into the room—but the resources of the English
> language would be much put to the stretch, and whole
> flights of words would need to wing their way
> illegitimately into existence before a woman could say
> what happens when she goes into a room.
> —Virginia Woolf, *A Room of One's Own*
> (cited in Probyn 1993:166)

In very concrete ways, for each Kalasha woman, the *bashali* is a room of one's own, a place at the same time set outside the pushing and pulling of everyday valley life and very much central to it. Far from being a prison where women are confined, the *bashali*, as Asmara Aya notes, is a place where *wã šíaw*, where there is space. The *bashali* is a place where women do things, say things, that would be difficult or inappropriate in other contexts, and the things they do here have consequences that emanate beyond the *bashali* ground itself.

- Here they relate directly with the goddess Dezalik and through their attention to her ensure the safe reproduction of the Kalasha community.
- Here women live as *jamilishír,* a community of Kalasha women with a common purpose. In the *bashali,* there is the opportunity to reconnect with women from other parts of the valley, women who otherwise would be known only superficially. Perhaps collective life inside the *bashali* serves as a basis for women's collective action in other contexts. Saras Gula Aya once told me, "You know, young men are like that—they don't listen to just one woman. If you want them to do what you want, you have to join together."
- Here young women escape the constant scrutiny of in-laws, parents, and anxious young husbands and have the opportunity to make reproductive and marital decisions away from the intense social pressure of the village.
- Here women receive a respite from day to day work at home and in their fields.
- Here there is space for laughter, affection, long lazy naps, extra cups of tea.
- Here they deliver babies and slay a few dragons.

In other words, the *bashali* is a space where women experience an expanded sense of themselves as effective agents, as free people.

Chapter 6

Marrying

You have told me to tell you of the things I remember from the very beginning. At first I remember this, my daughter, I think I was very small, maybe Zairah's age, maybe a little older, as old as Abida perhaps, my memories start. My fathers were five brothers. One of my father's sons, the oldest father's son, he was my brother [cousin], he played with me a lot. When shade fell across the valley, they would come home from the stable. One of them would pick me up and set me on his knee, then another one would pick me up. Then they would tease me, "you've already become a wife." "I'm not going to," I said, "I'm never going to." In the very beginning, I remember this. Then "she's Istroluk's wife," they'd say, "she's Istroluk's wife" [teasing her about an old and particularly randy man from Chetromagrom]. "I am not," I would say. "When, then, sing a song," they'd say. And I'd sit like this on their knees and sing apparently:

> *khē him, khē him, ónja, ne?*
> [What will I do (or what will I become), what will I do now?]
>
> *Then they'd all laugh, and cry, "sing again, sing again." So I apparently sang that song, "khē him, khē him, ónja, ne?" It went like this until Istroluk died, and then they all said, "oh, her husband has died." My earliest memories are these. "So, her husband has died," all my fathers went on saying.*
>
> —Saras Gula Aya[1]

Although it must have been sixty years since Saras Gula Aya (who was called Pilin Gul before the birth of her daughter, Saras Gul) was a toddler, I can picture her clearly because I have witnessed this familiar scene over and over again. A little girl, so small that she has started to grow only one tiny sprout of a forehead braid, is held as the cherished center in a circle of men from her patriline—her father and his brothers, her own brothers and male cousins. The men tease her that they have "given her away," all the while letting her know through their cuddles and smiles and obvious delight that they adore her, that she is theirs. Her beloved "fathers" tell her that she is married, and she exclaims that she is not, will never be—what will she do, what will she do?

In Saras Gula Aya's earliest memories, she had begun dealing with marriage or, rather what she would *do* about marriage. The right to elope with a man other than the one to whom your parents have "given" you, to go *alasíŋ* (or to choose not to), is the prototypic act that defines Kalasha women's freedom—a freedom that must always be balanced against an equally compelling ideal, respect for and devotion to one's family and patriline. By sorting out what is involved in making and living with this decision, I hope to outline what Kalasha mean when they say "our women are *free*"—to outline, in other words, a specifically Kalasha understanding of women's agency.

Freedom for Kalasha women is anything but detached from people and consequences. The deceptively simple act of "sitting" or "going" changes the direction of each woman's life, as well as her understanding of what sort of person she is. Each woman's decision is affected by many people and affects many more. To demonstrate how complex, difficult, and always contingent marital freedom is, I offer the life stories of two of my closest friends. Although I also draw on stories of many other Kalasha people, I begin and conclude this chapter with Saras Gula Aya's story. Nested inside her narrative is her daughter-in-law Bayda Aya's story of her romantic elopement with Saras Gula Aya's son. Their stories are complicated and rather long (although they were simplified and shortened for me, and I have further clarified them for you). I hope that unpacking them will allow me to provide a more nuanced understanding of women's agency, while giving you enough ethnographic detail to draw your own conclusions.

In the evenings around the fire, Saras Gula Aya told me stories about her life. She said I should tape them because there were so many words that I would surely forget most of them if I didn't. Even she had forgotten so much, she said.[2] Her grandchildren crowded around and hushed one another and took turns being my assistant by running the tape recorder. The next day they would ask if they could listen to the stories again. Saras Gula Aya's four daughters-in-law were also there for most of the recordings—interjecting commentary and reminding her, to her annoyance, of parts of the story that she had forgotten.

~

When she was small, Pilin Gul was very naughty. She made all the other children cry, she said. She was the oldest among her many cousins and siblings, though only two days older than her cousin (Father's brother's son, or FBS), Mizok. The little girls would be playing at making a belt, and she remembers taking their yarn and tying knots in it. She would go out into the fields and try to grab birds. Once she and her little sister were walking by the river on their way to a festival. A boy her age, now a respected ritual and historical expert, but then *"he was nothing—just a little puff—came along carrying a big stick."* So Pilin Gul *"took that stick from him, took it and wouldn't give it back."* She tossed the stick over his head to her little sister and told her to throw it in the river. The boy tried to grab the stick, fell in himself, and was carried downstream a short way. *"Oh, the water is taking him, I thought."* So she ran away, taking her sister with her. Because Pilin Gul was such a "cunning" child, she knew better than to admit to her family what had happened, so she and her sister sneaked up-valley the back way to the festivities. A little later her mother saw the boy standing naked on the riverbank while his father wrung out his shirt and pants. *"What happened? How did he get so wet?"* Pilin Gul's mother asked innocently. *"What happened? Your own daughter threw him in the river! Whatever else happened! Your daughter threw him in the river and ran away!"* Pilin Gul's mother was angry, *"like one who bitches at evil spirits. 'Well, then I'm going to throw this daughter of mine in, too!'"* she declared. She dragged Pilin Gul to the river and threw her in the water, pulled her out, and then dunked her again. Finally, she was rescued by one of her mother's sisters, who grabbed her mother's dress and pushed her out of the way, then pulled the drenched girl out of the river. Her aunt offered to take her to her house to warm up and change clothes, but Pilin Gul refused—she didn't want to miss the *gul parík* ritual at Sagigor (when infants would be blessed and their mothers' released from the restrictions they had undertaken since giving birth). Pilin

Gul was like that, she remembers—a naughty child, a clever child, a child with endless enthusiasm for singing and dancing and playing. *"They could scold me and scold me, but I wouldn't obey,"* she explained to me and her grandchildren, who were delighted to hear that their grandmother, who now scolds them for being naughty, was herself a naughty child.

~

From then on, memories rush in—she goes on growing older, remembering and knowing, she becomes herself. For the next twenty years, what she remembers, what seems memorable enough to tell about, is marriage.

How Kalasha Marriages Work

More specifically, Saras Gula Aya focuses her attention not on *being* married but on the process of marrying or *becoming* married. Marrying is a topic that never tires. It is an arena where values and interest intersect, a point of intrigue and romance and desire, alliance and betrayal and desperation. Jokes about marriage and elopement seem never to wear thin. Rumors about potential elopements sweep the length of one valley and jump the mountain into the next before the truth can catch up. Both men and women scheme and dream on behalf of brothers and sisters, friends and cousins, imagining possible matches and potential futures. It is an arena in which nothing is settled for years and years.

Kalasha marriages are interesting, both to them and to me, because there are so many variations. Some people get married quite young, some late, some once, and a rare few change partners four or five times. Some men have two wives. Some marriages are arranged, and some are elopements (*alaṣíŋ*).

One day Gekia Aya and I were talking with her young teenaged daughter Geki and Geki's girlfriends. Each girl was in a very different marital situation. Geki had been given in marriage when she was quite young, five or six, but had recently eloped with another man. Lilizar, one of her friends, had been promised by her family that she would not be "given" (would not have marriage arranged for her) and that she herself could fall in love and marry whom she pleased. Kosh

Begim, though only about nine years old herself, had been married for two years to Balaman, a man of about twenty-five. Balaman's first wife, with whom he claims to have been passionately in love, eloped with another man. Jam Gulu, who was thirteen years old, was not a wife and exclaimed defiantly that she would never marry (though no one believed her). Asham, also thirteen or fourteen, had just that week been given by her parents to Shah, a handsome young man liked by everyone (except at this point by Asham). Geki mercilessly teased Jam Gulu for saying she would never marry and teased Asham about her new husband. Later Gekia Aya scolded her daughter for teasing the other girls, saying, "This is our custom—we marry in different ways and at different times." Everyone has his or her own story, private and powerful.

Kalasha words for marrying do not refer to the relationship *between* partners but specifically to the transformation of a girl into a wife. When you refer to a woman's marriage, whether she was given by her parents or eloped with her husband, you say she *ǰa thi áau*, "became a wife." When you refer to a man's marriage you say he *ǰa kái áau*, "made a wife." The reverse construction, *berú thi áau* or *berú kái áau*, "became a husband" or "made a husband," is understandable but not used (i.e., I could use it and people understood what I meant, but I never heard anyone use it themselves). The act of getting married (for a man) is referred to as *ǰa nik*, or "taking a wife" (actually *leading* since a woman is an animate object). Parents "give" (*dek*) their daughters in marriage, *ǰa dek*. If you ask a woman who "gave" her, she will respond with the name of the person she holds responsible, almost always a man, usually her father, but possibly a mother's brother or grandfather or a community elder. Women always speak in the passive voice about their arranged marriages, saying of their husbands, *may aníu*, literally "he took me." In speaking of their elopements, women can choose whether to represent themselves as more active or more passive participants—one can say either *a alaṣíŋ páyam* (or *párim*) (I went *alaṣíŋ* or I am going *alaṣíŋ*) or *may alaṣíŋ aníu* (or *níu*) (he led me *alaṣíŋ* or he will lead me *alaṣíŋ*).

Most Kalasha girls are "given" when they are young, between about six and twelve years old, well before they "know their own choice" (*tása mi čit ǰhónen*). Often girls are given to men much older than they are, men whose previous wives had eloped with other men. But sometimes the husbands are also children—in a few cases the children had been promised to one another as infants. Table 7 documents marriage statistics among a sample of eighty-two Kalasha women from Rumbur Valley.

In every case, the boy's relatives "search" (khójik) for the girl, never the reverse. Male representatives from his family ask male members of hers to "give" them the girl. Her family member usually represent themselves as passive, coerced into whichever decision is made. If they agree, it is because the boy's family asked them, and—"what could they do?"—to refuse would be an insult. If they refuse, they almost always assert that, while they may be able to give their daughters as children, when she is older she would likely rebel and make her own "choice" anyway—that is, she would go alaṣíŋ with another man. Bayda Aya explains:

> First they say, "Will you give your daughter to me? I'll give her to my son." Then, if he [the father] likes the idea, he'll say, like, "I'll give her. What can I do? You've asked me, you've gotten under me (may nóa ata). I've given you my daughter." If [the father] doesn't like it, he says, "It's her own choice, when she's big she'll go alaṣíŋ. It's her mood. I can't give her to someone who is looking for a girl. If I give her, then she'll say later 'you gave me forcefully, you ripped my heart out.'"

As you can imagine, this simple schema has endless convolutions. It is also highly political, since it is not just the future of the girl but the future relations between families on which each potential match pivots. Since every male member of the family—uncles, older brothers, grandfathers, and mother's brothers as well as the girl's father—should be in agreement, underlying currents of division and dissension between male family members are brought to the surface. And, while most women I spoke with readily agreed with the dominant ideology that it is men who make decisions about marrying daughters, in fact women are consulted, and their opinions frequently affect the outcome,[3] either because they persuade male relatives to take their position or because they personally have enough influence to claim for themselves the authority to refuse or accept the proposal (as in the case presented in chapter 5, in which the match between Asham and Shah was delayed until Asham's paternal aunt could be persuaded). The process of negotiating a marriage is often contentious, and these

TABLE 7. Kalasha Marriages

Type	N	Percentage	Menstrual Age[a]	Relative Age of Husband[b]
First marriage				
Given	54[c]	66.7	−3.17	+11.49
Eloped	24	29.6	+.9	+4.35
Unclear	2[d]	2.47	+1.75	+7
Not married	1	1.23	+7	
	81[e]			
Second marriage				
Given	1[f]	3.8	+1	+10
Eloped	25[g]	86	+1.02	+5.04
Widowed (eloped)	1			
(Given to HyB)[h]	2			
	29			

Kalasha women who elope with a second husband: 31% (25 out of 80)
Kalasha women "given" as children who elope later: 42.6% (23 out of 54)
Kalasha women allowed to elope "from their father's house" (*dadas dur alaṣíŋ*) who elope a second time: 8.3% (2 out of 24)

Note: In addition, there was one woman who had been married three times and one who had been married four times (although two of those times she was with the man less than one month and bridewealth was not exchanged).

[a]Very few Kalasha people know how old they are in years, but they feel comfortable talking about their age in relation to one another and to significant life events. When I initially began asking women how old they were when they first married, most replied, "A year before I started going to the *bashali*," and so on. So instead of estimating each girl's age I have chosen to use the number of years relative to onset of menarche.

[b]"Relative age of husband" is the number of years older or younger each woman thought her husband was.

[c]Four women report being given as infants. These four are not included in age averages, nor are their husbands.

[d]Two women were not able to answer the question, "Were you given in marriage or did you elope?" They both said that they were coerced by their families into going *alaṣíŋ* but that it was not their "own choice." These women are the only ones who reported being "unhappy" after going *alaṣíŋ*.

[e]I surveyed 82 women. One didn't want to talk about her first marriage, so she is not included here. One young woman, Gul, has been menstruating for seven years and is not yet married. She lives in a complex, fragmented family. Her mother left her father when she was young and now lives in a different village and begs for a living. She is the only woman from any of the valleys who lives in this way. Her father's brother's wife died, leaving two small children, whom Gul cares for with the help of her elderly aunt (who is widowed and childless).

[f]This woman was "given" to her father's friend when she was two years old, but no bridewealth was exchanged. When her "husband" eloped with a woman his own age, she was "freed," and her father "gave" her a second time.

[g]The four women who reported having been "given" as infants all eloped with other men.

[h]HyB refers to late husband's younger brother.

decisions are often protracted and difficult (Parkes 1983; cf. Kratz 2000 for an interesting analysis of the agency of different actors as revealed through marriage negotiations among the Okiek).

The Khaltabár Relationship

After agreement has been reached that the girl will be given in marriage, a date is set when she will be sent to her husband's house. Accompanied by one or two male relatives, she will then be taken—usually kicking and screaming, though sometimes happily—to her in-laws' house. They will make a *marát*, a sacrifice and subsequent feast of an animal for the men who brought her, counted as the first of much bridewealth to follow. In a few days, or sometimes as much as a month or two later, her father will "call" for her, saying he misses his daughter and wants her to come home. This event is the first *khaltabarí*, in which the two patrilineages involved will "make *khaltabár*" with one another. All the available men in the girl's clan escort her home, bearing a showy procession of bridewealth—bulls and goats, guns, large assorted aluminum pots and pans, fancy woven coats, sugar and tea, large radio/cassette players, money, and huge basketfuls of walnut bread. Women say that it is always a happy occasion for girls, who love to go home. The girl is given bags of candy, for which little children mob her along the way. This is her only role. Once home, she will likely retreat with her girlfriends, sisters, and cousins to a place away from the men. Her family will have spent the day preparing a feast of bread and cheese and wine to greet their new *khaltabár*. Her husband need not be there. It is a celebration and affirmation of a link between families and lineages and has very little to do with the relationship between the couple itself.

On the day that Takat Jan's lineage made *khaltabarí* to celebrate the marriage of Takat Jan's brother to Kosh Begim, Takat Jan asked me what the English word for *khaltabar* was. I told him that my parents call my in-laws "Wynne's in-laws" and have no formal relationship with them. "What a pity," he said, explaining that in Kalasha the word *khaltabar* comes from the root *khal* (to taste) and *khaltabars* are thought to add sweetness, flavor, to life. Parents of both the bride and groom call each another *khaltabar* (a reciprocal term), and all other relations address one another as *bilahí*. As Takat Jan remarked, they are the sweetest of relations, extending from the closest to the most distant kin, depending on the situation. People wax poetic on the goodness of the *khaltabar* relationship, the best of all possible worlds—a relative who treats you always as an honored guest. The *khaltabar* relation is highly emotional and all about the desire to pull people into your life, to make a connection through the connection of your children. Calling someone *bilahí* or *khaltabar* is a gesture of affection, not just a term of address. It is always spoken as a call of welcome, with gusto and delight. Iraka Aya, an opinionated, emotional, funny neighbor, and her daughter Irak were telling me about Irak's elopement from the man her parents had given her to as a child. Iraka Aya is still disappointed about it. Irak insists that her former husband, Pundali, didn't want her, and this is why she left him. "It's not true," exclaims her mother, "He wants to marry his son to your daughter!" Pundali often pushes Irak to say she'll giver her daughter Diana (named after Princess Di) to his son Saktiar. He never failed to ask me how his *khaltabar* was. His desire to marry their children was proof to Iraka Aya that her former son-in-law is still in love with her daughter, a sort of second-generation consummation of desire (cf. Trawick 1990).

The alliance between the families of the young husband and wife is also important for pragmatic social and economic reasons: their houses are always open and wine and honey and all good things flow when you visit. As Parkes demonstrates, material and physical "assistance to wife-giving affines invariably outweighs that given to any other kin, irrespective of their relative wealth, their personal relationship of affection or their factional party" (1983:275). You rely on your *khaltabar* to support you, shelter you, welcome you, help you if you need extra labor, and offer any other assistance you might need. Yet this alliance is fragile because it lasts only as long as the marriage itself and therefore depends on the future cooperation of a child who may grow up and sever this relationship by eloping with another man.[4]

Pilin Gul's (Saras Gula Aya's) story continues.

She remembers when they were giving her as a wife. She was about eight years old. She remembers her "fathers" (her father and father's brothers) telling her, *"We're giving you as a wife."* She was thinking, *"they're just saying that."* *"Then it was evening. When it was evening the men who were 'looking for a girl' came."* Her family offered food to the men. "'We're giving you as a wife,' they said, and they gave them food." Pilin Gul was crying, crying as if she might break into pieces. Her oldest father told her that they hadn't given her away, her mother's brother had given her. But she didn't believe him. She knew that they had done this to her their own selves. The men ate and went away.

After some days, she was taken to her new in-laws' house. They lived only a few minutes' walk from her mother's brother's house, and so she ran away and went there. The next day her mother's brother took her home again. "*They took me home and my mother gave me food, gave me food, but I didn't eat it, the bread. My mother beat me.*⁵ *She beat me, and I left again; again I went to my* moa's [mother's brother's] *house.*" Her mother told her later, with annoyance, that she was a crazy girl to make so much trouble—if she didn't like her husband she knew she could go *alaṣíŋ* when she was grown.

"*So it went on and on like that* [living at her natal house]. *On and on as my memories become clearer. How many years was it like that? Maybe until I was as old as Lilizar. That old? Yeah, exactly as old as Lilizar* [about twelve]."

Finally, they really took Pilin Gul to her in-law's house. Her husband, who was a boy then, only two years older than Pilin Gul, is nowhere to be found in her narrative of this time. She formed new friendships with her sisters-in-law, and her mother-in-law was especially kind to her. "*My mother-in-law was so good to me, so good to me. They sought me when I was little—this little—and so my mother-in-law brought so many things to me. When I was older, and they had taken me to her house, she would go to Chet Guru* [her husband's family's summer fields, where she would go to work—long before Chet Guru became the tiny, lovely village it is today]. . . . *She would make jā̇ú* [special walnut bread] *just for me or come with tomatoes in her hand. When shade fell, she would bring tomatoes to me. Bibi Zar and I were the same age, and Nawshar was littler. So she would bring tomatoes.* . . . *'Here,' she'd say, 'steal this away and eat it.' She'd whisper, 'you eat this, eat this yourself, don't show them.' But I'd say, 'those are my sisters-in-law* [jómi], *we'll eat it together.' 'No, they're fine over there already, you eat it.' But I'd share it with them. We'd all eat it together.*"

∿

For two years, Pilin Gul shuttled back and forth between her father's and husband's houses. Then she started menstruating. For three more years, she was a nubile young woman (*moráy*), moving between the *bashali*, her fathers' house, and her husband's house.

Girls' Agency

Pilin Gul was typical in her fierce resistance to marriage. It is also typical that her resistance changed nothing. Almost all of the women who told me stories of being "given" as children (two-thirds of all Kalasha girls are married in this way) filled their narratives with brave defiance and narrow escapes. The songs my littlest girlfriends loved best were variations on the theme "my father adores me too much to give me away." Most little girls do not passively accept their parents' decisions—like Pilin Gul, they cry and scream, they run away, they refuse to speak or eat, and in general they behave abominably. Yet, because nothing is expected of them, nothing they do changes anything. Of course, the adults involved are angry—as Pilin Gul's mother was—but ultimately the fact that girls do not happily acquiesce to their parents' plans has few enduring consequences. Little girls are not *expected* to be responsible daughters-in-law, to stay put in their husband's home, or to have any sort of relationship with their husband while they are young (though the pressure does increase as they near adolescence). So the fact that there is no expectation that they will behave in certain ways makes all their running away, all their resistance, ineffective. If, as Knauft (1996) suggests, agency implies having an effect, then girls—for all they may resist—do not have agency. No matter what a young girl does, she is still married. So the *khaltabár* relationship between a girl's parents and her in-laws, which is generated *through* her, is in this sense also independent of her.[6] Girls are thus truly able to be treated as symbols in Lévi-Strauss's sense, as things, like words, which are exchanged as a means to binding others (1969:496).

I don't mean to imply that parents don't love their daughters or think about their future happiness and welfare when agreeing to arrange marriages for them. But, because every girl will have the opportunity to elope later if she is unhappy or in love with someone else, her parents, and especially the men of her family, are able to put the particularities of their *khaltabár* alliances ahead of thinking about what sort of life she will have with this particular husband or family. Thus, the freedom she will have later works against her as a child because her parents are able to disregard her feelings about the marriage by telling her (and themselves)—as Pilin Gul says her mother insisted—that she can always elope later if she wants to. By deferring effective agency until girls become women, Kalasha families who arrange marriages for young girls thus also defer the problem Lévi-Strauss refers to when he remembers that "insofar as she is defined as a sign, she must also be recognized as a generator of signs" (1969:496). Still, everyone involved is acutely aware that eventually a time will come when she will decide for herself whether to stay or whether to say to her parents, as Mayram put it: "I was little when you gave me away, and so you didn't ask my opinion. Now I am grown up, and I am telling you that I have different ideas about what I want." In fact, 43 percent of the women I surveyed who had been "given" as girls did have different ideas and eloped with another man as young women.

So, while little girls are not agentive in Knauft's sense of being *effective* in the present, they certainly fit Hobart's (1990) definition of agency as being "liable to act." And, while the marital freedom promised girls may work against them by making it easier for their parents to "give" them, it also works *for* them because husbands and in-laws know that they can leave later. Husbands and in-laws are therefore typically kind and generous in an attempt to win the loyalty and affection of their wives and daughters-in-law. Their future freedom means that Kalasha daughters-in-law enjoy a very different situation than young Taiwanese wives, as described by Margery Wolf (1968), or Kalasha stereotypes about the lives of young Chitrali wives, in which girls are under the thumb of their in-laws and there is little or no chance of escaping an unhappy situation. Older husbands of young girls are notoriously generous and kind to their "little wives," buying them shoes, clothes, beads, and candy or, like Zailun's first husband (in the upcoming narrative), by not pressuring them to have sexual relations. Pilin Gul remembers that her own mother-in-law slipped her special foods and did her special favors. In other words, although some girls might be "given" as children, the affection and loyalty of the women they will become must be won.

"You forgot to tell her how you went alasíŋ!" Lilizar Aya, the wife of Saras Gula Aya's (Pilin Gul's) oldest son, pointed out. Saras Gula Aya replied, *"Who is telling this? You? My daughter doesn't want to hear about*

that, that wasn't a 'real' alaṣíŋ that was just zit, just a couple of days, just retribution because I was angry. Bayda Aya can tell her about going alaṣíŋ, going alaṣíŋ with Bayda Dada." Saras Gul Aya told with a twinkle how her son, Miramin (who is now called Bayda Dada since the birth of his first daughter), had come to her three times, exclaiming that he was going to get married to this or that woman. The first one turned out to be a relative. *"She's too close,"* she told her son, *"don't take that one. Besides, she's lazy."* The next time he said, *"Mother, shall I show you my lover/friend? Shall I take this one?"* She told him not to take that one either, because *"she's weak and sickly."* Then, at a funeral for which many people from the other two Kalasha valleys had come to dance, Miramin said to his mother, *"Mother, shall I show you my friend/lover? This time you had better not say anything—one girlfriend is lazy, the next sickly—You won't let me marry anyone!"* She only glimpsed Bayda Aya (then called Zailun before the birth of her first daughter, Bayda) across the dance field briefly, but she said okay, you take that one. But it was four years before her son could bring the then Zailun to Rumbur as his wife.

A few days later I asked Bayda Aya and her husband's brother's wife, Nizara Aya to explain slowly, and in detail, how marriages are negotiated and the sequence of bridewealth prestations. As often happened, they quickly broke from the general to the particularities of their own lives. They began by explaining that girls cry when they first go to their new in-laws house, going *bring-brang* (making a ruckus).

"I was like that myself when I was sought and given (khóji dáyani). I was sought and given when I was my daughter's age [9]." Zailun had sobbed and sobbed. Her grandfather, then already an old man, said to her, *"No, my grandchild, that man was so in love with you, he was in love, so I gave you to him—I like that man so much. Later, you'll see, you'll also not be able to go anywhere* [you also will be in love, and so won't want to go alaṣíŋ]. *I am your grandfather, I've used my wisdom for you."* Zailun's grandfather told her that her husband was a good man, and from a good family, and that Zailun should respect her grandfather and do as

he said. But Zailun was a little girl—what did she know about wisdom? *"I'm not going!"* she proclaimed. Two years later, her own grandfather led her to her husband's house, and they made a *marát,* a sacrifice in her grandfather's honor. *"I was there, what, ten days or so, and again I cried, 'I'm leaving!' Every day I cried—'I'm leaving, I can't stay here.' My mother's brother's house was close. Every day I'd cry. Everyone said to me, 'Your husband is a good person. You sit there. He won't try to sleep with you.'"* Bayda Aya laughed and continued. *"'You're little still. You sit there.' That was right, sister. I was little, and he never tried to sleep in the bed. In his house, there was only one bed—he was only one single person. I slept on the bed, and he slept on the floor—until I was a young woman it was like that. He never touched me. As long as I was there as his wife, he never slept with me. So now I think, maybe I was wicked (gunagár háwis), I think. He, I never let him—how could he have slept* [a euphemism for sex] *with me? Even when I was a mature girl (moráy) I wouldn't let him. 'Don't ever let him sleep with me already!' I thought. My heart was not warm for him—I was given to him forcefully. . . . Maybe he thought, 'if I don't force her, she won't go aḷasíŋ.' I was afraid, afraid to sleep in his house, but he never asserted himself (wes ne árau). . . . I kept thinking, if only they hadn't given me to this man. My grandfather said to me, 'you sit, you sit, you sit'—urging me repeatedly to stay. It wasn't my fortune, maybe. I went aḷasíŋ with Bayda Dada."*

After she had been at her first husband's house only a few days, her father called for her to come back home, saying he missed her, saying his heart was breaking for her. Her husband and his lineage brought her back home, along with *"lots of bridewealth—seven goats, whatever, whatever bridewealth. It was like that. I spent most of my time at my father's house, only a little time at my husband's house. It was like that until I went aḷasíŋ,"* Bayda Aya concluded.

Bridewealth

Let me pause here for a moment to talk about bridewealth because understanding how bridewealth works in the Kalasha valleys is an important key to understanding Bayda Aya's and Saras Gula Aya's stories. The particular constellation of Kalasha bridewealth practices frame cultural understandings of women's marital freedom, as these "rules" simultaneously extend and limit women's opportunities to make economic choices and choices about marriage partners and sexuality.

Kalasha fit the economic and social profile of most bridewealth societies, which, as Bossen generalizes, typically

> have low levels of economic specialization and stratification, and sexual divisions of labor that assign the major part of agricultural production to women. They have the capacity to accumulate wealth, as evinced by the material transfers at marriage, but generally do not have highly concentrated or uneven distributions of private property, particularly in land. . . . Bridewealth is also associated with patrilineal decent and patrilocal residence after marriage. (1988:132; see also Goody 1973:50)

Bridewealth is also associated with polygyny and the exclusion of daughters from patrilineal inheritance (ibid.), and this, too, is true for the Kalasha. For all that is common, Kalasha bridewealth practices in their details, and these unique aspects are important for understanding gender relations.

Existing interpretations of Kalasha bridewealth are typical of anthropological literature on bridewealth generally. One gets the impression that women are sold into wifehood and that through this transaction men gain access to women's productive and reproductive labor and forge alliances between groups. Yet, as Laurel Bossen has wondered, such interpretations spark the question. "What are the advantages and disadvantages to women?" (1988:133). Before answering this question, let me detail what Kalasha bridewealth is and how it works.

Bridewealth is known simply as *mal,* or "property," and consists of a mix of ceremonial wealth objects and livestock (including grain and cheese and more recently sugar, tea, and biscuits). Major ceremonial wealth objects include some antique items such as large cauldrons that were manufactured at the end of the last century by a specialist caste of Tajik blacksmiths and among an offshoot of this caste living in the Shishi-Kuh Valley; precious metal cups; large, wrought iron tripods, which are much larger than those used in households for everyday cooking (these are used to support caldrons in which meat is cooked at feasts); guns, including antique firearms that no longer work as well as modern weapons; and gowns and woolen cloaks (Parkes 1983:535). Other bridewealth objects are very large, usually aluminum, cooking pots, plates, and vessels. Recent exchanges have also included large portable radios, tape recorders, and cash. Generally not much livestock is given as bridewealth, but each object and food item has a traditional value in goats. This becomes important in the event of an elopement, when many objects must be repaid in livestock "seized by the neck" (living animals).

The first few objects are given when the husband's party formally "seeks" the girl (at which point they have already ascertained that her family will agree to their request). The first time the wife is taken to her husband's house, his family will sacrifice an animal in their honor and perhaps offer one small object to each of the men who accompanied her. But the majority of the bridewealth, and the largest celebration of *khaltabarí*, takes place not when the girl is *given* but when she *returns* to her natal family's home after living for a short time at her new husband's house. The transfer of bridewealth is orchestrated so that there is never a direct exchange of girl for wealth and both parties can appear to be giving freely.

If a girl who has never been married before goes "*alaṣíŋ* from her father's house," meaning that the young couple elopes without the prior arrangement of their parents, a large *khaltabarí* will take place after both families have agreed to the marriage.

It is considered shameful for fathers to demand a certain amount of bridewealth, although everyone acknowledges that some unscrupulous men do "point out bridewealth." Mir Beck explained to me that most men do not like to place heavy demands on future sons-in-law: "It's the husband's own choice. He'll give as much as he is able to round up." Parkes notes that in the late 1970s the normal expectation was that at least sixty articles (*sóren*) would be given during the early stages of marriage, a third of which should be major wealth objects (1983:535). There does not appear to have been much inflation in this, as my friends agreed that this is still standard. However, a gift of cash is now common as well, usually around Rs 3,000 (U.S.$100). The husband's immediate household (and at this time in their life cycle of the household assets are still usually collective rather than divided among the brothers) is usually responsible for the major wealth objects. His mother's brothers are expected to give something equal in value to a cow (mother's brothers also receive a cow from their sisters' daughters' marriages). The other households in his patrilineage give the rest of the articles, and some (usually smaller items) are given by his maternal relatives.

Also potentially countable as bridewealth are animals slaughtered to feast a visiting member of the wife's lineage; food items given to the wife's household or households of her lineage in the event of a funeral; gifts of grain, cheese, grass, and livestock that are given to households of the wife's lineage; and items of bridewealth that are requested by distant affines (usually with the aim of collecting bridewealth for their own sons) (Parkes 1983:538). Additional bridewealth is given for each child born of the union in the form of an animal sacrificed for a celebratory feast for the woman's relatives and perhaps a few wealth articles as well. All this is silently noted by everyone involved (and, as you can see, almost everyone is involved). If the girl later goes *alaṣíŋ* with another man, the bridewealth given will be counted and her second husband (and his lineage) will return an amount double that which her father received from her first husband.[7]

Below is a list of the bridewealth that Kashdil (and his relatives) gave Sailun's ex-husband when the couple went *alaṣíŋ* (so this amount is roughly double what her first husband gave to her father). According to Kashdil's older brothers, most of the money and food items were borrowed from a friend's store. The wealth objects were borrowed from Sherzada Khan, a lineage mate, whose own wife had gone *alaṣíŋ* three months earlier.

Rs 6,500 cash
Rs 2,600 worth of sugar, biscuits, and candy
20 *batií* (1 *batií* = 2.5 kilograms) of wheat
10 *batií* of walnuts
20 *batií* of wine (totalling Rs 7,000 as they had to purchase it)
9 female goats
7 sheep
5 bulls (3 young bulls and 2 fully grown)
A total of 300 assorted bridewealth objects, including
> 12 *šoká* big woolen robes)
> 4 fancy shawls
> 8 guns

Altogether, they estimate that the bridewealth was worth about Rs 100,000 ($3,300), which is three times the yearly salary of a schoolteacher.

The basic rules are these:

- If a man divorces his wife (*ǰa hístik*), he forfeits any claim to the bridewealth given for her.
- If a married woman goes *alaṣíŋ,* her new husband (and his agnates) must compensate the ex-husband with double the amount of bridewealth her former husband (and his agnates) gave to her natal household.
- If she goes *alaṣíŋ* a second time, the amount given to the second husband is triple the original amount.
- If a married woman goes *alaṣíŋ* with a Muslim man, the woman's new husband must repay the original bridewealth (but the amount is *not* doubled). If one of the partners converts without remarrying, there is some ambiguity about what should happen to the bridewealth. Usually, if the husband converts and his wife won't, he simply loses the bridewealth he gave for her and she is free to marry someone else. If the wife converts and her husband does not, her family usually gives back the bridewealth her husband gave for her.
- If a woman's husband brings in a second wife, the first wife is "free" to leave him (if she chooses to) and he receives no compensation for the bridewealth his family gave to hers. But the first wife's children belong to and remain with her former husband and his family.
- It is possible for a father to return an equal amount of bridewealth to his son-in-law (and the son-in-law's family) in exchange for his daughter's "freedom." Although this is often threatened, it is exceptionally rare.
- After the marriage is well established, fathers often give *ǰhes* to their daughters and their husbands. *ǰhes* is a form of dowry. All items given by her father are subtracted from the amount of bridewealth given by her husband's family. Theoretically, if a woman went *alaṣíŋ* after her father had given *ǰhes,* her new husband would pay less compensatory bridewealth to her ex-husband.

There are two essential points to abstract from these details. First, the exchange of bridewealth is spread across time and space—given and received by many different people over the course of years. In other words, the "exchange" is never direct. Second, there is never a point at which a Kalasha man can be *certain* that his wife is *his* because she can *always* choose to go *alaṣíŋ*. It is also true that after the birth of children the probability that a woman will stay with her husband increases exponentially. Women in Rumbur were able to remember only seven cases in which women left their children with a former husband and eloped with another man (one of these seven left a second set of children with her second husband and eloped with a third man). But the *idea* that she might elope, even after having children, is still in the realm of the thinkable. So, the exchange is never complete. Ironically, instead of "securing" a wife, the particular configuration of Kalasha bridewealth puts men in a position of vulnerability and is seen as limiting the choices *they* can make about marriage. At the same time, as I'll explain in the following paragraphs, bridewealth affords women security for themselves and their children, greater sexual and expressive freedom (at least in comparison with neighboring Muslims), and the latitude to make choices that affect their economic and social positions.

Being married is a precondition to having what Saras Gula Aya, later in her story, terms a "purposeful life" (*maksát zindagí*). For both men and women, children, connection to place, authority, respect in the community, and future security all presuppose a successful marriage. The bridewealth system all but ensures each woman that, once married, the chance that her husband will divorce her (*ja hístik*, literally "to throw away the wife") is quite small and after she has had children almost unthinkable. In Parkes's sample, fewer than one in twenty marriages ended when men threw away their wives (1983:358). In looking through my own data, at first I could find no case of a woman who said she had been thrown away. Then I realized that the women whom I talked to were using a different word than Parkes's (presumably male) informants had. Men said they had thrown away their wives, but women said they had been "freed." In my sample, three out of eighty-two women acknowledged that their first marriage ended in this sort of "divorce."[8]

Before I understood how things worked, I worried about my friend Jan Bibia Aya. She had come *alaṣíŋ* from her father's house (*dādas dur alaṣíŋ*) with a young man she barely knew. Jan Bibia Dada, her husband, had been angry with his father for not allowing him to bring *alaṣíŋ* another woman with whom he was deeply in love (since she was the wife of one of his father's political supporters). One of his brothers said he knew of a beautiful unmarried girl from Bumboret, so "without thinking" he brought Jan Bibia Aya *alaṣíŋ* instead. She was young and impulsive, too, and he was very handsome and wealthy. But within a month of her arrival, the couple had stopped speaking entirely (her sisters-in-law told me how shocked they were at his behavior—he didn't even ask her to wash his laundry, the quintessential wife's responsibility). And she was already pregnant. By the time the baby was a year old, Jan Bibia Dada started talking incessantly about how he would either throw her away or take a second wife (knowing that Jan Bibia Aya would probably leave him if he did so). What would happen to her? Finally, when I asked whether his threats were real, I was roundly laughed at. "Who would let him do that?" his brothers and their wives reassured me. "Who would give him the bridewealth again? It's better to have a wife you don't like than no wife at all." If she didn't go *alaṣíŋ* (and she swore she would never do that, as she'd have to leave her baby, too), then he had no recourse.

Kalasha bridewealth is so expensive (and many of the necessary traditional wealth objects so rare) that no man can afford a wife without the contributions of other lineage households, friends, neighbors, and maternal relatives. As I mentioned earlier, a woman coming into a new household comes as a person valued not only by or for her husband but as an important contributing member of the community. One says *bumbarák* (congratulations) not only to a new husband but to every member of his extended family. Because so many others have "invested" in her, both emotionally and financially (and in many ways bridewealth does represent an investment since the wealth is doubled if she goes *alaṣíŋ*), to throw away (or set free) a wife is also to throw away the wealth of your family and friends, and this seriously jeopardizes a man's chances of remarrying. In fact, no one could recall a case in which a woman with children had ever been thrown away.[9] In Parkes's sample as well as my own, the only male-initiated divorces that did occur happened in the earliest stages of marriage. As there is no stigma against divorcees and no value placed on virginity, the girls were free to marry other partners.

Just as the exchanged bridewealth ensures a secure place for a wife in her husband's household, it also ensures that any children she bears will be legitimate members of her husband's lineage. Whom-

ever a woman is married to at the time she gives birth is the child's
father—even if he and everyone else knows that he is not the biologi-
cal father. "Bastards" (*jaróa*), children who were reputedly born of
adulterous affairs, are plentiful in Kalashadesh.[10] My friends liked to
point out children who were conceived while their fathers were away
at the high pastures or perhaps down-country in Peshawar. One man
reportedly returned from three years in Peshawar to find he had a
one-year-old son. But, while he will be a target for gossip, this boy
"belongs" to his father as much as any of his brothers and will inherit
his equal share of property and responsibility. It is certainly not the
case that there are no consequences of adultery or that it is encouraged. Women do risk being beaten. Hitting your wife if you suspect
her of adultery is acceptable, though beating her severely is not. They
certainly risk marital discord. They may gain a "bad" reputation. But
they don't risk their lives or the security of their children. Because
neither she nor her children risk being thrown away if a woman takes
lovers (let alone killed, as she would among some neighboring groups
[Keiser 1986]), Kalasha women enjoy sexual freedom as well—if such
freedom is defined as the ability to make choices about *whether or not*
to take lovers.[11]

It is my impression that this freedom extends into other areas of
expression. The security of women's marital situations means that
women don't *have* to work hard to endear themselves to their husbands and in-laws (it is rather the other way around). Young Kalasha
women thus worry little about pleasing their husbands. For example,
Kosh Begim, the girl in the last chapter who performed the *bashali*
purification ritual, didn't think twice about asking her husband's
permission—though he clearly would not have approved. I also witnessed one particularly tense (and particularly telling) argument between my friend Kosh Gul and her husband. As their disagreement
escalated, the husband shouted, "Just leave. Go back to your
brother's house." "You leave," she retorted, "This is my house. I have
sons." "Fine," he said, and left (though only for a few hours, returning as if nothing had happened).

Bridewealth also has economic and social advantages for women.
Women know, and seem to be proud of, the amount of bridewealth
they command—although to speak of it directly is considered crass.
In some ways, it does seem to be a measure of their value. In lullabies,
singers pay tribute to little girls as bringers of wealth, sentimentally

seeing the family's storehouses filling with priceless wealth objects and imagining a stream of livestock that fills the valley in a daughter's wake. The wealth she brings to her natal family entitles each woman to her "share" of the special bread that is baked on ritual occasions, to a share of fruit and meat, to take refuge in her father's house when she is angry with her husband, and to think of her natal house as home even after she has begun living continuously in her husband's house.

As Bossen noted for the women of Toj Nam, bridewealth, rather than limiting women's agency, also affords women the opportunity to make choices about economic and social position that aren't possible for men. Kalasha men are born into one family and remain in that household their entire lives. Their economic fate is more or less anchored to that of their natal family, as they will inherit land, house, and livestock from their parents. Women, on the other hand, are well aware that in marrying (in the case of *alasíŋ* marriages anyway) they are choosing an economic position as well as a spouse. Lilizar's family, as mentioned earlier, has decided to allow her to go *alasíŋ* on her own rather than choosing a husband for her. In weighing her suitors, she invariably cited their families' relative wealth, which for her included the quality, beauty, and accessibility (after all, she didn't want to spend her life with aching knees, she'd add) of their land, houses, and summer fields. Although I haven't the data to document this empirically, it appears that women who go *alasíŋ* almost invariably marry into wealthier families, wealthy enough, at least, to pay twice the bridewealth their first husbands gave.

Zailun's story is a good example. In leaving her first husband, Zailun left a man with no parents and no brothers (and hence no sisters-in-law either) to share the workload and eloped with a man who had been blessed with a wealthy family and many siblings. I asked her if she had thought about this when she fell in love with Miramin. "Of course not," she laughed, "I was young. Young people are crazy (*got*), they don't think about land and goats, only love." Then, dropping her voice, she pulled me toward her and whispered, "Well, maybe a little. Certainly I thought about that a little."

I have described how this particular constellation of bridewealth practices offers Kalasha women a secure base from which to make a number of economic and sexual decisions as well as the ultimate defining freedom of being able to exchange one husband for another.

And yet these same practices also limit the extent of their agency in precisely these areas. The limitations are different for each woman and vary especially depending on when she becomes pregnant and how much bridewealth her husband's family was able to give.

Marilyn Strathern has argued that in many bridewealth societies things come to be equated with persons or, more precisely with aspects of personhood that are thought to be split off, detachable (1985:197–200; see also 1984b). Among Kalasha, the most obvious aspect of female personhood that is split off and offered up in marriage (either by the woman herself, in the case of an elopement, or by her family in an arranged marriage) are rights to the children she bears. The children of a woman who goes *alaṣíŋ* belong to her husband: he paid for them, no matter how much or little bridewealth was given. Once Talimzar, angry with her husband for an alleged affair, lamented to me that her uncle once had eaten a goat sacrificed in his honor by her husband. Talimzar and her husband have an unusual marital situation in that her family never officially acknowledged her elopement and bridewealth had not been formally exchanged although the couple had been together for eight years. She explained that if only her uncle hadn't eaten that goat she would be free to leave him and take the children. As it was, if she left her husband she would lose her children utterly. The eating of this one goat, on this one occasion, constituted an exchange of bridewealth, and since bridewealth had been exchanged her children belonged to his family. She reminded me of Sherbek's mother, who eloped with the man next door when her son was three. Sherbek's father built a wall between their houses and refused to let her speak to the boy, refused to let him call her mother. Most women are bound to their husbands because of their devotion to their children.

This creates interesting marital politics for young couples. Perhaps you'll remember Geki, who in the last chapter began crying when she discovered that she had begun to menstruate. Her aunt and mother explained that it meant her husband would begin pressuring her to have intercourse with him. Yet, like other young men in his situation, Geki's husband walked a precarious line. A woman's husband at the time of birth of her baby is considered the baby's father, regardless of who her husband was at the time of conception. If Geki were to have a baby, the odds would be high that she would stay with her husband rather than leave the child. But if he pressured her to have sex against her will, she would be angry and unhappy, and thus likely to elope with someone else (even if she were already pregnant). (This is why, Zailun reasoned, her first husband never "touched" her: *"Maybe he thought, 'if I don't force her, she won't go alasíŋ.'"*) Older women claim that "girls these days" are foolish, that they have sex with their husbands and lovers too easily and too young. Mushiki claims that she and her girlfriends put men off for years and that way they could see what kind of men they were before they were bound to them with children. They would then have more time to decide whether they wanted to remain in the marriage or go *alasíŋ* with another man.

As I explained in the last section, a woman's freedom to elope is contingent on her ability to find someone to elope *with*. And the more bridewealth given the less likely it is that another man, however much in love with her he might be, will be able to round up the necessary double bridewealth payment. I once walked in on a conspiratorial conversation between two of the younger men in my village. Khan's wife had just converted to Islam. She had moved into her uncle's house. Because Khan did not choose to convert also, the marriage was dissolved and his bridewealth was returned. Khan and his lineage mate, Jamardin, were dreaming of prospective wives. They started pumping me for details about Geki. How much did she like her husband? Had I ever heard her mention either of them? Did I think she would go *alasíŋ* with Khan? How about with Jamardin? I told them that they were both crazy, that they knew she had already gone *alasíŋ* with her present husband. But that precisely, it seemed, was the beauty of their plan. "That's right," Khan exclaimed, "and I will pay three times for her, and then no one, ever, will be able to take her from me." Their plan came to nothing (resting as it did on Geki, who wasn't interested), but their logic explicitly underlies all bridewealth transactions. Bridewealth doesn't make women less free, since they are always *potentially* able to elope, but it does limit the ability of other men to pay the exorbitant compensation demanded by the first husband. Therefore, women are also *effectively* limited.

In addition to the exchange of bridewealth, most women receive a form of dowry (*jhes*) from their natal families. *jhes* seems to be expected, but it is certainly not required. It is given only once. The ceremony takes place after the birth of at least one child (sometimes after the birth of several children), when the marriage is securely established. Natal families organize the ceremony and a small feast and call their daughter and her relatives to come. It is a way of honoring beloved daughters and establishing equality between in-laws.[12] It also contributes to women's independence in important emotional and material ways.

Parkes (1983:543) noted that the normal quantity of *jhes* given in 1979 was:

5 to 10 sheep
15 to 20 *muti* (one-year-old goats)
1 to 2 cows or bulls (the *móa gak*—given by the maternal uncles)
Several woven, goat's hair rugs, which are used on beds
1 trunk (*tohón*)
1 valuable metal cup

Some wealthy families sometimes also give their daughters one or two walnut trees—the produce of which will make her life richer, both culinarily and materially (since she will be able to sell the walnuts and keep the money herself). This amount of *jhes* was still typical during my fieldwork (although I didn't see valuable cups given). Additionally, women usually received a new set of clothes—usually complete with expensive Power brand tennis shoes—and the trunk is filled with dishes and other small household items.

The ceremony in which *jhes* is given is touchingly sentimental. One the day on which my family gave *jhes* to Gumbas, the whole extended family had been preparing all morning for her arrival—cooking and collecting and displaying the items to be given to her. She finally arrived wearing her beautiful *kupás* headdress and carrying her newborn son, her older son in tow, accompanied by an entourage of men from her husband's lineage. There was a flurry of kissing as Gumbas greeted each of her family members in turn. Mir Beck stood up and offered her the small *hányak* stool he had been sitting on. Never before or since have I seen this man, arguably the most powerful and respected person in the valleys, offer his chair to a woman! There was a feast of bread and cheese and wine, and after everyone was pleasantly stuffed and slightly drunk the speeches began. In turn, each of Gumbas's brothers and cousins gave her *múti* (one-year-old goats) from their own herds. She knelt and kissed each goat's forehead, and as she did so she began weeping. I looked around and saw that all the other women were weeping, too, as were the more sentimental men. Later I was told that the goats are a token of the affection of her "brothers" for her, that women weep for joy, but it is a bittersweet joy, since the giving of *jhes* also symbolically marks the end of her childhood (during which she will shuttle back and forth between her husband's and father's houses, not quite belonging in either place) and the beginning of her life as an adult woman with her own nuclear family.

jhes gives women an important measure of economic independence from her in-laws (and indeed her husband). While the *jhes* given by each woman's family accounts for only a fraction of the bridewealth given by her husband's family, it is significant because it is usually the first productive property that is owned by her and her husband *as a couple*. The livestock forms the core of her husband's stock before he inherits his father's herd. Women have the right to request that these animals, and those born from them, be used for special sacrifices, to assist her family, or to make purchases she deems necessary. The other items given also symbolically provision her and her nuclear family for a life of their own—dishes, rugs for their family's beds, and especially the large trunk for storing her private things, the key to which she will hang from her beads.

There is another aspect of *jhes* that is equally important to a woman: the items given are deducted directly from the bridewealth originally paid for her should she choose to go *alasíŋ*. "Ah ha!" I exclaimed to Mir Beck, who had gone to some trouble to explain the ins and outs of bridewealth and dowry to me, "So you give *jhes* in order to make your daughters more free?" "Phhh. That's ridiculous," he said. "We give *jhes* to help our son-in-law." He reminded me that fathers give *jhes* to their daughters after they have had children, when there is little chance that women will go *alasíŋ*. Bayda Aya piped in, "*ṭu ta sahí mon des, bāba*. You're right sister. *jhes* does make us a little freer." Even though women rarely go *alasíŋ* after *jhes* has been given, it makes it more thinkable. "And also," she continued, "after our family gives *jhes* we can say to our husbands when they try to 'stand above' us, 'You think you're the only one who gave property (*mal*)? My family also gave property.'"

Let's go back to Bayda Aya's (Zailun's) story, where she is falling in love with her second husband, Miramin, and about to go *alasíŋ* with him. Like most *alasíŋ* stories, Bayda Aya's is filled with intrigue, danger, desire, humor, and some sadness. Her elopement is the point around which her life pivoted, a moment in time when she committed an irrevocable act that changed her future and the futures of those closest to her.

~

Zailun first saw Miramin at that funeral in Rumbur. They were both "heartstruck." Miramin would come to Bumboret and camp out along the river for days, just to get a glimpse of her sitting on the high porch at her parents' summer house. *"From the time I was small I was so in love. . . . He came all the time to Bumboret, we saw one another and fell in love*[13]*—just like you say—love at first sight. For three or four years we made love—not bad works* [they were not sexually involved], *no, only with words. We would look at one another and become happy. He'd bring me little gifts. In love. So, if I saw him far away, I would get so happy. My heart would bloom like a flower—I've seen my friend! He never asked to sleep* [have sex] *with me. He said to other people, 'I'll lead that girl* [elope with her].'" Miramin's friends started approaching Zailun, telling her that he was talking of bringing her *alaṣíṇ*. She would say, "Well, good. Later I'll see." Every twenty days or so, his friends would come back, urging her to "give straight words," telling her that Miramin liked her so much that he was becoming crazy, urging her to agree to elope with him. She also liked him, but she would say, "I'll see later. Now I can't come. I am a man's wife. One year later, two years later, three years later, we'll see." *"It was like that, sister. We were in love for four years. Then, finally, I came with him."*

Or rather she came *to* him with a friend of his, came over the mountain that divides Bumboret Valley from Rumbur Valley in the middle of the night, scrambling up steep scree slopes to the meadows and cedar forests above and descending, finally, in Rawelik, where Miramin and his friends were waiting for her. Miramin couldn't come for her himself, as the road was being watched. Zailun was being guarded, both by her husband and by a third man who was crazy in love with her (and hoped to bring her *alaṣíṇ* himself).

Ten days earlier, there had been a failed attempt. Mujika Dada, Khana Dada, and several friends, brothers, and other relatives of Miramin had come to Bumboret for her. It was night. They planned to go all the way to Ayun and then climb up the steep pass to Arigich—

"maybe they'd have to carry me on their backs!" noted Bayda Aya—and drop directly into Kalashagrom, Miramin's village. So they came to Bumboret and instructed Peshawar Khan, a friend of theirs, to tell Zailun of the plan. But Peshawar Khan's brother, the other man who was in love with Zailun, overheard. He had been after her for one or two years, pressuring her, following her. *"He had been saying, 'You absolutely have to be my wife. If you're not my wife* [he already had a wife and two daughters]. *. . . You absolutely come with me. You don't go with anyone else—If you go with anyone else, I'll kill myself.' I said, 'I can't come with you. I am a man's wife. If I go, I'll go far away. I can't come with you. Anyway, you have a wife, she'll get angry. And besides, my heart—even if your heart is stuck to mine, mine isn't stuck to yours. I am in love with someone else.'"* So when this man heard of the planned elopement he sent word to his friends to come, saying, *"the girl is going to run away tonight. You all come for me. Wait on the road and grab her and we'll take her for me."* So surrounding her father's house that night were ten or fifteen men, two groups, one waiting to lead Bayda Aya to her love, the other hoping to take her from them. *"I, well, I never even woke up from my sleep,"* Bayda Aya laughed.

"Then later, ten days later, I came alasíŋ." It was late summer, when nights are filled with "night dancing," an ongoing celebration leading up to the fall harvest festival, Uchau. Long nights of dancing to sweet love songs encourage the crops to mature. They are also a time when everyone is out of place, up until all hours, sleeping at friends' houses. Zailun took her little brother and cuddled with him in a bed on the porch of their house. No one was watching out for her, as everyone was dancing. When her brother fell asleep, she slipped away with two men from Rumbur and climbed over the mountain.

Zailun's grandfather was so angry. *"Bring her back as fast as spit,"* he said to her father. Her father's younger brother also held fast to the man to whom they had given her. *"You sit with him, you sit with him,"* he insisted. They had given her to a man of their choice, and now she should honor them, she should obey them and stay. *"What could I do? My heart was not warm for him. Going alasíŋ in love, I became another man's wife."* Her grandfather and her father's youngest brother fought with her father, accusing him of sending her *alasíŋ* himself. *"You sent her, you!"* her youngest uncle said, and he cut his brother with a knife, so that even today he has a scar on his nose. (No one told Zailun, knowing that this would make her *wam*—unable to move or respond because she would be so inconsolable.) For two years, her former husband and her grandfather refused to accept the bridewealth payment, as they were so angry. Her grandfather said that he would kill Miramin and his father. So Zailun could not visit her home for two years, and Miramin couldn't go near Bumboret or he'd be beaten by his wife's former husband and his friends. Finally, someone convinced them, saying *"Are you Muslims that you fight like this? No, we're Kalasha, we exchange bridewealth and resolve our differences."* Only ten days before they accepted the double bridewealth for Zailun, her grandfather died. *"What could I do? I wasn't able to go, and he died before, or I would have talked him into forgiving me. Even now my little father* [her father's younger brother] *doesn't speak nicely with me—fine, fine—but not loving words. Even now it's like that—if you're sought and given away, it's like that, sister."*

∼

"Going *alasíŋ*" turns Kalasha girls into women. One reason why young girls' resistance to marriage doesn't often work is that girls are not yet able to effectively organize social relations. The only way in which a girl can be free of one husband is to elope with another—and only when she is older will she be able to coordinate and inspire the actions of others. When, like Zailun, young women "go *alasíŋ*," they not only *agree* to elope but they always play an active role in planning and executing the elopement. They can (and often do) change their minds at any point. Going *alasíŋ* is physical. It is dangerous—or at least it always feels dangerous. And it has enduring consequences. When girls go *alasíŋ*, their actions have repercussions that ripple through the community. The people closest to them, parents, grandparents, in-laws, are most affected. But the act reverberates through the three Kalasha valleys as well. The choices women make about marriage are painful and real. By choosing to reject the marriage her grandfather made for her, Zailun jeopardized the warm and supportive relationship she had had with him. Her choice ended the *khaltabár* relationship her grandfather and father and uncles had cultivated, serving the economic and emotional bond they had built with her former husband and his family. Even now, more than ten years after Zailun came *alasíŋ* with Miramin, she still weeps when she thinks of the pain and anger she caused her grandfather.

After a girl has gone *alasíŋ*, she is taken seriously. As happens after every *alasíŋ*, Zailun's father (it could be any other close male relative) came to her new house and asked if she had chosen to go *alasíŋ* of her own will. "Did someone trick you, my daughter?" he asked. "Did he lie to you? Do you want to come back home?" "No," Zailun replied, "Coming with Miramin was my own choice. I want to stay here." Sometimes (as you'll see in Saras Gula Aya's story) girls are beaten and dragged back home by irate male relatives. But Kalasha girls know that if they are persistent they will have their way—in large part because marriage, both whom you marry and how you marry, is at the heart of "Kalasha *dastúr*," Kalasha custom.

Marrying and Being Kalasha

Like me, many of my Kalasha friends are fascinated with the details of other marriage systems. They often asked me questions about how Americans marry and whom and who decides and how old the bride and groom should be and who pays bridewealth (it is a common rumor that *aŋglís* women give bridewealth for the men they marry—why else would my husband do my laundry?). We spent long, cold, winter mornings trading stories and eating up the last evening's leftovers. The women in my family would tell me about their "customs" and how their community differed from neighboring Muslim communities. They would ask me to tell tales about marriage and divorce and polygamy in America—and in India, Japan, France, Canada, and the Punjab. They already knew all about Princess Diana's saga and told me how she had come from a poor family and married a prince (I said that I doubted Earl Spencer was all that poor, but they insisted he was). Diana had left Charles because he'd been unfaithful. She had the kids, and he was thinking of taking another wife, but the women all speculated that Diana wouldn't let that happen because she has a lot of *pawa* (power). Good anthropologists themselves, my friends felt that sorting through marriage systems was a way of classifying peoples, of understanding who's who and who values what and what kinds of agency are claimed by whom.

Through marriage, Kalasha set themselves apart from their Muslim neighbors in two ways—in whom they marry and how they marry. One of the few myths that are very widely shared (there are many known only to the *kazí*) explains the original split between Kalasha and Muslims.

Adam and Bibi Awa had seven boys and seven girls, born together on the same day in pairs. They didn't know how to marry them, so God told them they should marry the first boy to the last girl, and so on. But the youngest daughter was very beautiful, and her own twin wouldn't give her up. They were cast out and became the first Muslims.

This myth is one of the only stories I heard in which Kalasha claim to be God's chosen people—testifying to the fact that marriage strikes at the very heart of their ethnic identity. In few other circumstances, neither in songs nor stories nor conversations, are most Kalasha willing to speculate that they are right and Muslims wrong. Rather, they say simply, as Khana Dada often remarked, "Who has been to heaven and back to tell us if we are right or they are? Perhaps God is big enough for all of us. We'll each know in time."

Unlike their Muslim neighbors, Kalasha consider marriages between cousins, men and women born in the same patriline, or those clearly related through their mothers[14] to be incestuous or *máka*. In the time before the Nuristanis were forcibly converted to Islam, couples who violated similar marriage taboos automatically became *bara*, nonlandowning slaves to and craftsmen for the "true Kafirs" (Jones 1974). It does not seem that the Kalasha, who appear to have been the gentler and poorer neighbors of the Kafiristanis, ever had such a stratified system. But violation of the incest taboos has similar repercussions: young people sometimes do fall in love with a forbidden other, and the couple is automatically cast from the community and converted to Islam. Jan Bibi told me that when she and Rakmat Khan, distantly related members of the same patriline and therefore "brother and sister" to one another, fell in love and eloped together, the furor of their families lasted more than a year. Rakmat Khan's father immediately divided his land, giving his now Muslim son a place to build a house far from their home village near a group of other Muslim families. For months no one talked to them, but now they are reintegrated into their families, though of course as *šek*, converted Kalasha. "We knew what we were doing and what would happen," she told me, "but our love was too strong."

It is more than simply the practice of patrilineal exogamy that makes Kalasha marriage regionally unique, but especially the fact that young people have a culturally sanctioned pathway to escape the marriages their parents arrange for them. As I have said, the act of going *alasíŋ* is the prototypic act that defines women's freedom, and women's freedom is one of the central markers of Kalasha ethnicity. It is certainly not the case that neighboring Muslim women fail to assert agency or choice regarding marriage partners (cf. Tapper 1990). Indeed, my Chitrali friends loved to tell and retell stories of Chitrali women who had risked everything—security, status, connections to family, life itself—for the sake of love. And "love marriages"—marriages in which young women and men know and express an interest in one another before marriage—are becoming more common even in this conservative area of Pakistan. But the Kalasha are unique in this region in that women have a culturally acknowledged *right* to elope with another man.

When a young Kalasha couple goes *alasíŋ*, it always causes scandal and disorder. But no matter how great the opposition to the marriage of the young lovers, their act always elicits the comment, "Well, what can we do, this is Kalasha *dastúr*, Kalasha custom." And this "custom" is backed up by the very real threat that if young people are not allowed to make their own choices about marriage they can (and often do) convert to Islam (*šek thi an*). The neighboring Muslim community is eager to embrace—at least initially—converted Kalasha. By converting, the couple would escape the authority of their parents, and, although they would now be bound in a new moral community, they would be married by a mullah. As you'll see in Saras Gula Aya's story, her in-laws allowed her husband, Mir Beck, to take a second wife when he, their only son, threatened to convert. Converting to Islam is a desperate act because it is irrevocable—but for this very reason it is an effective threat that gives young lovers powerful leverage in these emotionally charged situations.

It is also Kalasha custom that disputes over marriages are settled through the exchange of bridewealth rather than deadly violence. When Kalasha women go *alasíŋ*, they risk the disappointment and disapproval of their families (although this itself is considerable), but they know that they are not risking their lives or endangering the lives of people they love. Zailun's male relatives, furious over her elopement with Miramin, were finally convinced to accept the double bridewealth payment customary after elopement after hearing, *"Are you Muslims that you fight like this? No, we're Kalasha, we exchange bridewealth and resolve our differences."* It is a point of pride, an aspect of Kalashaness, that elopements do not develop into the deadly blood feuds characteristic of this region. As Keiser notes, among the nearby Kohistani communities, "accepting such indemnity would be unthinkable. . . . Incidents like these require an instant exchange of gunfire. The passion for revenge aroused in the cuckolded husband demands that he at least attempt to kill his wife's lover" (1986:494–95; cf. Lindholm 1981). Kalasha women (and the young men who elope with them) can more boldly exercise their agency with regard to marriage decisions because the consequences, while certainly serious, are not lethal.

The Politics of Elopement

Going *alasíŋ* was the defining moment in Zailun's (Bayda Aya's) life, the point around which all her relationships turn. When I first came to Rumbur, I was attracted to stories of dramatic elopements like Zailun's. I thought bold women, women who chose "freedom" and took their lives into their own hands, made the decision to elope. But I came slowly to see that women's freedom involves more than that, that the decision *not* to elope, but to *stay*, is powerful and important as well. Saras Gula Aya could have gone *alasíŋ* many times—she had streams of men who were in love with her, according to her daughters-in-law. But, although she was "free" to go, she stayed. It is around her decision to stay that she narrates the story of her life. As well as illustrating many of the points I've already discussed, Saras Gula Aya's story (intertwined as it is with the stories of those closest to her) also offers a glimpse of the larger political ground on which elopements are enacted.

After Pilin Gul had been living in her in-laws' house for a couple of years as a young menstruating woman, her husband's sister (who had become Pilin Gul's good friend), Bibi Zar, went *alasíŋ* with Pilin Gul's cousin (FBS) Mizok (cousins are called *baya* [brother] or *baba* [sister] in Kalasha, and as children grow up in extended patrilocal families these relationships are especially close and siblinglike). Bibi Zar had been Gazi's wife, promised to him in her infancy although he was already a grown man. When Bibi Zar was only a tiny baby, Gazi had said, apparently, "I will make that one my wife." "*And he* [Gazi] *waited for her. And waiting and waiting, Bibi Zar grew up. She grew up and was a young woman. But when she was a young woman, Mizok led her alasíŋ.*" Pilin Gul herself had been a matchmaker, "running words" between her cousin and Bibi Zar. On that same day, Pilin Gul's husband, Mir Beck, led one of Pilin Gul's own cousins (mother's brother's daughter, or MBD), a girl from Bumboret Valley, *alasíŋ.* Although no one had seen them yet or knew where the two were staying, it appeared that her husband was bringing a second wife in on top of her head. "*I'm going, to my father's house I am going,*" Pilin Gul said, angrily. But her mother-in-law said, "*If you go, I will die. I will jump from a cliff and die. I will throw myself in a river and die.*" So Pilin Gul stayed.

Later that day, Pilin Gul went down to Badtet to braid her hair by the bridge. She kept a small wooden comb hidden there, halfway between her husband's house and her father's house. From her semi-hidden spot, Pilin Gul saw her father-in-law, Zada, storm down to the grassy area in the center of the village, where a small crowd had gathered. Apparently he had returned home from his work in the stable to find that both his son and daughter had been flagrantly disobedient. Furious, he swung his gun, shooting it off above the heads of the gathered people. "*In front of their faces, he shot the gun. 'I'll kill them* [his son and daughter]. *I'll also kill the matchmaker. I'll also kill myself. My son was persuaded to do this because of my daughter-in-law. They weren't able to take my daughter-in-law, so they persuaded my son.'*" The nephew of Zada's greatest rival in the valley, Mashara Shah, had long been in love with Pilin Gul. He once locked her in a storeroom until she swore she'd marry him. "*Of course I didn't do it. I just said the words so he would let me out,*" Pilin Gul explained. "*They persuaded my son—Mashara Shah and Nurjan Khan's father—they did it. 'I'll kill them. I'll kill my own self,' he said, swinging his gun around.*" Zada felt that his rival, Nurjan Khan's father, had convinced his son Mir Beck to bring in a second wife without his father's blessing so that his family relations, and especially his relations with his *khaltabár* (Pilin Gul's natal family) would be disrupted. He turned toward Nurjan Khan's father, ready to fight with him, but Nurjan Khan's father said, "*Oh my [categorical] father-in-law—Your own daughter has gone, and your son has led a woman.*

Why are you running around all angry now? In the beginning you must teach your children to behave." Zada glared at him. "You did this, you [You told him to do this, told him it was right.]" "About that you will have to produce evidence," Nurjan Khan's father said, "If you can produce evidence, then . . ."

At this point in her story, Pilin Gul has been married to Mir Beck for seven years. She has grown up shuttling back and forth between her in-laws' house and her natal house and has developed intimate relationships with her sisters-in-law and an affectionate tie with her mother-in-law and father-in-law. She glows when she talks about the romance between Bibi Zar and Mizok, and she herself facilitated their elopement by "running words" back and forth between the two young lovers. The very day on which Mizok and Bibi Zar first went *alasíŋ* Pilin Gul discovers that her own young husband is attempting to bring a second wife in "on her head." She is angry with him. (To this day, she becomes angry when she tells this story.) Knowing that his action has made her "free" to leave (and that her husband's family will forfeit the bridewealth they paid to her family if she does so), she declares that she is going. Her mother-in-law's desperate threat of suicide compels her to stay, at least for a while.

But beyond the immediacy of desire, rejection, anger, action, and intrigue felt by the young people themselves is a realm of politics and power in which these elopements, indeed all Kalasha elopements, are embedded. In his excellent dissertation, Peter Parkes (1993) argues convincingly that orchestrating elopements is the primary way in which important lineage elders garner power and prestige for themselves. From the perspective of male political leaders, the politics of elopement serve as public contests in which lineage elders demonstrate their relative power and influence through dishonoring political rivals and finessing the wealth and support needed to settle bridewealth compensation. Further, mediating or arbitrating elopement conflicts is the main occasion for elders to act as political leaders. "Indeed," Parkes notes, "without such hostilities to resolve, it is difficult to imagine what political leadership might entail in Kalasha society" (1983:591). In Parkes's construction—which I believe fairly represents the viewpoint of important male elders—women (and indeed young men, though Parkes does not comment on this) are seen as mere pawns in the political games played by older men.

From her semihidden spot near the river, Pilin Gul also glimpses this other level on which the elopement attempts of her husband, and of her cousin and sister-in-law, are being played out. She sees her father-in-law, Zada, enraged to find that on the same day his daughter has left the man to whom he "gave" her *and* his son is attempting to bring another woman *alaṣíŋ* (and both of these events jeopardize the *khaltabár* relationships he has cultivated over the years). His gunshots and threats of murder and suicide demonstrate both his anger and his self-control. They show that he could kill, that he is angry enough to do so, but since he is Kalasha he won't. Rather than ascribing intentionality and blame to his children, he sees them as having been tricked, "persuaded," by his political rivals—"*You did this, you!*"— especially Nurjan Khan's father, as a way of disgracing Zada himself. Indeed, Nurjan Khan's father's pointed jab, "*Why are you running around all angry now? In the beginning you must teach your children to behave*," is intended to slight the leadership abilities of the important and politically powerful Zada by suggesting that he can't even control the actions of his own children. I asked Saras Gula Aya (Pilin Gul) if it were true that these elopements were encouraged by Nurjan Khan's faction to humiliate Zada and break up his established *khaltabár* relationships. "Whatever else?" she replied. "But I thought that *women* made the choice of whether to go *alaṣíŋ* or not," I pressed. "That's right," she said, "It is women's choice."

Once again, I seem to have a harder time than Saras Gula Aya and my other Kalasha friends in believing that two seemingly contradictory things can be true at once. The question I wrestle with is this: does the fact that elopements are orchestrated by politically powerful older men as a way of garnering prestige for themselves and "pulling the pants down" (*bhut nihúji*) (Parkes 1983:584) on their rivals negate the conception that Kalasha women are free to make their own decisions about marriage? I think, finally, that Saras Gula Aya is right. Not only are both things true, but each makes it possible for the other to be true.

As Ivan Karp argues, "We really only 'know' agency when it fails—that is when it has to face it's own limits" (1995:7). Women's freedom, the fact that women are ultimately responsible for the decision to stay or go, defines the outer limits of elder men's political agency (which for them is the ability to coordinate the actions and mobilize the resources of others toward their own ends). Women disrupt the best-laid plans of fathers and lineage elders by saying, as Mayram put it earlier in this chapter, "Now I am grown and I have other ideas about what I want." Women are not simply traded. Elopements always involve the active collaboration of the women involved (and thus Parkes's use of the term *capture marriage* and his reference to the eloping husband as the "abductor" seem inappropriate). And, once married, women do not always stay put. Orchestrating marriages or facilitating elopements thus takes considerable finesse, charisma, material resources, more than a little luck, and a keen ability to respond immediately and decisively to shifting situations. It is exactly the fact that women are *not* the puppets of big men that makes marriage and elopement an interesting and appropriate ground for demonstrating men's political astuteness.

At the same time, the realm of politics defines the field in which women exercise their choices about marriage. I realize that in this chapter I have underplayed the importance of the ongoing "war of position" of lineage elders, partly because it is not where my own interest lies but also because I have been following the narratives of women, who are remembering what they saw and felt when they were barely more than children. But it is clear, to them and to me, that the choices they make about whether and with whom to elope are "loosely structured" (Ortner 1989:198; see also Ahearn 1994:40–41) by kinship and politics. As Karp, again, says, "agency itself can never simply mean the exercise of choice, or the carrying out of intentions. Choice itself is structured and is also exercised on people and matter" (1995:8). Freedom, for Kalasha women, does not mean limitless choice but crafting a "meaningful life" (*maksát zindagí*) out of present possibilities.

A Meaningful Life

A few days later, Pilin Gul again went to braid her hair, this time to her natal village of Maledesh. One of her fathers (father's brother, FB) called her to come to the house, to his house, which sat directly above her own, so that her roof formed his balcony. *"Let's go. Let's go to*

Rawelik [their summer land]. What else should you do, [now that] your husband has made a wife?" he said. Pilin Gul told him that her mother-in-law had said she would kill herself if she left. *"Let her kill herself already. Let her jump into the river. Your husband took a wife."* So then Pilin Gul left with her father (FB), left for Rawelik with her littlest father (father's younger brother, FyB). He had in mind that she would marry someone else, a friend of his, and it is this story of how she almost went *alasíŋ* that she refuses to tell despite all the pestering of her daughters-in-law. Her own father was there already. Bibi Zar and Mizok were also there [since Mizok is Pilin Gul's cousin, Rawelik is also his summer land], hiding in a small out of the way hut until Zada's wrath cooled. They had planned to cross the mountain into Bumboret in the morning, but that very evening Zada and his younger brother came to take Bibi Zar home. They forced Bibi Zar to accompany them back to her natal home, saying that she should stay with the man they had given her to.

Meanwhile, Mir Beck apparently had brought his new bride to his father's house, but Zada had not allowed them inside, so they had gone back to Bumboret. Thus, Mir Beck's first attempt to bring a second wife failed. His father, Zada, had said, apparently, *"I won't give him that one. She is the wife of one of my lineage members. Someone overpowered him and convinced him to do this. I won't give her to him."* Then Zada and one of Pilin Gul's mother's brothers came to Rawelik with a bull, a big bull (an important item of bridewealth and an apology for the insult of his son trying to take a second wife). Pilin Gul's father said to them, *"'Go on back.' My father was a simple, straightforward man, and he left, up the water channel up-valley he left. So it was like that, and I was there for a while."*

"Then she went again, Bibi Zar, went alasíŋ [a second time]." Her father sent his brother, a convert to Islam (*šek*) after her, saying apparently, *"'Go brother, Bibi Zar has gone again.' That šek old man said to Bibi Zar, 'Let's go, my daughter.'"* But this time she didn't agree, so he came back home along with one of Mizok's grandfathers. Zada is said to have asked, "Why didn't you bring her home?" And Mizok's grandfather is said to have answered, *"'My grandson went nowhere looking for a woman. Your daughter came here herself, looking for a man'*—those were bad words he had. He came there to say those words apparently, *'My grandson didn't go there looking for a woman, to your place. Your little daughter came herself—she's become a woman who looks for men!' My father-in-law was*

enraged. Enraged, he went and beat Bibi Zar, her beads on her kupás, he grabbed a stick and beat her, scattering the beads everywhere. Then he brought her home. Brought that one home, and then they brought me, too. Brought me here again. Brought me here and then Bibi Zar also. It must have been six or seven years she was here at our own house."

∼

Desire

In this segment of Saras Gula Aya's narrative, her father-in-law, Zada, is enraged to hear that his own daughter, Bibi Zar, has become "a woman who looks for men." According to Mizok's grandfather, Bibi Zar came to Mizok on her own initiative rather than waiting for him to come for her. In so doing, she violated the fundamental way in which desire is constructed in Kalasha society: men desire women and make advances and proposals to them. Kalasha women *choose* among the men who desire them, but they don't make the first move. Once, for example, Katie, one of the English schoolteachers who work in Chitral, was visiting, and I translated as she related a story about one of her friend's mothers who had fallen in love with another man and divorced her first husband after twenty-five years of marriage. Always fascinated with the details of marriage in other cultures, the women in my family listened attentively. Then Saras Gula Aya said the whole thing seemed very strange to her—especially the part about an old woman falling in love and pursing a man. "Women don't fall in love with men here," she said. "We never go looking for them. Men fall in love with us, and they come looking for us." This construction carries over into many aspects of courtship (and ritual life—as I'll elaborate in the concluding chapter). Families of boys come "looking for a girl," never the other way around. Women wait to go *alasíŋ* with their lovers rather than simply walking down the road to his house.

And yet, familiar as this construction might sound—women as objects of men's desire—Kalasha women's position of "being desired" is not passive but rather powerful and demanding and efficacious. Kalasha girls begin early finding that being desired demands an active response and a sometimes painful choice. One afternoon I accompanied my friend Shakar Shah as he went to retrieve his daughter Nisa Gul, aged three and a half, from her maternal grandparents'

house. After we had tea, Shakar Shah told Nisa Gul that we were
ready to go home. Her grandmother and aunts fawned over her and
jokingly pleaded with her not to go. "Of course, you should come
with me," said Shakar Shah, "You belong with your father." "Don't
go," they countered, "Haven't we been taking care of you? Don't we
love you? Don't you love us? Where will you go—there? Or will you
stay here with us just a few more days. . . . If you go, Nisa, we will
have no desire to live. Okay, go then, we don't like you any more!"
Meanwhile, Shakar Shah kept coaxing her to come with him. Nisa, for
her part, looked as if she wasn't sure how to respond. "I'm going,"
she said finally and began sobbing. Her aunts laughed and told her to
give them all kisses goodbye. On the way home, I asked Shakar Shah
if he didn't think that was too much pressure for a little girl. "Of
course not!" he said, "It will make her happy to feel so wanted."

In only a couple of years, Nisa Gul will have learned how to
respond appropriately to so much being wanted. By the time she was
five years old, Gulsambar had mastered the kind of flirting discourse
in which men and women constantly engage: women desired and
aloof, men bearing gifts and compliments. In this short conversation,
Pundali (a thirty-year-old male friend and neighbor whose sister is
married to Gulsambar's uncle) has been trying to talk Gulsambar into
coming over to his house:

> P: Come over, my daughter! Why do you never come over? I'll
> give you sugar . . .
> G: Go away, don't give me ashes! Don't give it to me! What do I
> need with your sugar? I have my own house. There is sugar at
> my own house.
> P: But I'll give you lots of sugar, as much as you want! (starts
> tickling her)
> G: You'll give me ashes, ashes! Ayo, aaaaaayooooo (Mommm-
> mmmy)—

Adult Kalasha women experience being desired as a powerful
position, a position in which there is more room to negotiate. When
my census of Balanguru village showed that there were forty more
men than women, one woman said—to the amusement of her
friends—"Great, if we don't like our husband, we'll just toss him
away and there will be another waiting." They are quite explicit that

not being in love with their husbands gives them the upper hand in the relationship. Bayda Aya explained that because she came *alasíŋ* with her husband she can no longer say to him (when she wants him to do something special for her or to agree to a request), "What, do you think I stay here because I am in love with you?" Likewise, her family's decision to let Lilizar go *alasíŋ* instead of giving her to a man of their choice, according to Nizara Aya, puts Lilizar in a position in which they (her natal family) are above her (*hóma lilizára pi tára*). If they choose a husband for her, she can say, "Look how unhappy I am! My husband is no good!" and her natal family will have to find a way to make her situation better. But if she chooses her own husband her natal family will be "above her" (i.e., they will be in the easier situation) because if she complains or is unhappy (unless of course her husband is violent, in which case they would act on her behalf) they will say, "What can we do? It was your own choice. You yourself went *alasíŋ* with that man."

For her part, Lilizar, now thirteen, is experiencing how demanding it is for a Kalasha woman to be desired. When I left the valleys, four different men were interested in her. She felt barraged by their persistent (though indirect) proposals. The men sent their female relatives to talk to her and asked me to slip cookies to her. One especially lovesick suitor rode his bicycle (the only bicycle in the valley) back and forth on the road in front of her house. Every advance demanded a reply, whether in the form of a brush-off or an indignant no. "I wish I were a boy," Lilizar lamented to me, "Then everyone would leave me alone."

Among Kalasha, the fact that women are desired, and that they make active, unpredictable choices about what to do, is powerful and efficacious. It changes the world in important ways. Parkes, for example, notes correctly that Kalasha do not have detailed ideas about the biology of conception. But he does say that the male "seed" (*bi*) is thought to "congeal" (*sínjik*) with the mother's blood in the same way that milk is congealed by rennet to make cheese (1983:443). A better gloss of *congeal*, however, is *tru'ik*, with the derived adjective *trúna* meaning "congealed" or "jelled." *sínjik*, on the other hand, means to persuade, convince, or apologize so as to bring the other person around to your way of thinking. It is then the active agreeing of women's blood with the persuasive sperm that makes a child. It is the active agreeing to go *alasíŋ* that changes not only a woman's own life

but the social and economic relations of so many others in the community. And, as we'll see in the last chapter, the desire generated by
women's ritual leaving of the valley (even as the men try to persuade
them to stay) even changes the weather, bringing back spring after
the interminably long winter.

Then finally, seven years later, Bibi Zar went *alasíŋ* with Mizok
again. This time, Mashara Shah (a clan mate of Gazi, the man Bibi Zar
was married to as a young child) led the wife of one of Pilin Gul's
brothers (who was of course also one of Mizok's cousins) *alasíŋ*. So
Mizok led Bibi Zar. Instead of counting and exchanging bridewealth,
the two lineages just said, *"'We're even.' So then she was that one's wife,
and she was that one's wife. And after that, I [Pilin Gul] was his [Mir
Beck's] wife, and I stayed right here."*

Negative Agency?

I'd like to interrupt Pilin Gul's story one last time, and then I will let
her finish this chapter herself. In her essay on Okiek marriage arrangement, Corrine Kratz introduces helpful theoretical refinements of the
concept of agency (2000). Of particular interest here is her claim that
young Okiek brides have "negative agency." At their weddings, in a
rare public moment of power, Okiek brides are asked to decide
whether they will "follow" or "refuse" the husband their families
have chosen for them. "Her right of choice recognizes her adult
agency, her ability to affect many others and responsibility for those
effects" (166). Yet a young Okiek bride's agency is "negative" because
she is accorded only the power to *disrupt* the plans of her family and
future husband. "Full recognition of adult capacity and responsibility
is accorded to young women in marriage as blame, imputing to them
the negative effects of their action and decisions. Credit for their
positive effects of young women's actions is shared with the families
who arranged the match and with her husband" (166).

Kalasha women's freedom resonates in interesting ways with the
"negative agency" Katz describes for Okiek brides. Kalasha women

clearly have the power to disrupt the best-laid plans of their elders, and, like Okiek brides, young Kalasha wives cannot create marriages themselves—as is evidenced by the violent squelching of Bibi Zar's second elopement attempt. What is clearly different about Kalasha women's agency is their understanding that positive choices, such as Pilin Gul's decision to stay with Mir Beck, are thought to be meaningful, to have consequences, and to contribute as much to a person's sense of individual identity as negative choices. Among Kalasha, deciding not to act is active, too, and not mere passive acceptance of authority, as we are often led to believe in our current theoretical "romance" with resistance (Abu-Lughod 1990). The story of Pilin Gul's life climaxes with a description of her wrenching decision to stay with Mir Beck after he makes another—and this time successful—attempt to bring in a second wife. Although Pilin Gul was free to leave, she consented to stay.[15] As you'll see, for Pilin Gul staying with Mir Beck was anything but a passive decision; rather it was a conscious act that transformed both her own life and the lives of those around her. It was a decision that had far-reaching economic consequences, consequences for which she herself assumes responsibility. It was a decision that transformed her sense of self—she became a person who is patient, who is not selfish, a person who has endured and has been rewarded with an abundant and purposeful life.

I asked Mir Beck about his marriages. Why did he feel compelled to have two wives in a community where polygamy is both exceptional and exceptionally difficult? Was it a way of demonstrating his political power, of displaying his wealth, of freeing himself of the authority of his powerful, respected father (who foiled his first elopement attempt and unsuccessfully tried to forbid the second)? Was he in love with Siaphat, his second wife? Once Siaphat told me that she had been in love with Mir Beck since she was a young girl and that now, as an "old" woman (of about forty-five), her heart still jumps a little when she sees him coming home. Mir Beck himself would never talk to me about his wives, saying simply that everything happened a long time ago. He would tell me, if I wanted to get my tape recorder out, about the merit feasts he has given or about how his father killed a snow leopard. This story, then, comes through Saras Gula Aya, and you should know that both Mir Beck and Siaphat would tell it differently, if they would tell it at all.

~

"I staaaaayed here. And my daughter, Saras Gul, was born. My son Sherayat was born. When he was Mirzada's size—no, a little bigger than that, as big as Gulabi perhaps—that's right, we were saying it was time to have his gostník ceremony [initiation/blessing ceremony] at Chaumos—then he [Mir Beck], so, he led Barayata Aya. He brought that other one as a wife." Barayata Aya (Siaphat) is ten years younger than Pilin Gul. She had been Tajikia Dada's wife. At first, Zada again refused to allow his son to take a second wife. Mir Beck and Siaphat lived for a couple of months at a distant relative's house. Finally, with Siaphat eight months pregnant, Mir Beck is said to have threatened to convert to Islam if his father didn't accept his second marriage and pay the double bridewealth as compensation to Tajikia Dada. Zada refused still, but Saras Gula Aya said that her mother-in-law wept and said that, although she was angry, too, she couldn't bear to lose her only son. A date was set to exchange bridewealth. And Saras Gula Aya was free. "I'm leaving," she said.

The story of her life spins now, as it must have then, through all the advice she received. Because he had brought in another wife, Saras Gula Aya was free to leave Mir Beck, and he was not entitled to repayment of the bridewealth his family had given for her. But their two children were "his" and would stay with his family.

Everyone had an opinion about what Pilin Gul should do. Her fathers (father and father's brother) and brothers and cousins were furious and said that she should come home. She was young, they reasoned, and would have plenty of other children. Her father came to try to persuade her, but she didn't leave. Her brothers came, but she didn't leave. They came two or three times, but still she didn't leave, still she couldn't decide.

Finally, it was time for them to exchange bridewealth, and men from Birir Valley had come to help count, along with Siaphat's father and brothers and her former husband and all his clan mates and all the men from Mir Beck's clan as well. They began to count the bridewealth, and Pilin Gul saw that her own bull, a bull given by her father, was among the animals to be given as bridewealth. "I'm going," she said. "I said, 'I'm going,' and I went upstairs and talked to my aunt [one of her aunts had married her father-in-law's brother]. I went to her, and I said, 'I'm going, Aunt, they're counting bridewealth. They're *exchanging bridewealth and I'm leaving.' 'Oh, my daughter, go ahead. It's time for your son's gostník ceremony. You've been saying you'll do gostník for him. It's a tragedy. Everyone's thoughts, everyone's plans, everyone's hopes—lost. Go.' Those were my Kabuli aunt's words, 'Everyone's thoughts, everyone's plans, everyone's hopes lost. Go.' What can I do? I see those two little packages [the two children] sitting around the hearth, and my heart breaks,"* she said. *"Then I stayed. So then the šek old man [her father-in-law's younger brother, who had converted to Islam] said, 'Oh my jan [body/ flesh—a sweet endearment], I can't say go, and I can't say stay. My tongue is tied. Which words could I say to you?' 'Then I'm going,' I said. Then my father-in-law came—he came and got on his knees in the dirt, rubbing ashes on his body, he crawled toward me. . ."* On three separate occasions, Saras Gula Aya got down on the ground and demonstrated for me how her father-in-law, one of the most respected men in the valley, in the three valleys, had fallen to the ground before her, before his friends and relatives, and rubbed ashes on his face and clothes. He begged her to stay. *"He crawled toward me, saying 'You don't go. You. You are the one I sought. You don't go. That's just his own choice of a wife.' Everyone—oh, there were so many people there, a congregation of people, so [in front of them] my father-in-law said, 'My act [Zada's decision to choose Pilin Gul as Mir Beck's wife], he, my son, didn't appreciate it/ like it. My, this grandson [Sherayat], to him I will give everything. Chet Guru, everything. You people are witnesses. To him [Mir Beck], I'll give one field. One field I'll give to him and his wife. The rest, everything—I have stables, I have much. Everything I have made is for my grandson, Sherayat, my son's son.' My father-in-law said [that] to all those people. So it was like that, and they gave a bull for Barayata Aya, and he [Mir Beck] made her [his wife]. That's all. . . . So I also stayed. He made a wife and I stayed."*

A short while later, Pilin Gul's father-in-law, Zada, brought a Patua (Chitrali) man to the house because this man knew how to write. Saras Gula Aya's cousin (father's brother's son, FBS) Mizok came to get her so that she would also be there when the man wrote down Zada's promise to give everything to her son and only one field to Mir Beck and his new wife. Mizok said to the man, *"'You write this down: my father-in-law said everything is hers—the stables are hers, the lower house is hers, Chet Guru is hers. My father-in-law gave all this to her, to her son. You write it down.' Then I said, 'It's done already, it's done. How would paper make it any different?' I didn't let them write it onto that paper. So Mizok got mad and left—'You didn't let this be written on paper.' If I hadn't grabbed that Patua's finger, if I had told him to write, Barayata Aya would have nothing today, would be nothing, they would have nothing—one field, that's all my father-in-law gave to them—one field. 'Don't do that,' I said, 'don't do that.'"*

"But," I interjected, "weren't you angry? Weren't you jealous?" Bayda Aya offered that she must *not* have been in love with Mir Beck or she wouldn't have stayed. If she had loved him, the jealousy would have been unbearable. Of course, she was angry, Saras Gula Aya acknowledged, and for a long time she wouldn't let him sleep in her bed, saying to him, *"What work do you have with me, now? Go crawl in your own wife's bed."* But by and by she realized that she had made her "choice." She had stayed, and he was her husband. She had three more sons and a daughter who died in infancy. *"Fifteen grandchildren because I endured, I was patient. I sat there, as if I was dumb. I staaaayyyed, my daughter. I didn't even argue with the woman. I stayed, stayed, stayed, and God did well by me."* She looked around, and she said, *"What is there, only a little bit in the world?"* By this, I think she means that the world is an abundant place, not a place to be stingy. *"Maybe that was his agreement, his fate. One single son, my father-in-law, and much riches. He* [Mir Beck] *wasn't able to fulfill his lust for fun—he made a wife, he went to Peshawar, he did one thing and another. Maybe there was an agreement that he should have another wife. . . . I was patient, my daughter. I was patient and agreed to it all—sat, sat, sat. Patua say, 'If you are patient, you will find results.' You are patient, quiet, don't say a thing, don't start a fight, you be still—Patua, that's what Patua say. So I was patient. Thanks be to God. Look around here, my full life—my patience has been rewarded. širín-šarán zindagí, a sweet life. . . . God saw my patience, and for me cooked aluá* [a sweet, comforting pudding made out of slightly fermented wheat]. *Who else in the world has more than this? Whose life has more meaning/ purpose (maksat) than this, what, my daughter, among us humans. . . . So Yasira Awas sang a song for me, 'Saras Gula Aya's life has meaning/purpose,' she goes. That's right, it's like that."*

Conclusion

Bringing Back the Sun

Each fall, the first snow brings the shepherds home from the high pastures. Families return from their summer fields. The same villages that seemed abandoned during the height of the summer season now overflow with people and produce. Children spill from one house to the next. Storehouses are filled with fruit, grain, dried tomatoes, walnuts, bottles of wine, pumpkins. Looms are set up outdoors, and women begin weaving belts and headdresses for the coming Chaumos (winter solstice) festival. Old folktales are dusted off and told and retold around the evening fire.

Winter reaches its climax with Chaumos, and then, exhausted by two weeks of dancing and singing, feasting and praying, there is quiet. Winter, in the Kalasha valleys, is a time of drawing inward and a time of rest. Snow makes travel difficult. It is an *onjesta* time, and extra care is taken to separate *onjesta* and *pragata* things. Mornings are long, and people sit inside drinking extra cups of tea, waiting for the world to warm up before going out. Men take the livestock to graze in the nearby holly oak forests or offer fodder dried last summer. Women weave and spin, sort and grind grain. By early afternoon, the tall mountains above the valleys cast their cold, dark shadows over the villages, and people move indoors again. There is more talking. Night comes early, as does sleep.

By the time of the *ístam sáras* festival (in mid-March), the ceremony blessing the "first blossoms of spring" (Morgenstierne 1973:171) and marking the beginning of farming and the relaxation of *onjesta/ pragata* customs, winter—once enjoyable—has grown wearisome. Everyone—men, women, children, anthropologists—is ready for spring, ready to plant, ready to work again, to move again. Yet winter drags on. There is more snow. It is still cold. Worse yet, cold rain sets in. The weather becomes unbearable.

I remember thinking I would go crazy if the sun didn't come out soon, if I were trapped inside one more day, if I had to drink one more cup of tea. And I was not alone. Mothers complained that their children were "eating their heads" (driving them crazy). People started grumbling that they were in foul moods. Steve and I left for a two-week vacation, thinking that surely when we returned spring would also.

But the beginning of April saw more rain, more snow. "This must be unusual," I complained. My family agreed: it was unusual, and what was more, they said, almost every year was unusual like this. On April 10, it rained all night. It rained all morning and was bitterly cold. Mid-morning, Steve came running to the downstairs house. We all went out to see what the commotion was about. From our vantage point high up in Kalashagrom village, we saw a procession of women streaming down the road in the center of the valley. At first, I worried that the women had organized yet another political march to Chitral, but then I noticed that they were singing and laughing. I bolted to catch up, but Saras Gula Aya caught my arm and reminded me that I couldn't go: I was going to the *bashali* that evening. She told me not to worry, that she would tell me all about how women, every spring, bring out the sun after an interminably long winter. Here, then, is Saras Gula Aya's description (and my paraphrasing) of going Hawyashi (*hawyáši*):

> Women, when it rains a lot, if the rain won't stop, they go. It's our custom. Every year they go. We're going to *ṭsiám góra kóṭa* [to the white castle/fort of Tsiam], they say, and go.

Every spring, if the weather is unseasonably bad (and almost every year it is), Kalasha women go Hawyashi. As they leave the villages, they proclaim that the weather is terrible and so are their moods. One woman takes a *khawá* basket. She fills it full of rags and declares that she is going to drown herself in the river. The men follow after her and try to prevent her from leaving, saying "don't go, don't go, the sun will come back." The women say, "No, no, the sun won't come back. I'm going, I'm going to Tsiam. The sun isn't coming." The men say, "No, no, don't go, don't go, the sun will come. If you go there you will get cold." "No," say the women, "let us get cold, let us die (*nášik-oría*). I have no desire to stay here (*may da ne háwaw*). My sheep and goats are freezing. It's cold here. We're going." And the women take off. They take the basket and go. "Don't drown, don't drown," say the men, "The sun will come." The women leave, singing:

yáši párim day-o, hawyáši
[I'm going *yashi*, oh, Hawyashi]

may tábiat ásta ṭúkur-búkur-o-, hawyáši
[My mood is also awry (higgledy-piggledy), oh, Hawyashi]

tsiám góra kóṭa párim day-o, hawyáši
[I'm going to the white castle/fort in Tsiam, oh, Hawyashi]

a ta ne báta him, o, hawyáši
[I'm not coming back, oh, Hawyashi]

bi zhe bat ást ṭúkur-búkur háwan-o, hawyáši
[Seeds and stones have also become awry, oh, Hawyashi]

tsiam góra kóṭa parím day-o, hawyáši
[I'm going to white castle/fort of Tsiam, oh, Hawyashi]

may ta bátyak améyak ásta čilá háwan-o, hawyáši
[My kids (young goats) and sheep have become cold, oh, Hawyahsi]

bačúyak ásta čilá háwan-o, hawyáši
[Calves have also become cold, oh, Hawyashi]

tsiám góra kóṭa parím day-o, hawyáši
[I'm going to the white castle/fort of Tsiam, oh Hawyashi]

a ta tsiám parím day-o, hawyáši
[I'm going to Tsiam, oh Hawyashi]

So the women leave the villages singing, and the men follow, also singing and begging them to return. They walk out of the valleys toward Tsiam, the mythical Kalasha place of origin. Once, it is said, ten women did not respond to the men's pleas that the women return, to their promises that the sun would come out again soon. These ten reached Tsiam, and there they married dogs. The dogs there are big and fierce, and won't allow Kalasha men to return. But women are always welcome. "But these are old words," comes the cautious refrain, "Who knows if they're are true?" "They go, go, go, go, go. The men try to bring them back at Kort Desh [the Kalasha settlement that lies furthest down-valley], but they don't obey. Finally, the men catch up. They gather lots of wood, gather lots and lots of wood. They light a big fire to make smoke, and the smoke reaches the sky, reaches the sky. The smoke reaches to cloud brother-in-law [*jamó*]. Then he talks to the sky, the smoke talks to the sky, saying, 'don't rain, don't rain! The women are leaving, leaving all by themselves. Please let the sun shine.' Then the sun shines, and they all come back together."

Unlike most Kalasha rituals, going Hawyashi is spontaneous, and people agree about when the time is right. Often the women think to do it, though sometimes a man might suggest it. Like the *bashali* rituals, going Hawyashi is lighthearted and fun, but it is also important. To the Kalasha, going Hawyashi is important because this practice causes the seasons to turn, shifting the world of winter into the fertility and possibility of spring. To me, this ritual is important because, like the women's march to Chitral with which this book began, it serves as an embodied metaphor of what Kalasha mean when they say, "our women are free."

When women go Hawyashi, they say they are returning to Tsiam, the mythical place from which Kalasha believe they came. Although they may never make it there ("Who knows where that is? Who has ever been there and returned?"), in a way the very *act of going* is a return to the heart of Kalasha ethnicity, an enactment of women's freedom that is one of the most significant markers of Kalashaness. As its most basic level, Kalasha women's freedom is freedom of movement, a freedom that is always in implicit comparison to surrounding Muslim women, who never travel unescorted and who take great pride in the comfortable lives they make for themselves and their families within the high walls of Chitrali family houses. Kalasha women also value their freedom to be seen in a world where neighboring women take care to conceal themselves. Most critically, Kalasha women's freedom is the right to exit an intolerable situation, freedom to disregard—once in a while—the authority of families, husbands, custom. And it is the expectation that their actions will have real effects.

Going Hawyashi, then, is a ritual enactment of the agency—as well as the complexities of and limits to agency—Kalasha women claim across other arenas of their lives. Women leave their villages, wearing the very *khawá* baskets that I argued in chapter 3 are emblematic of women's freedom of movement and their essential economic contribution. The women leave knowing that there are significant risks—indeed, they might drown in the icy river. They disobey the men who try to call them back. They are indifferent to both men's attempts to bring them back physically and their persuasive rhetoric and promises of better tomorrows. And in the end the idea that the women might leave is effective: the sun comes out.

Like other acts that demonstrate women's freedom, women actively *go* Hawyashi (*hawyáši parík*)—just as they *go alasíŋ* (*alasíŋ parík*) and *go* to the *bashali* (*bašáli parík*). While men may make speeches, give their word, and issue orders, women act—and in fact usually they *walk*. Women shape the invisible *onjesta/pragata* landscape by means of their physical movement through it, by their conscious decisions to go here but not there. They walk, sometimes alone, and sometimes long distances, to care for the fields for which they are responsible. They make and wear the clothing that represents Kalasha ethnicity. So women's freedom almost always involves embodied action or at least potential action.

And, to refine this further, Kalasha women's freedom is expressed through the power to act, not the power to speak. In the 1970s, feminist scholarship was stimulated by Edwin Ardener's (1975a) theory of "muted groups," in which he argued that dominant groups control the dominant form of expression, silencing those over whom they have authority or forcing them to communicate through a model of reality that does not adequately express their experience or worldview. Since then, a major objective of feminist ethnography and theorizing, both within and beyond anthropology, has been "rediscovering women's voices" (Smith-Rosenberg 1985:26, cited in Gal 1991). Recent works have looked beyond speech to consider both silence and action (Gal 1991). Maureen Mahoney has criticized Carol Gilligan's influential notion of "voice" as the site that "connects body and psyche as well as psyche and culture" (Mahoney 1996:610). She argues that silence "should not be understood unidimensionally as the condition of disempowerment, or 'being silenced,' but carries the potential for strength and resistance" (622). Sometimes, then, silence makes authentic action possible.

Although there are many situations in which Kalasha women *do* speak, and many women whose words carry significant weight, "freedom of speech" isn't part of the Kalasha conception of women's freedom. They don't, for example, say "our women are free because they have equal say with men." Rather, women are free because they do things, make choices, go here or not, elope or not, wear this or that. And in the face of women's action men's words have little weight. So part of what women's freedom involves is the recognition that male spoken authority—while real—is nonbinding.

Once, for example, a coalition of elders was called together by Taksina's husband. Taksina had been seen with a lover in her mother's brother's guesthouse. She claimed that her husband was cruel to her. He claimed that he was fed up with trying to convince her to stay, to behave. He wanted her father to return his bridewealth and "free" Taksina (a quite unconventional but not altogether unthinkable solution to their marital problems). The elders instead decided to direct Taksina to stay with her husband, to work hard in his fields and not take lovers. For an entire afternoon, the most influential men in the valley sat in Taksina's father's house instructing her with their most eloquent (if somewhat didactic) speeches about how she should behave. Finally, they asked her, point blank, whether she would stay with her husband. "I'll stay," answered Takina firmly. Later I asked her if she had told the truth, if she really intended to stay. She replied, "Who knows, sister? Probably I'll go *alaṣíŋ*. I'll see later what I'll do." (And in fact I learned in a recent cassette-tape letter from my Kalasha family that she has gone *alaṣíŋ*). She insisted that she hadn't lied, but the truth for her would be in the action she would take, not in spoken promises.

Similarly, the proclamations (chapter 2) issued by valley elders that Kalasha women should no longer wear shawls that cover their headdresses, that they shouldn't keep chickens, that they should always go to the *bashali* when menstruating rather than sometimes staying at home, all these spoken mandates and many others are meaningful and compelling—to Kalasha women as well as other Kalasha men—but they are not completely *binding*. Because each woman chooses for herself which customs to observe and how far to follow them, the social and religious landscape of the valley is constantly shifting—slightly but perceptibly.

And yet I have tried not to give the (false) impression that Kalasha women's freedom is an ideal women cultivate at men's expense. Men play a critical role in the Hawyashi ritual, were involved in the political march to Chitral, benefit from and encourage women's agricultural productivity, and make elopements possible. The concept of "our women are free" is an ethical model, embraced by Kalasha men as well as women, of the way the gendered social world *should* work. But this model does not exist in isolation. The cultural emphasis on women's freedom always coexists with an equally powerful and deeply felt model of respect for patriarchal authority—again, an ethical value in which women as well as men are invested.

These two values compete as models for how men and women ought to relate to one another, how social relations ought to progress. Parents and husbands line up on the side of patriarchy and conspire to coerce a girl into staying in a marriage that benefits them, even if it makes her unhappy. Young male lovers are exuberant in their support of the culturally sanctioned freedom of women to leave their husbands in their favor. Women who have taken one path and not the other have a stake in seeing that others do as they have done, in pushing their own choices as the more moral or righteous or courageous. A woman may support freedom of choice when she is young and in love and switch lines when her own daughter wants to leave her favored son-in-law. Or, just as likely, she may choose to stay married to the man to whom her father gave her—citing loyalty to her natal family—but encourage her own daughter to elope.

In fact, these two discourses not only coexist, but each presupposes the other. The assumption of male authority/control is the ground against which women's freedom is configured—it is this, after all, that the women are "not obeying" when they don't heed men's calls to return to the villages rather than marching to Tsiam, when they decide not to follow *onjesta/pragata* customs, when they elope with another man. And, conversely, women's freedom—and the assumption that Kalasha women are, as Hobart puts it, "liable to act"—defines the limits of male authority.

As Bradd Shore notes in *Culture in Mind* (1996), when incompatible models exist for the same domain of experience, conflict and ambivalence are necessarily generated. At the same time, the collision of these ethical models, these different ways of making sense of and being in the world, makes ethical dilemmas poignant and the outcome of each situation unpredictable. I have a sense that this ambiguity at the very heart of Kalasha culture contributes to the ethos of flexibility and dynamism that, in part, has enabled them to survive for hundreds of years, and against all odds, as a despised minority.

Certainly Kalasha women don't see themselves as creating their lives out of nothing. They do the most they can with the options available to them. In this way, women's choices illustrate cultural innovation and cultural reproduction at the same time. For example, a woman has the right to reject the authority of her former husband and natal family in favor of another man she prefers. So, while she throws off authority, she embraces it in the same act, since she must elope with another man to be truly "free" of the first. Freedom therefore means choosing between available options rather than generating completely new possibilities herself. Women's choice operates in a similar way in other arenas. When women "threw off" some old customs of the *bashali*, they did not reject the cosmological symbolism of *onjesta/pragata* but instituted a new set of customs. This is not to minimize the radical nature of such choices, as each woman's life, relationships, and indeed the lives of many of the community change according to the decisions she makes. And it goes further than this. I think that these small, culturally sanctioned acts of rebellion make other things thinkable—allowing women to imagine that there are no absolutes, that they can do something about oppressive and intolerable situations, and that what they do might make a difference. They know spring can return after the interminable winter.

I asked Saras Gula Aya if the Hawyashi ritual really works, if it really brings back the sun. "What do I know, my daughter?" she said. "Sometimes it does, sometimes it doesn't." Then, looking up at the gathering clouds, she said that she guessed this time it hadn't. "Tomorrow or the next day," she said, "we'll go again."

Glossary

ačhámbi	A ceremony celebrating the birth of a baby. On the fifth day after the birth, young girls gather at the *bashali* to purify the new mother with water and smoke. Then they run to the temple of Jestak, make a small fire, and take turns jumping over it while shouting, *"ačhámbi aaaaa."*
alagúl	Chaotic, noisy confusion (often used to describe a large, happy household).
aluá	A sweet, comforting pudding made of slightly fermented wheat.
aḷasíŋ	Elopement.
amátak	Means you have left the period of holiness and reentered the everyday world. The *amátak sáras* ceremony at the end of Chaumos marks the end of ritually proscribed sexual abstinence. If you touch a Muslim person during Chaumos, you become *amátak* and may no longer participate in the festival. *amátak* is also applied to the prohibition on eating walnuts before Uchau, the fall harvest festival.
aŋgár-bat	"Fire rocks," quartz crystals.
aŋglís	English, a reference to Westerners in general, and including Japanese people. Kalasha from Bumboret say *aŋgrís*.
áya	Mother. The only Kalasha kinship term reserved for just one person. *Fathers, brothers,*

	sisters, grandparents, aunts, and so on are terms that name relationships with many others (e.g., one's father's brothers are all called *dáda*), but *mother* refers only to one's birth mother.
azát	Free.
azát masaháp	Free tradition; free religious practice; free culture.
barabár	Equal, the same, good. A name children born in the *bashali* call each other (also *burubér*).
bas hik	To spend the night somewhere.
bashali (bašáli)	Community menstrual house where Kalasha women live when they are menstruating or giving birth.
batií	A measure of about 2.5 kilograms.
beŕu	Husband.
bešárum	Without shame; embarrassing.
bilahí	Relative-in-law; used as a kinship term for the relation of ego to all relatives of a child's spouse except the child's spouse's parents (who call one another *khaltabár*).
biramór	A large and important feast of merit.
boniátyak	Diminutive form of *boníak,* a swaddling cloth.
bronzíkik	A little (term uses the diminutive form) grassy spot for resting, chatting, or relaxing.
bumbarák bo	Many congratulations!
čaumós	Chaumos, the Kalasha winter solstice festival.
čičílak	Fresh corn. Roasted in coals, it is a fall treat.
čiš	An ornament traditionally made of pheasant feathers (now usually peacock) and woven wheat and beads. Traditionally, only women whose fathers are "big men" wore them on their *kupás.* Now they are common as mere decoration.
čit	Choice, will, intention, thought. Used often in the phrase, *may cit,* "it's up to me, it's my choice, my decision."
čot	Decoration.

čet krom	Fieldwork, agricultural work.
čhir āya	Milk mother. A name for a woman (not your own mother) who nursed you one or more times when you were a baby.
dáda	Father, father's brother.
dádas dur alaṣíŋ	To elope from one's father's house (a girl who has not been married and elopes without her parents' permission).
dasmán	Muslim priest.
dastúr	Tradition, custom.
dastúr hístik	To "throw away" a tradition, to give up a custom.
dáim hútala	High pomegranate tree. The sun travels down the valley and rests there for the shortest seven days (*dič*) of the year before making its way up the valley again.
déwa dur	House of the spirit/god Sajigor, the ritual altar at Sajigor Torn.
dič	The purest part of the Chaumos festival, a time when many ritual prohibitions, including sexual abstinence, are carefully observed.
dubáč	The government check post at which all visitors stop on their way into the Rumbur and Bumboret valleys. (*dubajá* means "the confluence of two streams," and this check post is located at the point where the rivers from Rumbur and Bumboret join.)
dupáṭa	Many Muslim women in the North West Frontier Province wear this large, usually white shawl to cover their heads, faces, and shoulders when they are in public places.
dur	House, household.
dúray krom	Housework or work around the house.
dúray moč	People of a household, people who share their economy.
dušmán	Enemies.
dak bónyak	The (back-swaddling) ceremony for a newborn at one month. The midwife who delivered the baby is called to swaddle him or

	her. Babies have their first tiny taste of solid food at this ritual.
gáḍa āya	"Great (or big) mother," the name children call the midwife who delivered them.
gaḍérak	A respected male elder.
gadoḷái	A special necklace made of four to six strands of beads held together with pieces of carved bone.
ga̲ ačók	Bare necked, an insult thrown at a woman who doesn't have many beads.
ghóna saǰigór	Great Sagigor, a spirit being honored in Rumbur.
gonǰ	A storeroom located (usually beneath) the family house where grain and other shared resources are stored.
goṣṭník	A ceremony that takes place during the winter solstice festival in which two- to three-year-old boys and girls are dressed for the first time in traditional Kalasha clothing by their mothers' brothers. Boys celebrate a similar rite of passage again when they are five, called *bhut sambiék*, "putting on the pants." Before this time, little boys traditionally didn't wear pants, only a long shirt. During *bhut sambiék*, boys are dressed in traditional men's clothing and pose as stiff, fierce warriors at Sajigor, the most sacred altar in the valley.
goṣṭník-ani ma̲ík	Beads girls receive during their *goṣṭník* ceremony.
goṭ	Crazy, insane.
gul parík	"Going with/to the flowers," a blessing ceremony for an infant at three or more months that releases women entirely from their association with the intense *pragata* of childbirth.
hányak	A short, four-legged stool with a seat of woven leather.
hawyáši	A spontaneous spring ritual enacted when winter has become unbearably long.

hóma istríža azát ásan	"Our women are free."
hóma pi tára	"On top of us," "better than we are."
ístam sáras	A ceremony celebrating the first blossoms of spring and marking the beginning of farming.
istę̃ink kárik	To divine using a bracelet dangled from a thread.
istóngas	To ritually purify by sprinkling goat's blood (always performed by men).
istrižan čit	Women's choice, a decision left to women.
išpónyak	A thick porridge made from wheat flour and topped with walnut oil.
ja	Wife.
ja hik	To marry (of a woman).
ja nik	To marry (of a man).
jamíli	Female patrilineage members; clan sisters.
jamilishír	Community of women (lit. community of *jamili* but used to refer to all women in the Kalasha community).
jangalí	From the jungle, wild.
jaṛọa	Bastard; a child whose mother has no husband or a child thought to have a biological father not married to his or her mother.
jhes	Dowry given to one's married daughter or married sisters.
kalašadéš	Kalashadesh, the "place of the Kalasha." Currently only the three valleys of Birir, Rumbur, and Bumburet.
káḷun	Traditional soft-soled shoes once commonly worn and still important for burial dress.
kam	A group of Kalasha people related through their common patriline.
kapabán	A choker made of multiple strands of colorful beads and dividers carved from cow bones.
kásik	To walk, move.
kawaḷíak istríža	A single woman (meaning the only woman in her household).
kazí	A ritual expert (always a man) with special

	knowledge of Kalasha history and religious traditions; also a judge.
khaltabár	Relationship between a bride and bride-groom's parents.
khaltabarí	A marriage alliance; a ceremony/party celebrating and arranging a marriage.
khawá	A conical basket woven of wool on a wooden frame. These baskets are made by Nuristani women.
khẽ kárik, ása čit	"What can we do? It's her or his choice."
khójik	To search; also "to look for a wife."
krom	Work or, more specifically, necessary activity.
kupás	The elaborate cowrie shell and bead-laden headdress used by Kalasha women on special occasions.
kušún	A household; also people with a shared economy, who usually, but not always, share the same house or cluster of houses.
kušuší	A "try-er"—someone who tries hard at what he or she does and is earnest, especially in observing Kalasha traditions.
máka	Ritually impure; said of people who marry forbidden partners.
maksát zindagí	A purposeful, fulfilling life.
marát	A sacrifice of an animal and subsequent feast.
may de, may de	"Give it to me," what little children say when they want something.
may khalí del	"I feel lazy"; "I don't feel like doing it."
méher	Kindness, love.
mezbút	Sturdy, strong, solid.
mišári	Mixed.
mišári moč	A person who is half-human, half-fairy.
móa	Maternal uncle.
moráy	Nubile young woman; woman of marriageable age.
nazúk	Precious, sweet, cute (like a baby).
onǰáaw	Things of this time, modern; lit. "It came now."

onǰeṣ marát	A pure sacrifice.
onjesta (ónǰeṣta)	Ritually pure, holy, sacred, taboo.
ónǰeṣta wão	The *onjesta* space in every house that runs from the back of the stove to the far wall. Women don't step over this space.
páček	An embroidered white cotton head covering worn under their beaded headdress by women from the Urtsun Valley before they converted to Islam.
pastí	Wooden shed for storing food. These are tiny buildings separate from the family house and belonging to one woman.
pátua	Kalasha term for Chitrali Muslims.
páwa	Kalasha use this English word, *power*.
paysadár	A wealthy person, someone with lots of money.
pragata (prágata)	Ritually impure.
pruṣt	Good, better; okay.
rumiš	If a married man or woman finds his or her spouse has a lover, these gifts of compensation can be demanded and are offered to assuage anger.
sadá	Simple, straightforward, honest.
sahí istríža	A "real" woman.
sariék	A merit feast (*namús*) given to one's married daughter or sister. Young goats are given to the woman as well as a chest filled with clothes, jewelry, cups, plates, and so on. Guests (from the whole valley, and sometimes all three valleys) are invited for one to three days of feasting and dancing.
saw kaḷáša	Completely Kalasha.
son	The high pasture where goats are taken in the summer.
súda uṣṭawáu	A midwife; lit. a person who "lifts" children.
ṣiṣ áu sučék	A purification ceremony for women using specially baked bread and juniper smoke.
ṣiṣ istóŋgas	A sacrifice that solemnifies the bonds between husband and wife. This ritual often takes place years after the couple has

	married. If this ceremony is not performed, children of the couple are considered illegitimate.
ṣumbér-áu	From past times, old-fashioned (adj.).
ṣuṣútr	A small headdress covered with beads and cowrie shells. Kalasha women wear their susútr whenever they are awake, except in the menstrual house, where it is optional.
šalwár kamíz	The long shirt and loose trousers that are the national dress of Pakistan.
šaydár bo	"Congratulations on the birth of your daughter." *šay* means "a valuable person"; *dar* is a suffix meaning "you own something." I think the phrase means "you have someone very valuable."
šek	Kalasha who have converted to Islam.
šok	Mourning period when a relative has died.
tasíli	The staple pancakelike bread of wheat or corn flour made by spreading batter on a convex griddle.
tiriwéri	A horrible snakelike dragon.
trómiš	Evening.
wã	Space; place.
waḷ moč	Shepherds, men whose main occupation is herding goats.
wasiát	A testimonial, usually in the form of an elaborate stylized praise song, that traces the heroic deeds of ancestors, generation by generation, to the living elders.
wẹ́i	The pouch of fabric above the tightly belted waist of Kalasha women's dresses. All sorts of small things are carried there.
zánti	A woman who is ready to give birth or has just given birth.
zarúri	Necessary.
zit	A dispute or a small act of stubbornness to show how angry you are.

Notes

Introduction

1. *Aya* (*áya*) means "mother." Wasiar's mother is called Wasiara Aya. His father is called Wasiara Dada (*dáda*), "Wasiar's father." Throughout this book, I have used pseudonyms, although it is a decision that has caused me agony. Remembering people's names is important to Kalasha people, a sign of respect. I hope that my friends will understand that I have changed their names only to protect their privacy. They know how important they are to me. I have reserved quotation marks for speech that was recorded with a tape recorder or (more frequently) reconstructed in field notes immediately. More loosely paraphrased dialogue is not in quotes. All quotations longer than a couple of sentences are transcribed from tape-recorded interviews.

2. In March 1997, the residents of Rumbur Valley won the court case for timber rights (and the right not to have their forests logged by outside parties) and were also awarded royalties for all timber cut in the past fourteen years. The money was distributed equally to all the male members of the valley (Birgitte Sperber, personal communication).

Chapter 1

1. The kingdom of Chitral, ruled for three hundred years by the Katur dynasty, was incorporated as district of Pakistan in 1969. The last *Mehtar* now lives comfortably in Peshawar, and his family members continue to have considerable influence in the area as contractors for development projects, owners of hotels and travel agencies, heads of aid programs, and excellent polo players.

2. Steve and I were fortunate to be befriended by a wonderful Chitrali man who welcomed us into his family, and so we were able to experience the warmth of Chitrali family life. His household became a haven for us whenever we passed through Chitral. Without this glimpse behind the walls of Chitral, it would have been much more difficult to dispel Western stereotypes of women in purdah as passive or oppressed.

3. Henrietta Moore (1985:21–24) succinctly reviews debates about the analytical appropriateness of dividing the social world into a public realm where men operate and a private realm for women. See also Rapp 1979; Rogers 1978; Rosaldo 1980; Strathern 1984a; and Yanagisako 1979.

4. *Kalash* is the Khowar term for *Kalasha,* but it has come to have very offensive connotations. It is used in southern Chitral as some people in the United States use ethnic slurs such as *nigger* or *Polack* (Alb. Cacopardo 1991:279).

5. Michael Hutt writes about local reactions to the Western perception of Himalayan countries as magical realms (1996).

6. In fact, Peter Parkes's Ph.D. dissertation places "sexual antagonism" on center stage, arguing that it is interrelated with the economy and social order and forms a "tensile structure of solidarity and controlled conflict in reaction to a hostile environment" (1983:ii).

7. For a review of Kalasha literature, see Maggi 1998:55–57.

8. These are to be found now mostly in homes of fashionable European collectors. The beautiful carvings having been chopped unceremoniously out of doorways or off of the walls of Nuristani houses and smuggled out of the country.

9. The Durand Line defined the limit for Afghans, although under the terms of the treaty the British could still go forward into Afghanistan (Nigel Allan, personal communication).

10. Because Kafiristan was converted so quickly and so utterly, Robertson's work remains the "Bible" for scholars interested in pre-Islamic Nuristan. Also useful is appendix C of Elphinstone's *An Account of the Kingdom of Cabul* (1819), which is based on a report by "Moolah Nujeeb," whom Elphinstone sent to Kafiristan with "a long list of queries" in 1809. As Jones (1966) notes, until Robertson's account this appendix constituted virtually everything known about Kafiristan. Readers interested in Nuristan should consult the work of LaRiche (1981), whose master's thesis masterfully condenses most of the available literature that deals with Nuristan both before and after its conversion to Islam. Schuyler Jones, perhaps the best-known scholar of Nuristan, has compiled two painstakingly annotated bibliographies (1966, 1969). A condensed review of the literature on Nuristan can be found in Maggi 1998:58.

Only a handful of scholars have conducted research on post-Islamic Nuristan. Those who have written extensively include Schuyler Jones (1963, 1966, 1967, 1969, 1970, 1974), Louis Dupree (1971, 1973), Max Klimburg (1999), and Richard Strand (1974a, 1974b). Strand currently maintains an informative web site, "Richard Strand's Nuristan Site," at <http://users.sedona.net/ ~strand/Nuristani/nuristanis.html>. Fredrik Barth and Lincoln Keiser have written studies on the Kho, a people who live in northwestern Pakistan bordering the Swat River and the upper regions of the Indus River (Barth 1956; Keiser 1986). Since these people converted to Islam only 200 to 250 years ago, they are interesting to compare to the more recently converted Nuristanis.

The war, and now the civil war, in Afghanistan have made it impossible for anthropologists to conduct extensive field research since the mid-1970s.

11. Augusto and Alberto Cacopardo, Italian anthropologists who wrote dissertations about the Kalasha of Rumbur, recently conducted a survey of the converted Kalasha throughout the Chitral region. Their survey confirms a widespread Eastern variety of Kalasha culture, possibly closer in form to that of Birir (and certainly more similar in dialect) than to that of Rumbur and Bumboret (Alb. Cacopardo 1991; Aug. Cacopardo 1991).

At the time of Morgenstierne's visit to the Chitral area in 1929, there were five Kalasha valleys, all located to the west of the main Kunar Valley. From north to south, they were Rumbur, Bumburet, Birir, Jinjeret Kuh, and Urtsun. The valleys of Jinjeret Kuh and Urtsun were progressively converted between 1910 and 1920 and in 1940. Before this time, these two valleys were involved in the Kalasha intervalley community. People from these communities attended one another's festivals, invited one another to feasts of merit and important funerals, and married their children to one another as the peoples of the three remaining Kalasha valleys do today (Alb. Cacopardo 1991). An old woman, Mranzi, who was born in Urtsun and married in Birir, died during my field-work during the summer of 1995. Although she told me that she had never gone back after her natal family converted, she continued to wear the distinctive Urtsuni *páček*, an embroidered white cotton head covering, under her Kalasha headdress (*susútr*) (Aug. Cacopardo 1991:332). Kalasha continues to be spoken in these valleys, as well as in a number of other previously Kalasha communities, by the older generation (though most do not admit to speaking it because of its associations with "paganism").

12. Tak and Shamlar's answers about their own religious beliefs demonstrate that even in 1835 the Kati were clearly aware of the Muslim world around them. They framed their answers in such a way as to make them more acceptable to Islam (Holzwarth 1993).

13. Kalasha have a rich oral tradition concerning the history of the various lineages, and these are given in testimonials (*wasiát*), usually in the form of elaborate stylized praise songs that trace the heroic deeds of ancestors, generation by generation, to the living elders (Parkes 1991:77; Parkes 1994:172–74; Cacopardo 1992). They also have a fairly rich corpus of myths surrounding the origin of most ritual practices. This is in contrast to a rather vague cosmology (Jettmar 1975:338; Cacopardo 1992:1). Kalasha deities, while certainly important, are quite underdetermined figures. As Parkes has noted, the various gods and goddesses in the Kalasha pantheon seem barely differentiated beyond the epithets directed in their prayers to, for example, the "great" Sajigor (*ghóna sajigór*) or the "powerful" goddess Jach (*balíma jač*) (1991:76).

14. Linguistic data also point to separate origins of the peoples of Nuristan and the Kalasha. Early linguists classed them together, but Morgenstieren argued that they should be classed separately, since almost all aspects of Kalashamun (and Khowar, the language of Chitral to which Kalasha is quite similar both in structure and in much common vocabulary) can be derived

from early Sanskrit (Indo-Aryan), while many features of the Nuristani languages are "decidedly un-Indian" (Parkes 1983:7–10). See also Bashir 1988 and LaRiche 1981:21–28. Karl Jettmar (1975) has hypothesized that the "original" religion of the Kalasha was probably much closer to other Dardic-speaking peoples in pre-Islamic times and has now been "overlaid" by borrowings from Kafiristani religion (cited in Parkes 1983:9).

15. Kalasha women do not envy the Nuristani sexual division of labor (in which, it seemed to them, women do everything, men next to nothing). And both men and women seemed to consider the ethos of Nuristani life to be rather too violent.

16. Little is known about these first Muslim kings, known as the Rais (Biddulph 1986:150; Alberto Cacopardo 1991:273; Parkes 1983:21; Schomberg 1938:262; Siiger 1956:33).

17. They appear to have retained some political influence during this time—Kalasha were believed to have great skill at divining the future (Parkes 1995) and played pivotal roles in political intrigue. In the mid–eighteenth century, Kalasha spies helped Mehtar Mohtaram Shah Katur regain Chitral after it had been overtaken by a rival branch of the royal family. Kalasha spies arranged for the ambush of the rival Mehtar Khairullah as he returned from a campaign in Bashgal. For this, the Kalasha were awarded control of the neighboring Bashgal Valley, then part of Chitral (Parkes 1983:22; 1995). Many Kalasha ancestors are remembered as having held prominent positions in the court of the Mehtars in Chitral (Parkes 1995).

18. I didn't conduct a demographic survey of Birir or Bumboret, but there are clearly more Chitrali Muslims and more Kalasha šek in these valleys than in Rumbur.

19. Pakistani tourists, mostly groups of young male college students from the Punjab, also vacation in the valleys. Many (though not all, of course) are disrespectful of the valleys and the Kalasha people. Some are looking for sex with Kalasha girls, whom they have heard (falsely) are available. They make vulgar comments and gestures, and a few follow about or otherwise harrass Kalasha women (and foreign female tourists and anthropologists). Others seem to be on a quest for wine, which most Kalasha refuse to sell them. I have seen some young men posing for photographs with skulls they have removed from coffins in the graveyard in Bumboret.

20. Rumbur has two quite uncomfortable hotels. The largest, the Exlant Hotel, was leased to and managed by a Pukhtun entrepreneur. The other, even less successful, is owned by a Kalasha family, though mainly used as a place where local Kalasha and Muslim men play cards. There is one private guesthouse where anthropologists and extra-savvy foreign tourists stay. The larger valley of Bumboret had thirteen small hotels in 1995, the two most successful of which were owned and managed by "down-valley" (one Punjabi and one Pukhtun) businessmen. In 1999, the Pakistan Tourism Development Corporation (PTDC) opened a hotel in Bumboret. The new hotel, which features bathrooms and beds with sheets, caters to tourists looking for a less rustic travel experience.

21. For example, tourists can't possibly navigate the complex and unmarked geography of pure and impure spaces, and so sacred places are often defiled as tourists trek about the valleys. Kalasha leaders also worry that their community is becoming dependent on foreign aid to rebuild altars, irrigation canals, and menstrual houses, all processes that built solidarity within the community when local people organized the effort and everyone participated. While only a handful of Kalasha men have been even marginally successful in cashing in on tourism and development money, these few have begun accumulating markers of wealth and privilege like cement floors and glass windows in their houses. Two men have jeeps, and some have traveled outside of the Chitral region. These amenities are nearly unthinkable for those who have no access to foreigners and their money.

There is a new collection of stories that most Kalasha know, and love to retell, about silly things foreigners do. For example, one English woman is said to have named her dog Pooch, which, in Kalashamon is a slang word for penis. She went all about the valley calling, "Pooch! Pooch! Has anyone seen my Pooch?"

22. To be fair, some Kalasha do find small ways to sell their culture to tourists. Occasionally, some unscrupulous elder convinces women to dance for the pleasure of some visitor or another (and usually he pockets most of the money himself rather than dividing it among the dancers). And some women are beginning to find ways to sell Kalasha handicrafts to tourists. But, at least so far, such transactions are infrequent and not very lucrative.

23. Most anthropologists now accept the idea that contemporary tourism is largely a "quest for the Other," as van den Berge (1994) has called it. See Selwyn 1996 and Adams 1996 for excellent reviews and refinements of the literature on tourism.

24. LaRiche writes that the former non-Muslim inhabitants of Nuristan also apparently felt a curious link with Europeans (1981:41–43). In the winter of 1839, the Kafirs sent a deputation to see Sir William McNaughten, secretary to the government of India. McNaughten was in winter quarters in Jalalabad with Shah Shuja, whom the British had recently installed as ruler of Afghanistan. Maj. H. C. Ravery was told the following anecdote by an old member of his corps:

In the end of 1839, in December, I think it was, when the Shah and Sir W. McNaughten had gone down to Jalalabad for winter quarters, a deputation of the Si-ah-Posh Kafirs came down from Murgal to pay their respects, and, as it appears, to welcome us as relatives. If I recollect right, there were some thirty or forty of them, and they made their entry into our lines with bagpipes playing. An Afghan peon [orderly] sitting outside Edward Connolly's tent, on seeing these savages, rushed into his master's presence, exclaiming, "Here they are, Sir! They are all come! Here are all your relations." Connolly, amazed, looked up from his writing, and asked what on earth he meant, when the peon, with a very innocent face, pointed out the skin-clad men of the mountains, saying "There! Don't you see them? Your relatives, the

Kafirs?" I heard Connolly tell this as a good joke, he believing at the same time that his Afghan attendant was not actuated by impudence in attributing the blood connection between his master and the Kafirs. The Kafirs themselves certainly claimed relationship, but I fear their reception by poor Sir William was not such as pleased them, and they returned to their hills regarding us as a purse-proud people, ashamed to own our country cousins.

Raverty claims that the Afghan attendant was only acting on the commonly held fact that the Kafirs claimed European descent (cited in LaRiche 1981:42).

25. Parkes notes that this description resonates with Kalasha conceptions of their own communal identity, in that Kalasha repeatedly emphasize that "all Kalasha are poor, all are equal," in contrast to the finely graded status hierarchies of surrounding Chitral (1994:160). During the "women's march," the women were offered a jeep ride, but they refused it, saying that they were "poor Kalasha" and they would walk.

26. There are interesting parallels between Kalasha and the Maya of Guatemala. Maya culture, of course, is surrounded by the politically and numerically dominant Ladino culture. Like Kalasha women, Maya women wear distinctive, elaborate clothing, while Maya men are difficult to distinguish from Ladino men. Carol Smith argues that Maya women also have greater latitude to make decisions about their sexual and marital lives than do Ladino women—as long as they remain within the Maya community (1995).

27. For a review of recent ethnographies that deal with the ways in which gendered disempowerment provides a connection point to other inequalities, see Knauft 1996.

28. For example, Judith Butler writes, "If one 'is' a woman, that is surely not all one is; the term fails to be exhaustive, not because a pre-gendered person transcends the specific paraphernalia of its gender, but because gender is not always constituted coherently or consistently in different historical context, and because gender intersects with racial, class, ethnic, sexual, and regional modalities of discursively constituted identities. As a result, it becomes impossible to separate out 'gender' from the political and cultural intersections in which it is invariably produced and maintained" (1990:3). And Bourdieu writes: "Sexual properties are as inseparable from class properties as the yellow of a lemon is from its acidity" (1984:107).

29. *ásan* is the "proper" third-person-plural conjugation. In the Rukmuli dialect (spoken by those from Rumbur Valley), everyday speech contracts *ásan* to *an*. Morgenstierne noted that the change was beginning to take place when he studied the language in 1929 (1973). *ásan* is still used in more formal contexts, such as speeches or in formulaic pronouncements. Using *ásan* in this context marks this phrase as special and proper, a well-known expression rather than the casual speech of one person.

30. I'm not saying that there are no differences between the behavior of Kalasha women and the various communities of Muslim women who are their neighbors—all this talk is about practices that *are* real and that *do* have consequences for the way lives are lived. But the differences are relative ones

that are not nearly so disparate as the stereotyping discourse (on both sides) would lead us to believe.

31. See, for example, Bohannan 1954; Mead 1928; Faithhorn 1976; Fernea 1969; Hurston 1990; Underhill 1934; Weiner 1976; Wolf 1968; and Shostak 1983, among many others. In a special issue of *Critique of Anthropology* (1993, vol. 13, no. 4), which focuses on "women writing culture,'" the significance of some of these works are discussed. See also Behar and Gordon 1995.

32. Ethnographies that deal with women's "agency as resistance" include Comaroff 1985 and Raheja and Gold 1994. See Abu-Lughod 1990 for an important critique.

33. Certainly the association between agency and community identity is not unique to Kalasha. Many Indian feminists focus on the "question of 'Woman's' and 'women's' discursive and strategic location in the emergence of national, racial, religious and other community identities" (Gedalof 1999:29). Zoya Hasan (1994:32) argues that in contemporary India, even in times of conflict, when religious identity is heightened and gender identity seems muted, there is still much concern about what women do because "community identities are often defined through the conduct of women." See also Chhachhi 1994, Mann 1994, Chakravarti 1990, Mani 1990, and Sangari and Vaid 1990 for historical and ethnographic accounts of the ways in which gendered agencies are enmeshed in other identities in India. Carol Smith (1995) makes a similar argument for Mayan communities in Guatemala.

34. See, for example, Kratz 2000, Ahearn 1994, Finn 1995, Hobart 1990, Tsing 1993, Ortner 1996, and Wardlow 2000.

Chapter 2

1. The complicated relationship between space and identity has long been an important topic for many social theorists. Early social-theoretical works that addressed relationships between space and identity include Durkheim 1915; Goffman 1959; Barth 1966; Douglas 1966; Bourdieu 1971, 1977; and Foucault 1979, 1980, 1986, among many others. In recent years, cultural geographers have taken this compelling discussion to new levels of complexity. Soja, for example, has demonstrated the ways in which "human geographies become filled with politics and ideologies" (1989:6), and Massey reads the spatial as "an ever-shifting social geometry of power and signification" (1994:3). Perhaps because we all share fundamental embodied understandings of life in a three-dimensional universe "space" captures our imagination: it's good to think with. Many recent studies of space have taken wing, soaring above the intricacies of life on the ground to new conceptual heights, pulling us along so that we, too, can glimpse Pratt's "contact zones" (1992), Jameson's "world space of multinational capital" (1991), and hooks's, "space of radical openness" (1991:149, quoted in Keith and Pile 1993:5), among many others. Ethnographers have this to offer to discussions about "space": by slowing down and attending to the details of how people move in and understand the

landscapes they live in, attending to spaces with a small *s* rather than Space with a big *S* (Knauft 1996:135), we can trace not only what spaces do or mean but how they change in particular cultural contexts, and why—what Foucault has called "the little tactics of the habitat" (1980).

2. *azát* is an adjective. It is also possible to use it as a noun, *azatí*, but this form seems to be less common.

3. According to A. Raziq Palwal, another different version of this myth was recorded by Peter Snoy in 1970 (1972:34).

4. The *onjesta* status of a woman who has given birth to twins means that she is especially vulnerable. Baraman's wife, for example, is thought to have lost her voice after giving birth to twin sons. A woman who has borne twins will not drink from a cup that has first touched the lips of another woman. She also doesn't take food from Muslim neighbors (this is interesting because men, who are also said to be *onjesta*, often eat with Muslim friends). While she is said to be *onjesta*, such a woman does not reap male privileges. As Pirdaus' Aya put it, "No matter how pure we become, they will never let us eat the meat of male goats (*bíra mos*)."

5. As Margaret Mills commented (personal communication), perhaps the Kalasha example can serve as a starting place for a general critique of purity theory that dislodges (or at least nudges) hierarchy as a logical implication of dichotomy.

6. For a structuralist interpretation of *onjesta-pragata* dualism, see Cacopardo and Cacopardo 1989.

7. Spatial segregation and gender have been considered with increasing nuance by feminist anthropologists and geographers (cf. Rosaldo 1974; Ardener 1981; McDowell 1983; Moore 1986; Rose 1993; Spain 1992; Massey 1994). The best of these interpretations look beyond the social outcomes of an already existing spatial order, recognize space as both the "product and producer" of existing social and economic relations (Moore 1986:89), and ask how women themselves participate in the creation of the spatial worlds in which they live (cf. Abu-Lughod 1995: Wikan 1982).

8. The man transgressing the *bashali* boundary would have to wash thoroughly on the spot and later provide a goat to be sacrificed at a Sajigor altar for an *onǰés marát*, a "pure sacrifice."

9. Kalasha talk about modernity with the same nuance they give to other complicated topics. Things and ideas that are *onǰáaw* (from right now) are not necessarily better than things that are *sumberáw* (from before). Things that are *sumberáw* are not unquestionably right because they are traditional. Sometimes when Kalasha discuss development in the valleys they use the words *tarakí*, "upwardness." But a person can also improve his or her status, *tarakí káru*, through traditional means like giving feasts of merit.

10. Margaret Mills tells me that *wāo* means "old woman" or "grandmother" in Khowar.

11. For women who are menstruating or have recently given birth, this *onjesta* part of the house expands still further, and they avoid touching or even reaching into the entire rear section of the house.

12. I have, however, had cocky younger men like my friend Nisarge respond to my questions about why women don't go to ritual altars by saying, "We don't let them." So perhaps this is a more contentious point than either women or ritual elders led me to believe.

13. Several women claim to have been the first to "stay the night" (*bas hik*) at home instead of going to the menstrual house. There is a certain valued boldness in being on the leading edge of cultural changes.

14. Although men can "pass" since they dress like other men in the North West Frontier Province, Kalasha dancing, wine making, religion, and especially women's distinctive, colorful clothing and beads, lack of a veil, and assertion of freedom of movement mark them as different in almost every context.

15. When I admitted to Saras Gula Aya that Westerners are more like Muslims than Kalasha in that way—that we cook for our families when we are menstruating and have our babies in the presence of husbands and male doctors, she said, "What can I tell you, Wynne? *aŋglís* are like us, something like us. Muslims are *bo warék,* very different."

16. For excellent descriptions of Chaumos, see Cacopardo and Cacopardo 1989; and Loude and Lievre 1984, 1988.

Chapter 3

1. Of the 114 Kalasha or Kalasha *šek* (converted Kalasha) households in Rumbur in 1995, 30 owned no goats. Among those households that did own goats, average herd size was 55. Fourteen households owned more than 100 goats, 2 owned 200, and one owned 250. Of 104 Kalasha families, 17 owned no livestock (cattle, sheep, or goats) whatsoever. Of 10 families of converted Kalasha, 4 families owned no livestock, 6 owned no goats, one family owned 5, one 10, one 20, and one 50. While the great differences between average goat ownership of *šek* and Kalasha households could be due to the small number of *šek* households, it could also be a reflection of the different sexual division of labor among converted Kalasha: women do less agricultural work, so men are less able to pursue pastoral work that takes them away from family crops during the growing season.

2. Families with no girls old enough to watch the sheep may take in a neighbor girl to do this work.

3. Margaret Mills, who did fieldwork in Ishkoman, told me that this description is only partially true for Kho women in that community. They do travel back to natal homes in adjacent villages to help with births. While they don't necessarily need a male escort, they always travel with children or other women, never alone.

4. For example, one middle-aged man lives alone. One household consists of a single middle-aged woman, said to be "crazy," whose brother has moved to Peshawar. In one household, an elderly brother and sister, both widowed and childless, live together and care for their dead brother's children.

5. I am unable to figure out why there are so many fewer women than men in Rumbur, and don't know if this is true in the other two Kalasha valleys of Birir and Bumboret. Conversion rates appear similar, and I did not notice signs of neglect of female children. Clearly, this would be an important issue for further research.

6. I conducted this economic survey of Rumbur Valley by means of a method known as rural participatory appraisal. I surveyed each village with the help of a Kalasha friend who knew each family in the village well. We spent two to three days working in each village, asking interested residents to provide economic data on their own and their neighbors' households. I cross-checked this information by interviewing individuals about their personal livestock, grain harvests, and other assets and found that assessments provided by the group of friends and neighbors corresponded well. Nevertheless, all numbers provided are estimates of average years.

Chapter 4

1. In particular, there have been rich debates about the multiple meanings of the veil (Jacobson 1970; Sharma 1978; Nanda 1976; Thompson 1981; Mills 1985; Tapper 1990; Grima 1992; Raheja and Gold 1994) and the role of clothing in women's rituals (Fruzzetti 1982).

2. Boys celebrate a similar rite of passage again when they are five, called *bhut sambiék*, "putting on the pants." Before this time, little boys traditionally didn't wear pants, only the long *kamiz*. During *bhut sambiék*, boys are dressed in traditional men's clothing and pose as stiff, fierce warriors at Sagigor, the most sacred altar in the valley.

3. This is also true of women in many other communities in Pakistan and indeed all over South Asia. Gandhi hoped that Indian women would put aside their beloved bright colors and adopt plain, white, Indian cotton (*khadi*). Such unmarked dress, he thought, would erase divisions and enable women to enter the public, political sphere without appearing immodest. Most Indian women objected that *khadi* (besides being heavy) threatened their aesthetic sense and their very identity as women (Tarlo 1996:110).

4. Interesting parallels can be found in Alfred Gell's account of how the Muria Gonds of Madhya Pradesh invent their own uniforms for public occasions, revealing the dynamism of what he calls "collective styles" (1986:120; discussed in Tarlo 1996:7).

5. Jackson and Karp comment "No one makes the world from nothing or escapes the contingencies of his or her birth, upbringing and culture. But each person strikes to live the 'found' world as though it were of his or her own making. . . . [T]he integrity and perpetuation of every collective order depends in the last analysis on the initiatives and actions of individual persons" (Karp and Jackson 1990:29). Kalasha fashion is exciting and compelling because each woman is actively engaged in personalizing the "found" world, in making it their own, and in so doing in changing it for others.

6. As Berlo suggests for Latin American women, "One of women's funda-mental roles is to creatively transform alien objects, influences, materials and ideas in order to appropriate them into indigenous culture" (1991:462).

7. James Clifford reminds us that "art collecting and culture collecting now take place within a changing field of counterdiscourses, syncretisms, and reappropriations, originating both outside and inside 'the West'" (1988:236).

8. The material to make a new dress costs about Rs 600, or U.S.$20, and each women and girl needs at least one, ideally two, every year. Yarn for a new belt costs about $20. Until about fifteen years ago, women spun the wool for their own dresses and belts, but now only very old women (and one middle-aged woman who proclaims that she is "dedicated" to Kalasha tradi-tion) wear woolen dresses, and woolen belts are also becoming less common, replaced by synthetic yarn. My own beads, less than a third of what most women wear, cost well over $100. A laborer in the valleys can expect to earn Rs 50 ($1.70) per day.

9. A woman's dress used to represent the prestige of her father (though not her husband). If he were a "big man," having held feasts of merit, she would wear a special configuration of cowrie shells on her *susútr* and was entitled to wear a *čiš,* a feathered ornament, on ceremonial occasions. Now such ornaments can be worn by anyone, regardless of the status of her father.

Chapter 5

1. Had Graziosi realized that it is Kalasha women themselves who are responsible for the creation and maintenance of their menstrual house cul-ture, he could have made a valuable contribution, as *bashali* customs have changed greatly in the forty years since his "expedition" and many Kalasha people (as well as scholars) are interested in their history.

2. In the introduciton to their edited volume, *Blood Magic,* Thomas Buckley and Alma Gottlieb write:

> To our knowledge there have been no detailed studies of women secluded in menstrual huts, and a great many questions go largely unexamined in re-ceived ethnographies and cross-cultural studies. Are most secluded women in "solitary confinement," or is seclusion more often communal . . . ? Do women usually "resent" their seclusion . . . ? Or do they . . . usually "enjoy this break from their normal labors"? Do they widely perceive it as a "break" from men as well? What do women do during this time? Some, at least talk and weave, meditate, cook—do others just mope? (1988:2)

I looked for answers to questions such as these by comparing existing ethnographic information about menstrual houses drawn primarily from the Human Relations Area Files.

Although the descriptive data available are not at all satisfactory, menstrual houses can be divided into two ideal types. In the first type, which I have termed "closed," menstruating women are isolated from one another and are not allowed to receive visits from anyone but a designated person or group of persons who bring food to her. Menstrual huts in which women are relatively more free to receive other women as visitors and situations in which all women from a community share one menstrual house are categorized as "open." It appears that the way menstrual huts are organized, whether they are open or closed, has a great deal to do with whether women look forward to menstrual seclusion with joy or simply resignation.

Closed menstrual houses isolate women from the social life of the village. A young Gond woman exclaims, for example, "You feel as if you were in jail; why has God sentenced us girls to such a punishment as this?" (Elwin 1947:81). Khanty women report finding menstrual seclusion unpleasant (Balzer 1981), and Maroon women dislike being isolated from (and therefore out of control of) village happenings (Price 1984). There are no subjective data available on the other three societies (Nahane, Micmac, and Creek), which I coded as having relatively more "closed" menstrual house practices. But it seems true that in Gond, Khanty, and Maroon society menstrual seclusion is just that, seclusion.

In contrast there are societies such as the Yurok, Papago, Yap, and Kalasha in which the menstrual house can hardly be thought of as a way of isolating menstruating women from the group, as in these four societies the menstrual house itself is a focus of women's community. Buckley suggests that Yurok women could even synchronize their periods so that they could share an important ritual life with one another (1988:190–91). The Papago menstrual hut was a place where women gathered to gamble, sing and tell stories and where no man dared go (Underhill 1936). In these cases, women are not really "secluded"; they just move to a different and special realm. In fact, it might be more correct to say that the world of men is secluded from them.

The menstrual houses in these communities all have an open structure, and they therefore come closer to realizing Michelle Rosaldo's dream that "Pollution beliefs can provide grounds for solidarity among women. Women may, for example, gather in menstrual huts, to relax or gossip, creating a world free from control by men" (1974:38). Because open menstrual houses afford women the opportunity to be together in an extended and intimate way, and because this space is free of overt male influence, it can become a center for female culture and community.

3. My thanks go to my colleague Birgitte Sperber, who brought this myth to my attention and conducted the joint interview in which this story was told. See Fentz 1994:74 for an alternative version told by Kasi Khosh Nawaz.

4. Graziosi reports that when he was attempting to elicit census data and asked men "Where were you born?" (meaning "What is your natal village?") they would often reply "In the bashali!" (1961).

5. The Rumbur bashali construction saga continues. Birgitte Sperber informed me that Maureen Lines, a British woman who has also set up her own

NGO, has constructed a second *bashali* building right next to the one Renata Hansmeyer had builit.

6. Although I asked many times what could be revealed and what was secret, I received almost no guidance. Women don't talk to men about what goes in the *bashali,* and men don't ask. Women don't seem interested in what goes on at men's ritual altars, but I know that some women have seen films made by foreigners of men's rituals. I think that it is the separation of ritual *spaces* by gender, rather than ritual *knowledge,* that is most important in Kalasha cosmology.

7. The few fields that fall inside the *pragata* areas of the valley (see chapter 2) are areas in which *bashali* women can work. Often, owners of these fields will invite *bashali* women to come and help with the fieldwork, and the work party of women will be provided with tea and good food. It becomes a social time when people who live nearby come to visit with the *bashali* women. Women whose families own such fields often *do* go there to help out, but they are not required to do so.

8. Adam Nayar told me that the menstrual house was also previously an important institution in the mountain community of Astor, as it was throughout much of northern Pakistan and across the Hindukush into Afghanistan. When Nayar did his fieldwork in Astor in the 1970s, old people remembered the menstrual house, the remains of which were then still standing in the village. Although the custom hasn't been practiced for many decades, their word for "menstrual house" had become a synonym for "lazy," so that men whose buttons weren't sewn on, and so on, would tease one another, saying, "What? Is your wife in the menstrual house?"

9. Every Kalasha person I talked with believed that there is only one God, one *khodaí* (the Chitrali word for God), and that traditional Kalasha gods and goddesses are manifestations of God.

10. Dezalik figurines also stand watch over the menstrual houses in Rumbur. In Birir, the goddess is worshiped, but there is no physical representation of her.

11. I had intended to tape-record conversations in various social arenas to use for comparative discourse analysis. The fact that everything that goes into the *bashali* must be thoroughly washed made bringing recording equipment with me impossible. I also found that I felt uncomfortable taping women's private conversations. It felt like spying, and the presence of my machines seemed to make my friends self-conscious.

12. Relationships between close female friends are similar in many ways to relationships between young heterosexual lovers. They exchange small gifts, look forward to seeing one another, and feel a "lack" when they have been apart for a long time. They like to sit close together and hold hands and engage in intimate conversation. "But I don't think women ever think of sleeping together like husband and wife," Wasiara Aya told me. "Of course, we haven't seen much of the world like you have, so who knows?" Other women echoed her sentiments, saying that female friendships were charged

with warmth and emotion but were never explicitly sexual in nature. Male homosexuality was not unfamiliar, but the Kalasha word for it is a terrible insult and it is claimed no Kalasha men (in contrast to men from surrounding communities) engage in homosexual behavior.

13. I'm reluctant to argue that the basis for women's community in the menstrual house is rooted in the body, especially the reproductive body. Feminists have rightly deconstructed long-standing Western associations between women and body, men and mind/idea/spirit. Western women, as Simone de Beauvoir has said, have been "weighed down" by being cast in the role of body, "by everything peculiar to it" (see Bordo 1993). Teasing apart the conflation of biology and gender, then, has been politically important as well as theoretically liberating.

14. I'm not sure that men *really* don't know these words. It would have been embarrassing and inappropriate to ask. Certainly, as skilled herdsmen, they understand the details of reproduction and birth.

15. Paternity appears to be far less important to Kalasha men than it is to Dogon men, as Strassmann describes. While Kalasha men certainly do talk about it, there are a number of children in the village who are known "bastards" (*ǰaróa*), conceived and born while their fathers were away from the valleys. These children are still considered the children of their mother's husband, with an equal right to inherit property.

Chapter 6

1. The stories relayed in this chapter were recorded on a number of occasions over the course of my stay in the Kalasha valleys. Those words and sentences that are direct translations from tape are italicized. The rest is paraphrased from the tapes or my field notes.

2. This story is a compilation of the "life history" Saras Gula Aya gave for my tape recorder, as well as conversations we had across the span of my fieldwork. As in other parts of this book, I have used pseudonyms and attempted to change details that would make the identities of the people in the story more obscure. I worry that for Saras Gula Aya these changes would constitute "lying" since so much of what is meaningful hangs on the connections between real people and their locatedness in specific places.

3. Women commonly said that while they recognized that it was possible for them to choose their own son-in-law it was not desirable because if something went wrong with the match (if, for example, he beat his wife) the girl's father would say, "He's your son-in-law. You chose him. You deal with him."

4. I have seen Kalasha people trying to extend their *khaltabár* relationship beyond the marriage of their children. Mir Beck's son had once been married to Mir Beck's good friend from Bumboret. After a feast, the two men spent a long, wine-warmed evening toasting to still being *khaltabár*.

5. While I often heard Kalasha threaten their children with physical violence, I very rarely saw or had direct evidence that these threats were acted

upon. One time I did see a woman—frustrated and insecure—slap her one-year-old child. Everyone present roundly chastised the young mother. I have no way of knowing whether Pilin Gul's mother really beat her, but I believe she is telling the story this way to emphasize her mother's intense anger.

6. On the other hand, as Laura Ahearn pointed out to me, girls do have agency in the sense of others acting through them.

7. As you can imagine, the process of enumerating bridewealth items in the case of an elopement is extremely contentious, as the new husband's lineage tries to minimize the amount while the ex-husband's lineage attempts to maximize it (in order to exact the highest possible payment from their "enemies" [dušmán]). As Parkes, who has an extraordinarily informative and well-documented chapter on bridewealth in his 1983 doctoral thesis, explains, "'Bridewealth' is therefore partly a question of classification: the verbal ascription of any gift between non-agnatic households as partial 'payment' for a bride transferred between their respective lineages. Such problems of classification only arise in the event of subsequent elopements, but these are sufficiently common to underwrite effectively all assistance outside one's lineage as a well-placed 'bet' that will return with double increment in the future (i.e. from the lineage of an eloping husband). It is the duty of the bride's father, assisted by mediating elders, to ensure that bridewealth enumerated in cases of elopement is restricted to genuine objects that were overtly transferred to his lineage on behalf of his daughter's marriage—most parents being anxious to relieve the load of double bridewealth that will be demanded of their future affines (to whom their daughter has eloped)" (539–40).

8. These husbands (and their families) would have forfeited the bridewealth paid for the young wives they threw away or freed.

9. Robertson claims that among other "Kafir" groups (before Kafiristan was converted to Islam) divorce was easy, and men could sell their wives or send them away. Women, he wrote, had no right to leave if a man took a second wife or a fourth or fifth (1896:536). If this is true, one wonders whether Kalasha marriage rules have changed over the last century or if they were always so different from those of neighboring Kafir communities.

10. Indeed, all children whose parents have not performed the sis istóŋgas ceremony, which consecrates the marriage, are jokingly referred to as bastards. Yet many people never bother to perform this ceremony at all (often it is only performed when, after an illness or some other misfortune, it is divined that this ceremony is needed).

11. Both men and women are liable to pay compensation (rumíš) to the offended spouse if caught in flagrante delicto in an affair. Women give jewelry—beads or expensive metal bracelets—to their lover's wife, while men are required to pay bridewealth items or livestock to their lover's husband.

12. I think (but I am not sure) that after this ceremony the parents of the couple call one another bilahí instead of khaltabár.

13. ogoék páši ašék háwimi, "We saw one another and were ašék" (in romantic love). The Kalasha language distinguishes between many types of love that English lumps together. ašék (romantic love) derives from the Persian ashiq.

Also commonly used is the phrase *hárdi šáti šíaw,* which translates as "to be heart stuck," from the verb *saṭék,* which is used in cases of active joining together.

14. Patrilineages can be divided after seven generations, after which time children of the two new lineages are allowed to marry. Also, as with most "rules," Kalasha have a way of softening the boundaries between maternal relatives. If a woman marries a man who is uncomfortably close in relation to her mother, she can perform a ceremony called *pos tára biórten,* in which she jumps over a cowhide three times. The rules about whom you can marry on your mother's side seem to be relaxing. Sarawat's mother said of her new daughter-in-law, who is also a distant relative of hers, that far from feeling like the marriage was improper she and Sarawat's wife felt *tíčak ásta rákum* (even more familial love).

15. In her life narrative, she demonstrates that she clearly understands that, as John Hoffman puts it:

[C]onsent, although the relatively passive moment of a relationship with another, is never simply a fatalistic acceptance of what 'is.' To consent is also to transform, for in 'consenting,' the individual enters into a relationship and by participating in such a relationship, social reality becomes something other than what it would have been, had the act of consent not occurred. (Hoffman 1984:124–25, quoted in Ahearn 1994:229)

References

Abu-Lughod, Lila
    1986   *Veiled Sentiments: Honor and Poetry in a Bedouin Society.* Berkeley: University of California Press.
    1990   The Romance of Resistance: Tracing Transformations of Power through Bedouin Women. *American Ethnologist* 17:41–55.
    1995   A Community of Secrets: The Separate World of Bedouin Women. In *Feminism and Community,* edited by Penny A. Weiss and Marilyn Friedman, 21–44. Philadelphia: Temple University Press.

Adams, Vicanne
    1996   *Tigers of the Snow and Other Virtual Sherpas: An Ethnography of Himalayan Encounters.* Princeton: Princeton University Press.

Ahearn, Laura
    1994   Consent and Coercion: Changing Marriage Practices among Magars in Nepal. Ph.D. diss., University of Michigan.
    1995   Agency. Paper presented at the annual meetings of the American Anthropological Association, Washington, DC.

Allan, Nigel J. R.
    1987   Ecotechnology and Modernization in Pakistan Mountain Agriculture. In *Western Himalaya, Environment, Problems, and Development,* edited by Y. P. S. Pangtey and S. C. Josh, 2:771–87. Nainital, India: Gyanodaya Prakashan.
    1990   Household Food Supply in Hunza Valley, Pakistan. *Geographical Review* 80 (4): 399–415.

Appadurai, Arjun
    1990   Disjuncture and Difference in the Global Cultural Economy. *Public Culture* 2 (2): 1–24.

Ardener, Edwin
    1975a Belief and the Problem of Women. In *Perceiving Women,* edited by Shirley Ardener, 1–17. London: Dent.
    1975b The Problem Revisited. In *Perceiving Women,* edited by Shirley Ardener, 19–27. London: Dent.

Ardener, Shirley, ed.
    1981   *Women and Space.* London: Croom Helm.

Balzer, Margorie
    1981   Rituals of Gender Identity: Markers of Siberian Khanty Ethnicity, Status, and Belief. *American Anthropologist* 83:850–67.

Barth, Fredrik
    1956   *Indus and Swat Kohistan: An Ethnographic Survey.* Oslo: Forenede Trykkerier.
    1959   *Political Leadership among Swat Pathans.* London: Athalone.
    1966   *Models of Social Organization.* Royal Anthropological Institute Occasional Papers, no. 23. Republished in Fredrik Barth, *Process and Form in Social Life.* London: Routledge and Kegan Paul, 1981.
    1981a   *Features of Person and Society in Swat: Collected Essays on Pathans.* London: Routledge and Kegan Paul.
    1981b   *Process and Form in Social Life: Selected Essays of Fredrik Barth.* Vol. 1. London: Routledge and Kegan Paul.
    1985   *The Last Wali of Swat as Told to Fredrik Barth.* Oslo: Norwegian University Press.
    1987   *Cosmologies in the Making: A Generative Approach to Cultural Variation in Inner New Guinea.* Cambridge: Cambridge University Press.
    1993   *Balinese Worlds.* Chicago: University of Chicago Press.
    1994   A Personal View of Present Tasks and Priorities in Cultural and Social Anthropology. In *Assessing Cultural Anthropology,* edited by Robert Borofsky, 349–61. New York: McGraw-Hill.

Barth, Fredrik, ed.
    1969   *Ethnic Groups and Boundaries.* Bergen: Universitetsforlaget.

Bashir, Elena
    1988   Topics in Kalasha Syntax: An Aereal and Typological Perspective. Ph.D. diss., University of Michigan.

Bateson, Gregory
    1958   *Naven: A Survey of the Problems Suggested by a Composite Picture of the Culture of a New Guinea Tribe Drawn from Three Points of View.* Cambridge: Cambridge University Press, 1936. 2d ed., Stanford: Stanford University Press.

Bayly, C. A.
    1986   The Origins of Swadeshi (Home Industry): Cloth and Indian Society, 1700–1930. In *The Social Life of Things: Commodities in Cultural Perspective,* edited by Arjun Appadurai, 285–321. Cambridge: Cambridge University Press.

Bean, Susan S.
    1989   Ghandi and Khadi: The Fabric of Independence. In *Cloth and Human Experience,* edited by Annette Weiner and Jane Schneider, 355–76. Washington, DC: Smithsonian Institution Press.

Behar, Ruth, and Gordon, Deborah, eds.
    1995   *Women Writing Culture.* Berkeley: University of California Press.

Berghe, Pierre van den
    1994   *The Quest for the Other.* Seattle and London: University of Washington Press.

Berlo, Janet Catherine

    1991 Beyond Bricolage: Women and Aesthetic Strategies in Latin American Textiles. In *Textile Traditions of Mesoamerica and the Andes: An Anthology*, edited by Margot Blum Schevill, Janet Catherine Berlo, and Edward B. Dwyer, 437–75. New York: Garland.

Biddulph, John

    1986 *Tribes of the Hindu Koosh*. Lahore: Ali Kamran. Originally published in 1880.

Bohannan, Laura [Elenore Smith Bowen]

    1954 *Return to Laughter*. New York: Harper Brothers.

Boissevain, Jeremy

    1996a *Coping with Tourists: European Reactions to Mass Tourism*. Oxford: Berghahn.

    1996b Ritual, Tourism, and Cultural Commoditization in Malta: Culture by the Pound? In *The Tourist Image: Myths and Myth Making in Tourism*, edited by Tom Slewyn, 105–20. Chichester: Wiley.

Bordo, Susan

    1993 *Unbearable Weight: Feminism, Western Culture, and the Body*. Berkeley: University of California Press.

Bossen, Laurel

    1988 Toward a Theory of Marriage: The Economic Anthropology of Marriage Transactions. *Ethnology* 27 (2): 127–44.

Bourdieu, Pierre

    1971 The Berber House. In *Rules and Meanings: The Anthropology of Everyday Knowledge*, edited by Mary Douglas, 98–110. Harmondsworth: Penguin.

    1977 *Outline of a Theory of Practice*. Translated by Richard Nice. Cambridge: Cambridge University Press. Originally published in 1972.

    1984 *Distinction: A Social Critique of the Judgement of Taste*. Translated by Richard Nice. Cambridge: Harvard University Press.

    1990 *The Logic of Practice*. Translated by Richard Nice. Stanford: Stanford University Press.

Brush, Stephen B.

    1977 *Mountain, Field, and Family: The Economy and Human Ecology of an Andean Valley*. Philadelphia: University of Pennsylvania Press.

Buckley, Thomas

    1988 Menstruation and the Power of Yurok Women. In *Blood Magic: The Anthropology of Menstruation*, edited by Thomas Buckley and Alma Gottlieb, 187–209. Berkeley: University of California Press.

Buckley, Thomas, and Alma Gottlieb

    1988 A Critical Appraisal of Theories of Menstrual Symbolism. In *Blood Magic: The Anthropology of Menstruation*, edited by Thomas Buckley and Alma Gottlieb, 3–53. Berkeley: University of California Press.

Buddruss, Georg

    1960 Zur Mythologie der Prasun-Kafiren. *Paideuma* 7, no. 4–6: 200–209.

Butler, Judith
    1990   *Gender Trouble: Feminism and the Subversion of Identity.* New York and London: Routledge.

Cacopardo, Alberto
    1991   The Other Kalasha: A Survey of the Kalashamun-Speaking People in Southern Chitral. Pt. 1: The Eastern Areas. *East and West* 41 (1–4): 273–310.
    1992   Historical and Mythic Past among the Kalasha of Chitral (Pakistan). Paper presented at the Sixth Annual South Asia Conference, Madison.

Cacopardo, Alberto, and Augusto Cacopardo
    1989   The Kalasha (Pakistan) Winter Solstice Festival. *Ethnology* 28 (4): 317–29.

Cacopardo, Augusto
    1991   The Other Kalasha: A Survey of the Kalashamun-Speaking People in Southern Chitral. Pt. 2: The Kalasha of Urtsun. *East and West* 41 (1–4): 311–50.

Castile, George Pierre, and Gilbert Kushner, eds.
    1981   *Persistent Peoples: Cultural Enclaves in Perspective.* Tucson: University of Arizona Press.

Chakravarti, Uma
    1990   Whatever Happened to the Vedic Dasi? Orientalism, Nationalism, and a Script for the Past. In *Recasting Women,* edited by Kumkum Sangari and Sudesh Vaid, 27–87. New Brunswick, NJ: Rutgers University Press.

Chhachhi, Amrita
    1994   Identity Politics, Secularism, and Women: A South Asian Perspective. In *Forging Identities: Gender, Communities, and the State in India,* edited by Zoya Hasan, 74–95. Boulder: Westview.

Clifford, James
    1988   *The Predicament of Culture: Twentieth-Century Ethnography, Literature, and Art.* Cambridge, MA: Harvard University Press.

Clifford, James, and George E. Marcus, eds.
    1987   *Writing Culture: The Poetics and Politics of Ethnography.* Berkeley: University of California Press.

Cohn, Bernard
    1989   Cloth, Clothes, and Colonialism: India in the Nineteenth Century. In *Cloth and Human Experience,* edited by Annette B. Weiner and Jane Schneider, 303–53. Washington, DC: Smithsonian Institution Press.

Comaroff, Jean
    1985   *Body of Power, Spirit of Resistance: The Culture and History of a South African People.* Chicago: University of Chicago Press.

Castile, George, and Gilbert Kushner, eds.
    1981   *Persistent Peoples: Cultural Enclaves in Perspective.* Tucson: University of Arizona Press.

Darling, Gillian
1979 Merit Feasting among the Kalash Kafirs of Northwest Pakistan. Master's thesis, University of British Columbia.
Denker, Debra
1981 Pakistan's Kalash: People of Fire and Fervor. *National Geographic* 160 (4): 458–73.
Douglas, Mary
1966 *Purity and Danger: An Analysis of Concepts of Pollution and Taboo.* London: Routledge and Kegan Paul.
1993 *Into the Wilderness: The Doctrine of Defilement in the Book of Numbers.* Sheffield: JSOT Press.
Douglas, Mary, and Baron Isherwood
1996 *The World of Goods: Towards an Anthropology of Consumption.* Harmondsworth: Penguin, 1978. Rev. ed., with a new introduction. New York: Routledge.
Dupree, Louis
1971 Nuristan: "The Land of Light" Seen Darkly. *American Universities Field Staff Reports* 15 (6):1–24.
1973 *Afghanistan.* Princeton: Princeton University Press.
Durand, Agernon
1899 *The Making of a Frontier: Five Years' Experiences and Adventures in Gilgit, Hunza, Nagar, Chitral, and the Eastern Hindu-kush.* London: John Murray.
Durkheim, Emile
1915 *The Elementary Forms of the Religious Life.* London: Allen and Unwin.
Edelberg, Lennart
1984 *Nuristani Buildings.* Moesgaard, Aarhus: Jutland Archaeological Society.
Edelberg, Lennart, and Jones, Schuyler
1979 *Nuristan.* Graz, Austria: Akademische Druk-u. Verlasanstalt.
Elphinstone, Mountstuart
1819 *An Account of the Kingdom of Caubul and Its Dependencies in Persia, Tartary, and India, Comprising a View of the Afghaun Nation and a History of the Dooraunee Monarchy.* 2d ed. London. Printed for Longman, Hurst, Rees, Orme, and Brown, and J. Murry.
Elwin, Verrier
1947 *The Muria and Their Ghotul.* Bombay: Oxford University Press.
Faithorn, Elizabeth
1976 Women as Persons: Aspects of Female Life and Male-Female Relationship among the Kafe. In *Man and Woman in the New Guinea Highlands,* edited by Paula Brown and G. Buchbinder, 86–95. Special Publications, no. 8. Washington, DC: American Anthropological Association.
Fentz, Mytte
1994 Kalasha kvindens røde perler. *Jordans Folk* (2): 73–79.

Fernea, Elizabeth
  1969 *Guests of the Sheik: An Ethnology of an Iraqi Village.* New York: Doubleday.
Finn, Janet
  1995 Crafting the Everyday: Women, Copper, and Community in Butte, Montana, USA, and Chuquicamata, Chile. Paper presented at the annual meetings of the American Anthropological Association, Washington, DC.
Flueckiger, Joyce Burkhalter
  1987 Land of Wealth, Land of Famine: The Sua Nac (Parrot Dance) of Central India. *Journal of American Folklore* 100 (395): 39–57.
Foucault, Michel
  1979 *Discipline and Punish: The Birth of the Prison.* Translated by Alan Sheridan. New York: Vintage.
  1980 *Power/Knowledge: Selected Interviews and Other Writings, 1972–1977,* edited by Colin Gordon. New York: Pantheon.
  1986 Of Other Spaces. Translated by Jay Miskowiec. *Diacritics* 16:22–27.
Friedl, Ernestine
  1975 *Women and Men: An Anthropologist's View.* New York: Holt, Rinehart and Winston.
Fruzzetti, Lina
  1982 *The Gift of a Virgin: Women, Marriage, and Ritual in Bengali Society.* New Brunswick, NJ: Rutgers University Press.
Gal, Susan
  1991 Between Speech and Silence: The Problematics of Research on Language and Gender. In *Gender at the Crossroads of Knowledge: Feminist Anthropology in the Postmodern Era,* edited by Micaela di Leonardo, 175–203. Berkeley: University of California Press.
Gardiner, Judith Kegan
  1995 Introduction to *Provoking Agents: Gender and Agency in Theory and Practice,* edited by Judith Kegan Gardiner, 1–20. Urbana: University of Illinois Press.
Gedalof, Irene
  1999 *Against Purity: Rethinking Identity with Indian and Western Feminisms.* New Brunswick, NJ: Rutgers University Press.
Gell, Alfred
  1986 Newcomers to the World of Goods: Consumption among the Muria Gonds. In *The Social Life of Things: Commodities in Cultural Perspective,* edited by Arjun Appadurai, 110–38. Cambridge: Cambridge University Press.
Giddens, Anthony
  1971 *Capitalism and Modern Social Theory.* Cambridge: Cambridge University Press.
  1977 *New Rules of Sociological Method.* New York: Basic Books.
  1979 *Central Problems in Modern Social Theory: Action, Structure, and Contradiction in Social Analysis.* Berkeley: University of California Press.

1984 *The Constitution of Society: Outline of the Theory of Structuration.* Berkeley: University of California Press.

Goffman, Erving
1959 *The Presentation of Self in Everyday Life.* New York: Doubleday/Anchor.

Goody, Jack
1973 Bridewealth and Dowry in Africa and Eurasia. In *Bridewealth and Dowry,* edited by Jack Goody and S. J. Tambiah. Cambridge: Cambridge University Press.

Graziozi, Paulo
1961 The Wooden Statue of Dezalik, a Kalash Divinity, Chitral, Pakistan. *Man* 61:148–51.

Greenwood, Davydd J.
1989 Culture by the Pound: An Anthropological Perspective on Tourism. In *Hosts and Guests: The Anthropology of Tourism,* edited by Valene Smith, 171–85. 2d ed. Philadelphia: University of Pennsylvania Press.

Gregorian, Vartan
1969 *The Emergence of Modern Afghanistan, 1880–1946.* Stanford: Stanford University Press.

Grima, Benedicte
1992 *The Performance of Emotion among Paxtun Women.* Austin: University of Texas Press.

Harrison, John
1995 *Himalayan Buildings: Recording Vernacular Architecture, Mustang, and the Kalash.* Islamabad: British Council.

Hasan, Zoya
1994 Introduction: Contextualising Gender and Identity in Contemporary India. In *Forging Identities: Gender, Communities, and the State in India,* edited by Zoya Hasan, vii–xxiv. Boulder: Westview.

Heath, Deborah
1992 Fashion, Anti-fashion, and Heteroglossia in Urban Senegal. *American Ethnologist* 19 (1): 19–32.

Herdt, Gilbert
1987 *The Sambia: Ritual and Gender in New Guinea.* Fort Worth: Harcourt Brace Jovanovich.

Hobart, Mark
1990 The Patience of Plants: A Note on Agency in Bali. *Review of Indonesian and Malaysian Affairs* 24:90–135.

Hoffman, John
1984 *The Gramscian Challenge: Coercion and Consent in Marxist Political Theory.* Oxford: Blackwell.

Hogbin, Ian
1970 *The Island of Menstruating Men.* London: Chandler.

Holzwarth, Wolfgang
1993 Auguste Court's Questionnaire on the Kafir Way of Life Answered by Tak and Shamlar from Kamdesh (about 1835). Paper presented at the Conference of European Kalash Researchers, Moesgard.

hooks, bell
  1991   *Yearning: Race, Gender, and Cultural Politics.* London: Turnaround.
Hornsby, Jennifer
  1993   Agency and Causal Explanation. In *Mental Causation,* edited by
          John Heil and Alfred Mele, 161–88. New York: Oxford University
          Press.
Hurston, Zora Neale
  1990   *Mules and Men.* Philadelphia: J. B. Lippincott, 1935. 1st Perennial
          Library Ed., New York: HarperPerennial.
Hutt, Michael
  1996   Looking for Shangri-La: From Hilton to Lamichhane. In *The Tourist
          Image: Myths and Myth Making in Tourism,* edited by Tom Selwyn,
          49–60. Chichester: Wiley.
Jackson, Michael, and Ivan Karp.
  1990   Introduction. In *Personhood and Agency: The Experience of Self and
          Other in African Cultures,* ed. Ivan Karp and Michael Jackson. Wash-
          ington, DC: Smithsonian Institution Press.
Jacobson, Doranne
  1970   Hidden Faces: Hindu and Muslim Purdah in a Central Indian
          Village, Ph.D. diss., Columbia University.
Jameson, Fredric
  1991   *Postmodernism or the Cultural Logic of Late Capitalism.* Durham: Duke
          University Press.
Jeffrey, Patricia, and Roger Jeffery
  1994   Killing My Heart's Desire: Education and Female Autonomy in
          Rural North India. In *Women as Subjects: South Asian Histories,* ed-
          ited by Nita Kumar, 125–71. Charlottesville: University of Virginia
          Press.
Jettmar, Karl
  1961   Ethnological Research in Dardistan, 1958. *Proceedings of the Ameri-
          can Philosophical Society* 105 (1): 79–97.
  1975   *Die Religionen des Hindukusch.* Stuttgart, Berlin: W. Kohlhammer.
  1986   *The Religions of the Hindu Kush.* Vol. 1: *The Religion of the Kafirs.*
          Warminster: Aris and Phillips.
Jettmar, Karl, and Lennary Edelberg, eds.
  1974   *Cultures of the Hindukush.* Wiesbaden: Franz Steiner Verlag.
John, Mary
  1989   Postcolonial Feminists in the Western Intellectual Field: Anthro-
          pologists and Native Informants. *Inscriptions* 5:49–73.
Jones, Schuyler
  1963   A Rare Look at Remote Nuristan. *National Geographic School Bulletin*
          41 (16): 250–53.
  1966   *An Annotated Bibliography of Nuristan (Kafiristan) and the Kalash Kafirs
          of Chitral (Part One).* Copenhagen: Munksgaard.
  1967   *The Political Organization of the Kam Kafirs.* Copenhagen: Munks-
          gaard.

1969   *An Annotated Bibliography of Nuristan (Kafiristan) and the Kalash Kafirs of Chitral (Part Two)*. Copenhagen: Royal Danish Academy of Letters.

1970   The Waigal "Horn Chair." *Man* 5 (2): 253–57.

1974   *Men of Influence in Nuristan*. London and New York: Seminar.

Jones, Schuyler, and Peter Parkes

1984   Ethnographic Notes on Clan/Lineage Houses in the Hindukush and "Clan Temples" and Descent Group Structure among the Kalasha ("Kalash Kafirs") of Chitral. In *Proceedings of the Sixth International Symposium on Asian Studies*, 1155–76. Hong Kong: Asian Research Service.

Karp, Ivan

1995   Agency, Agency, Who's Got the Agency? Paper presented at the meetings of the American Anthropological Association, Washington, DC.

Karp, Ivan, and Michael Jackson, eds.

1990   *Personhood and Agency: The Experience of Self and Other in African Cultures*. Washington, DC: Smithsonian Institution Press.

Keesing, Roger

1985   Conventional Metaphors and Anthropological Metaphysics: Problematic of Cultural Translation. *Journal of Anthropological Research* 41:201–18.

Keiser, Lincoln

1971   Social Structure and Social Control in Two Afghan Mountain Societies, Ph.D. diss., University of Rochester. University Microfilms 32/06–B, p. 3126, 72–00728.

1986   Death Enmity in Thull: Organized Vengeance and Social Change in a Kohistani Community. *American Ethnologist* 13 (2): 489–505.

Keith, Michael, and Steve Pile

1993   The Politics of Place. In *Place and the Politics of Identity*, edited by Michael Keith and Steve Pile, 1–21. London and New York: Routledge.

Kipling, Rudyard

1953   The Man Who Would Be King. In *Maugham's Choice of Kipling's Best*, edited by Somerset Maugham, 162–92. New York: Doubleday.

Klimburg, Max

1995   Status Imagery of the Kalasha: Some Notes on Culture Change. Paper presented at the Third International Hindu Kush Cultural Conference, Chitral, August 26–30.

1999   *The Kafirs of the Hindu Kush: Art and Society of the Waigal and Ashkun Kafirs*. 2 vols. Stuttgart: Franz Steiner Verlag.

Knauft, Bruce

1996   *Genealogies for the Present in Cultural Anthropology*. New York and London: Routledge.

Kratz, Corinne A.

2000   Forging Unions and Negotiating Ambivalence: Personhood and Complex Agency in Okiek Marriage Arrangement. In *African*

Philosophy and Cultural Inquiry, edited by Dismas Masolo and Ivan Karp, 136–71. Bloomington: Indiana University Press.

Kristiansen, Knut

1974 A Kafir on Kafir History and Festivals. In *Cultures of the Hindukush: Selected Papers from the Hindukush Cultural Conference Held at Moesgard, 1970,* edited by Karl Jettmar and Lennart Edelberg, 11–21. Wiesbaden: Franz Steiner Verlag.

Lamphere, Louise

1995 Feminist Anthropology: The Legacy of Elsie Clews Parsons. In *Women Writing Culture,* edited by Ruth Behar and Deborah A. Gordon, 85–103. Berkeley: University of California Press.

LaRiche, Jeffrey Todd

1981 Nuristan: Pre-Islamic Past to Islamic Present. M.A. thesis, University of Pennsylvania.

Lessing, Doris

1987 The Catastrophe. *New Yorker* 63 (March 16): 74–90.

Lévi-Strauss, Claude

1969 *The Elementary Structures of Kinship.* Boston: Beacon.

Levy, Robert

1984 Emotion, Knowing, and Culture. In *Culture Theory: Essays on Mind, Self, and Emotion,* edited by Richard A. Shweder and Robert A. LeVine, 214–37. Cambridge: Cambridge University Press.

Lindholm, Charles

1981 The Structure of Violence among the Swat Pakhtun. *Ethnology* 20 (2): 147–56.

1982 *Generosity and Jealousy: The Swat Pukhtun of Northern Pakistan.* New York: Columbia University Press.

Lines, Maureen

1988 *Beyond the North-West Frontier: Travels in the Hindu Kush and Karakorams.* Sparkford: Oxford Illustrated.

Loude, Jean-Yves, and Vivian Lievre

1984 *Solstice Päien.* Paris: Presses de la Renaissance.

1988 *Kalash Solstice.* Translated by Grahame Romaine and Mira Intrator. Islamabad: Lok Virsa.

Lovibond, Sabrina

1993 Feminism and Postmodernism. In *Postmodernism: A Reader,* edited by Thomas Docherty, 390–414. New York: Columbia University Press.

Lurie, A.

[1981] 1992 *The Language of Clothes.* London: Bloomsbury.

MacCannell, Dean

1976 *The Tourist: A New Theory of the Leisure Class.* New York: Schocken.

1992 *Empty Meeting Grounds: The Tourist Papers.* London: Routledge.

MacLeod, Arlene

1992 Hegemonic Relations and Gender Resistance: The New Veiling as Accommodating Protest in Cairo. *Signs: The Journal of Women in Culture and Society* 17 (3): 533–57.

Maggi, Wynne
    1992   Inside the Menstrual House: A Cross-Cultural Exploration. Paper
            presented at the annual meetings of the American Anthropologi-
            cal Association, San Francisco.
    1998   Our Women Are Free: An Ethnotheory of Kalasha Women's
            Agency, Ph.D. diss., Emory University.
Mahoney, Maureen
    1996   The Problem of Silence in Feminist Psychology. *Feminist Studies* 22
            (3): 603–10.
Mani, Lata
    1990   Contentious Traditions: The Debate on Sati in Colonial India. In
            Recasting Women, edited by Kumkum Sangari and Sudesh Vaid,
            88–127. New Brunswick, NJ: Rutgers University Press.
Mann, Elizabeth
    1994   Education, Money, and the Role of Women in Maintaining Minor-
            ity Identity. In *Forging Identities: Gender, Communities, and the State
            in India,* edited by Zoya Hassan, 130–68. Boulder: Westview.
Mann, Patricia
    1994   *Micro-politics: Agency in a Postfeminist Era.* Minneapolis: University
            of Minnesota Press.
Mannheim, Bruce
    1995   Agency, Grammar, and Pragmatics. Paper presented at the annual
            meetings of the American Anthropological Association. Washing-
            ton, DC.
March, Kathryn
    1983   Weaving, Writing, and Gender. *Man* 18:729–44.
Martin, Emily
    1987   *The Woman in the Body: A Cultural Analysis of Reproduction.* Boston:
            Beacon.
    1988   Premenstrual Syndrome: Discipline, Work, and Anger in Late In-
            dustrial Societies. In *Blood Magic,* edited by Thomas Buckley and
            Alma Gottlieb, 161–86. Berkeley: University of California Press.
Marx, Karl
    1965   *The German Ideology.* London.
Massey, Doreen
    1994   *Space, Place, and Gender.* Minneapolis: University of Minnesota
            Press.
Mayberry-Lewis, David
    1967   *Akwe-Shavante Society.* Oxford: Clarendon.
McDowell, Linda
    1983   City and Home: Urban Housing and the Sexual Division of Space.
            In *Sexual Divisions, Patterns, and Processes,* edited by Mary Evans
            and Clare Ungerson, 155–200. London and New York: Tavistock.
Mead, Margaret
    1928   *Coming of Age in Samoa: A Psychological Study of Primitive Youth for
            Western Civilization.* New York: W. Morrow and Co.

Messer-Davidow, Ellen
  1994 Acting Otherwise. In *Provoking Agents,* edited by Judith Kegan
        Gardiner, Urbana: University of Illinois Press.
Mills, Margaret
  1985 Sex Role Reversals, Sex Changes, and Transvestite Disguise in the
        Oral Tradition of a Conservative Muslim Community. In *Women's
        Folklore, Women's Culture,* edited by Rosan Jordan and Susan
        Kalcik, 187–213. Philadelphia: University of Pennsylvania Press.
Mohanty, Chandra
  1985 Under Western Eyes: Feminist Scholarship and Colonial Dis-
        courses. *Boundary* 2:333–58.
Moore, Henrietta
  1985 *Feminism and Anthropology.* Minneapolis: University of Minnesota
        Press.
  1986 *Space, Text, and Gender.* Cambridge: Cambridge University Press.
  1994 *A Passion for Difference.* Bloomington: Indiana University Press.
Morgenstierne, Georg
  1951 Some Kati Myths and Hymns. *Acta Orientalia* 21 (3): 161–89.
  1973 *Indo-Iranian Frontier Languages.* Vol. 4: *The Kalasha Language.* Oslo:
        Universitetsforlaget.
  1974 Languages of Nuristan and Surrounding Regions. In *Cultures of the
        Hindukush: Selected Papers from the Hindu-Kush Cultural Conference
        Held at Moesgard, 1970,* edited by Karl Jettmar and Lennart Edel-
        berg, 1–10. Wiesbaden: Franz Steiner Verlag.
Nanda, Bal Ram, ed.
  1976 *Indian Women from Purdah to Modernity.* Delhi: Vikas.
Ortner, Sherry B.
  1984 Theory in Anthropology since the Sixties. *Comparative Studies in
        Society and History* 26:126–66.
  1989 *High Religion: A Cultural and Political History of Sherpa Buddhism.*
        Princeton: Princeton University Press.
  1996 *Making Gender: The Politics and Erotics of Culture.* Boston: Beacon.
Palwal, A Raziq
  1972 The Mother Goddess in Kafiristan: The Place of the Mother God-
        dess in the Religious Dualism of the Kafir Aryans, Afghanistan.
        M.A. thesis, Department of Geography and Anthropology, Louisi-
        ana State University.
Parkes, Peter
  1983 Alliance and Elopement: Economy, Social Order, and Sexual An-
        tagonism among the Kalash (Kalash Kafirs) of Chitral. Ph.D. diss.,
        University of Oxford.
  1990a Kalasha: Rites of Spring. *Anthropology Today* 6 (5): 11–13.
  1990b Livestock Symbolism and Pastoral Ideology among the Kafirs of
        the Hindu Kush. *Man* 22:637–60.
  1991 Temple of Imra, Temple of Mahandeu: A Kafir Sanctuary in

Kalasha Cosmology. *Bulletin of the School of Oriental and African Studies* 54 (1): 75–103.

1994 Personal and Collective Identity in Kalasha Song Performance: The Significance of Music-Making in a Minority Enclave. In *Ethnicity, Identity and Music: The Musical Construction of Place*, edited by Martin Stokes, 157–183. Oxford and Providence: Berg.

1995 Chitral 1895: Minority Historical Perspectives. Paper presented at the Third International Hindu Kush Conference, Chitral.

1997 Kalasha Domestic Society: Practice, Ceremony, and Domain. In *Family and Gender in Pakistan: Domestic Organization in a Muslim Society*, edited by Hastings Donnan and F. Selier, 25–63. New Delhi: Hindustani Publishing.

2000 Enclaved Knowledge: Indigent and Indignant Representations of Environmental Management and Development among the Kalasha of Pakistan. In *Indigenous Environmental Knowledge and Its Transformations: Critical Anthropological Perspectives*, edited by Roy Ellen, Peter Parkes, and Alan Bicker, 253–91. Amsterdam: Harwood Academic Publishers.

Parkin, David J.
1982 Introduction to *Semantic Anthropology*. London: Academic Press.

Pratt, Mary Louise
1992 *Imperial Eyes: Travel Writing and Transculturation*. London: Routledge.

Price, Sally
1984 *Co-wives and Calabashes*. Ann Arbor: University of Michigan Press.

Probyn, Elspeth
1993 *Sexing the Self: Gendered Positions in Cultural Studies*. London: Routledge.

Raheja, Gloria, and Ann Gold
1994 *Listen to the Heron's Words: Reimagining Gender and Kinship in North India*. Berkeley: University of California Press.

Rapp, Rayna
1979 Anthropology: A Review Essay. *Signs* 4 (3): 497–513.

Robertson, George Scott
1896 *The Kafirs of the Hindu Kush*. London: Lawrence and Bullen.

1898 *Chitral: The Story of a Minor Siege*. London: Metheun.

Rogers, Susan Carol
1978 Women's Place: A Critical Review of Anthropological Theory. *Comparative Studies in Society and History* 20:123–62.

Rosaldo, Michelle Z.
1974 Woman, Culture, and Society: A Theoretical Overview. In *Woman, Culture, and Society*, edited by Michelle Z. Rosaldo and Louise Lamphere, 17–42. Stanford: Stanford University Press.

1980 The Use and Abuse of Anthropology: Reflections on Feminism and Cross-Cultural Understanding. *Signs* 5 (3): 389–417.

Rosaldo, Michelle, and Louise Lamphere, eds.

   1974   *Women, Culture, and Society*. Stanford: Stanford University Press.

Rose, Gillian

   1993   *Feminism and Geography: The Limits of Geographical Knowledge*. Minneapolis: University of Minnesota Press.

Rozario, Santi

   1992   *Purity and Communal Boundaries*. London: Zed.

Saifullah, Jan

   1995   Some Problems Facing the Kalasha Community. Paper presented at the Third International Hindu Kush Cultural Conference, Chitral, August 26–30. Forthcoming as "Development and Self-Determination: A Kalasha Point of View." In *Proceedings of the 3rd International Hindu Kush Cultural Conference*, edited by Elena Bashir and Israr-ud-Din. Karachi: Oxford University Press.

   1996   History and Development of the Kalasha. In *Proceedings of the Second International Hindu Kush Cultural Conference*, edited by Elena Bashir and Israr-ud-Din, 239–42. Karachi: Oxford University Press. (Kalasha language text, transcribed by Peter Parkes, 242–45.)

Sangari, Kumkum

   1993   Consent, Agency, and Rhetorics of Incitement. *Economic and Political Weekly*, May 1, 867–82.

Sangari, Kumkum, and Sudesh Vaid

   1990   Recasting Women: An Introduction. In *Recasting Women*, edited by Kumkum Sangari and Sudesh Vaid, 1–26. New Brunswick, NJ: Rutgers University Press.

Scheibe, Arnold, ed.

   1935   *Deutsche im Hindukusch, Bericht Der Deutschen Hindukusch-Expedition 1935 der Deutschen Forschungsgemeinschaft*. Berlin.

Schevill, Margot, Janet Catherine Berlo, and Edward B Dwyer, eds.

   1991   *Textile Traditions of Mesoamerica and the Andes: An Anthology*. New York: Garland.

Schneider, Jane

   1980   Trousseau as Treasure: Some Contradictions of Late Nineteenth-Century Change in Sicily. In *Beyond the Myths in Culture*, edited by Eric Ross, 323–58. London: Academic Press.

Schomberg, Reginald Charles Francis

   1938   *Kafirs and Glaciers*. London: Hopkinson.

Selwyn, Tom

   1996   *The Tourist Image: Myths and Myth-Making in Tourism*. Chichester: Wiley.

Sharma, Ursula

   1978   Segregation and Its Consequences in India: Rural Women of Himachal Pradesh. In *Women United, Women Divided*, edited by Pat Caplan and Janet Bujra, 259–82. London: Tavistock.

Shore, Bradd
    1996   *Culture in Mind: Cognition, Culture, and the Problem of Meaning.* New York: Oxford University Press.

Shostak, Marjorie
    1983   *Nisa: The Life and Words of a !Kung Woman.* New York: Vintage.

Siiger, Halfdan
    1956   Ethnological Field Research in Chitral, Sikkim, and Assam: A Preliminary Report. *Historiskfilologiske Meddelelser udgivet af Det Kongelige Danske Videnskabernes Selskab* 36 (2): 12–33.

Simmel, Georg
    1950   *The Sociology of Georg Simmel,* edited and translated by Kurt Wolff. New York: Free Press.

Smith, Carol
    1995   Race-Class-Gender Ideology in Guatemala: Modern and Anti-Modern Forms. *Comparative Studies in Society and History* 37:723–49.

Smith-Rosenberg, Carroll
    1985   *Disorderly Conduct: Visions of Gender in Victorian America.* New York: A. A. Knopf.

Soja, Edward
    1989   *Postmodern Geographies: The Reassertion of Space in Critical Social Theory.* London: Verso.

Spain, Daphne
    1992   *Gendered Spaces.* Chapel Hill and London: University of North Carolina Press.

Sperber, Birgitte Glavind
    1992   Nature in the Kalasha Perception of Life and Ecological Problems. *Nordic Proceedings in Asian Studies* 3:110–30.
    1993   Kalasha Development Problems. Paper presented at the Conference of European Kalasha Researchers, Aarhus University, Denmark, March 25–27.

Strand, Richard
    1974a A Note on Rank, Political Leadership, and Government among the Pre-Islamic Kom. In *Cultures of the Hindu-Kush: Selected Papers from the Hindu-Kush Cultural Conference Held at Moesgard, 1970,* edited by Karl Jettmar and Lennart Edelberg, 57–63. Wiesbaden: Franz Steiner Verlag.
    1974b Principles of Kinship Organization among the Kom Nuristani. In *Cultures of the Hindu-Kush: Selected Papers from the Hindu-Kush Cultural Conference Held at Moesgard, 1970,* edited by Karl Jettmar and Lennart Edelberg, 51–56. Wiesbaden: Franz Steiner Verlag.

Strassmann, Beverly
    1991   The Function of Menstrual Taboos among the Dogon: Defense against Cuckoldry? *Human Nature* 3 (2): 89–131.

Strathern, Marilyn

1984a Domesticity and the Denigration of Women. In *Rethinking Women's Roles: Perspectives from the Pacific,* edited by D. O'Brien and S. Tiffany, 13–31. Berkeley: University of California Press.

1984b Subject or Object? Women and the Circulation of Valuables in Highlands New Guinea. In *Women and Property,* edited by R. Hirshon, 158–75. London: Croom Helm.

1985 Kinship and Economy: Constitutive Orders of a Provisional Kind. *American Ethnologist* 12:191–209.

Tapper, Nancy

1990 *Bartered Brides: Politics, Gender, and Marriage in an Afghan Tribal Society.* Cambridge: Cambridge University Press.

Tarlo, Emma

1996 *Clothing Matters: Dress and Identity in India.* Chicago: University of Chicago Press.

Thompson, C.

1981 A Sense of Sharm: Some Thoughts on Its Implication for the Position of Women in a Village in Central India. *South Asia Research* 2:39–54.

Trail, Ron L., and Gregory R. Cooper

1999 *Kalasha Dictionary—with Urdu and English.* Islamabad, Pakistan: National Institute of Pakistan Studies, Quaid-i-Azam University, and the Summer Institute of Linguistics.

Trawick, Margaret

1990 *Notes on Love in a Tamil Family.* Berkeley and Los Angeles: University of California Press.

Treloar, A. E., R. E. Boynton, B. G. Behn, and B. W. Brown

1967 Variation of the Human Menstrual Cycle through Reproductive Life. *International Journal of Fertility* 12:77–126.

Tsing, Anna Lowenhaupt

1993 *In the Realm of the Diamond Queen: Marginality in an Out-of-the-Way Place.* Princeton: Princeton University Press.

Underhill, Ruth

1936 *The Autobiography of a Papago Woman.* Memoirs of the American Anthropological Association, no. 46. Menasha, WI: Memoirs of the American Anthropological Association.

Urry, John

1990 *The Tourist Gaze: Leisure and Travel in Contemporary Societies.* London: Sage.

Wardlow, Holly

2000 Passenger Women: Gender, Sexuality, and Agency in a Papua New Guinea Modernity. Ph.D. diss., Emory University.

Wazir Ali Shah

1974 Notes on Kalasha Folklore. In *Cultures of the Hindukush: Selected Papers from the Hindu-Kush Cultural Conference Held at Moesgaard,*

1970, edited by Karl Jettmar and Lennart Edelberg, 69–80. Wiesbaden: Steiner.

Weber, Max
[1921] 1978 *Economy and Society.* Edited by Guenther Roth and Claus Wittich. Berkeley: University of California Press.

Weiner, Annette
1976 *Women of Value, Men of Renown: New Perspectives in Trobriand Exchange.* Austin: University of Texas Press.

Weiner, Annette, and Jane Schneider, eds.
1989 *Cloth and Human Experience.* Washington, DC: Smithsonian Institution Press.

Werbner, P.
1990 Economic Rationality and Hierarchical Gift Economies: Value and Ranking among British Pakistanis. *Man* 25 (2): 266–86.

Wikan, Unni
1982 *Behind the Veil in Arabia: Women in Oman.* Baltimore: Johns Hopkins University Press.

1990 *Managing Turbulent Hearts: A Balinese Formula for Living.* Chicago: University of Chicago Press.

1992 Beyond the Words: The Power of Resonance. *American Ethnologist* 19 (3): 460–82.

Wilson, Elizabeth
1985 *Adorned in Dreams: Fashion and Modernity.* London: Virago.

Wolf, Margery
1968 *The House of Lim: A Study of a Chinese Farm Family.* New York: Prentice-Hall.

Wolff, Kurt, ed.
1950 *The Sociology of Georg Simmel.* New York: Free Press.

Woolf, Virginia
1929 *A Room of One's Own.* New York: Harcourt, Brace and World.

Yanagisako, Sylvia Junko
1979 Family and Household: The Analysis of Domestic Groups. *Annual Review of Anthropology* 8:161–205.

Index

Abu-Lughod, Lila, 209
Agency, 42–43, 72, 177–78, 202–3, 238n. 5, 244n. 15; and community identity, 32, 235n. 33; ethnographic approaches, 43; gendered, 41–42, 202–3; Kalasha theories of, 34–40, 216–20; and practice theories, 40–42. *See also* Ethnicity, Kalasha; Freedom, Kalasha women's
Agricultural productivity, 85–86
Ahearn, Laura, 243n. 6, 244n. 15
Allan, Nigel, 85
Anthropologists: ethnographic research in Kalasha valleys, 27; impact on Kalasha community, 28–30, 36–37
Ardener, Edwin, 217
Authenticity, 28
Ayun, 3, 13

Barth, Fredrik, 16, 40, 154
Bashali (menstrual house): anthropology of, 117–18; attendance as evidence of menstruation, 161; changes in traditions, 61, 66, 146–47; Dezalik (*bashali* goddess), 139–41, 241n. 10; facilitating women's agency, 161–65; foreign intervention in customs, 66, 121–24, 240n. 5; as retreat, 159–60; solidarity within, 154; work in, 128, 241n. 7. *See also* Festivals, rituals, and ceremonies

Beads, 97–98, 107–8, 110–11
Berlo, Janet, 102, 239n. 6
Bordo, Susan, 95, 242n. 13
Bossen, Laurel, 181, 188
Bourdieu, Pierre, 40, 58, 234n. 28
Bridewealth: anthropology of, 181; basic rules, 184; and women's freedom, 185–89
Butler, Judith, 234n. 28

Cacopardo, Alberto and Augusto, 20, 231n. 11, 236n. 6
Ceremonies. *See* Festivals, rituals and ceremonies
Childbirth, 62–63, 142
Child care, 77, 96
Chitral, 3, 11–12; historical relation to Kalasha, 22–24, 229n. 2
Clifford, James, 239n. 7
Cowrie shells, 107

Darling, Gillian, 106, 122
Desire, 205–8
Dezalik (menstrual house goddess), 139–41
Divorce, 185
Dowry (*jhes*), 190–92
Durand Line, 20, 230n. 9

Elopement: from the *bashali* (menstrual house), 163–65; difficulty of, 190, 195; prototypic enactment of women's freedom, 168, 199; statistics on, 178

Ethnicity, Kalasha: and
anthropologists/tourists, 28–30,
37, 94, 113–16; and fashion, 95–
96, 99, 102, 104, 115; and gender,
31–33, 36–38, 42, 61, 71, 81, 95,
99, 102; and marriage system,
196–99; and neighboring Islamic
communities, 31, 38, 69–70, 81,
102, 196–99; related to *onjesta* and
pragata (purity and impurity), 47,
57, 61, 69–71. *See also* Freedom,
Kalasha women's; Kalasha culture; Religion, Kalasha

Fashion: anthropology of, 94–95,
111, 238nn.3, 4; changes in, 108–9;
description of women's clothing,
97–101; as ethnic marker, 95–96,
99, 102, 104, 115; pleasure of, 103;
as self-expression, 107, 110; value
of visibility, 103–4
Festivals, rituals, and ceremonies:
ačhámbi (first blessing of new
baby), 149; *bhut sambiék* (putting
on the pants), 238n. 2; *biramór*
(merit feast), 106, 122; Chaumos
winter solstice festival, 2, 153, 213;
goṣṭník ceremony (children
dressed in traditional clothing for
first time), 96, 111; *hawyashi*
(*hawyáši*), 214–16; *ístam sáras* (first
blossoms of spring), 213; *khaltabarí*
(celebrating a marriage arrangement), 174; purification of *bashali*,
151; ritual during childbirth, 144–
45; ritual for first menstruation,
141–42; *sariék* (wedding feast), 106
Flueckiger, Joyce, 39, 95
Freedom, Kalasha women's, 17–18;
and anthropological concept of
"agency," 35, 42–43, 72, 177–78,
202–3, 216–20; in the *bashali* (menstrual house), 161–62, 165–66; and
bridewealth, 185–89; and dowry,
190–92; elopement as prototype of,
168, 199; enacted rather than

spoken, 217–18; and ethnicity, 31–
33, 36–39, 71, 81; and fashion, 102–
3; girls' agency, 177–78, 195–96; as
gloss of Kalasha word *azát*, 34;
Kalasha woman's description of,
33–34; limitations on, 35, 38–39,
113, 116, 189; men's role in, 36, 161,
219; of movement, 81, 216–17; negative agency, 208–9; and *pragataness*
(impurity), 46, 57, 72; and
"women's march," 35–40; and
work, 74, 81, 83, 93. *See also* Agency
Friedl, Ernestine, 91

Gal, Susan, 217
Gell, Alfred, 238n. 4
Gender ideology, 38–39; and desire,
205–8; and ethnicity, 31–33, 38,
42, 61, 81; separation of men's and
women's knowledge, 62, 138–39,
153, 159, 241n. 6; and spatial segregation, 236n. 7; women as *pragata*
(impure), 47
Gender status, 39, 78
Giddens, Anthony, 40
Gifts, 78, 112; of compensation, 112,
155, 243n. 11
Girls: role in arranged marriages,
177–78; role in elopements, 195–
96; work, 79–81
Graziozi, Paolo, 117

Hall, Ken, 99–100
Harrison, John, 59
Hobart, Mark, 178
Hoffman, John, 244n. 15
Holzworth, Wolfgang, 21, 231n. 12
Households, 84
Hutt, Michael, 230n. 5

Islamic neighboring communities:
converted Kalasha (*šek*), 25–27; position in Kalasha cosmology, 69–
71; relations with Kalasha, 24–25,
30, 113–14. *See also* Chitral;
Nuristan; Purdah

Jettmar, Karl, 104–5

Kafiristan. *See* Nuristan
Kalasha culture: changing traditions, 61, 66, 71–72; dynamism of, 105; as enclave community, 30–31; resurrected traditions, 106. *See also* Ethnicity, Kalasha; Religion, Kalasha
Kalasha history, 232n. 17
Kalashamon (Kalasha language), 231n. 14
Kalasha valleys: landscape, 14–16; map, 15
Karp, Ivan, 72, 202, 203, 238n. 5
Kenoyer, Mark, 107
Kipling, Rudyard, 19
Knauft, Bruce, 177, 234n. 27
Kratz, Corrine, 208–9

Lamphere, Louise, 42
LaRiche, Jeffrey, 19, 233n. 24
Lévi-Strauss, Claude, 178
Love, 243n. 13
Lullabies, 83

Mahoney, Maureen, 217
Marital relationships, 178, 189
Marriage: arranging marriages, 172; disputes settled nonviolently, 198–99; divorce, 185, 243n. 9; as ethnic marker, 196–99; gifts of compensation for infidelity, 112; Kalasha words for marriage, 171; khaltabar relationship (between families of husband and wife), 174–75, 242n. 4; patrilineal exogamy, 197, 244n. 14; and political leadership, 201–3; value of women's work, 86; variation in marriage type, 170, 173. *See also* Bridewealth; Dowry; Elopement
Martin, Emily, 158
Massey, Doreen, 71
Medicinal knowledge, 25
Men's houses, 153

Menstrual house, cross-cultural research on, 128, 239n. 2. See also *Bashali*
Mills, Margaret, 236nn. 5, 10, 237n. 3
Modernity, Kalasha conception of, 28, 236n. 9
Moore, Henrietta, 41, 230n. 3, 236n. 7
Morgenstierne, Georg, 16, 234n. 29

Names, 106
Nanga Dehar, 21
Nayar, Adam, 241n. 8
Nuristan: ethnographic literature about, 230n. 10, 231n. 11, 243n. 9; history of, 18–20, 106, 223n. 24; Kalasha relationship to, 20–22, 73, 232n. 15

Onjesta and *pragata* (purity and impurity): altitude hypothesis, 45–46; description of, 45, 67–68, 118, 138; and ethnic boundaries, 47, 57, 69–71; gendered nature of, 48–49, 71; nonhierarchical, 48; *pure* and *impure* as gloss, 45, 48; and women's agency, 49–50, 57–60, 63, 118
Ortner, Sherry, 39–42

Palwal, A. Raziq, 162, 236n. 3
Parkes, Peter, 18, 19, 21, 23–24, 30, 45, 85, 105, 175, 182–83, 201, 230n. 6, 231n. 12, 232n. 17, 234n. 25, 243n. 7
Power (*pawa*), 37
Public vs. domestic space: in Chitrali culture, 12; in Kalasha culture, 160
Purdah, 12, 81, 160; foreigners' (mis)understanding of, 114–15
Purity and impurity. See *Onjesta* and *pragata*

Religion, Kalasha: Dezalik (menstrual house goddess), 139–41; history, 21; and Kafiristani religions, 21–22;

Religion, Kalasha: (*continued*)
mythology, 21, 47, 118, 119–20, 140, 231n. 13; *onjesta* and *pragata* (purity and impurity), 47–49, 69–71, 138; and surrounding Muslim world, 4, 36, 231n. 12. *See also* Festivals, rituals, and ceremonies
Reproductive life histories, 133–38; Experience of reproductive selves, 158; first menstruation, 141
Robertson, George Scott, 19–20, 243n. 9
Romanticism, 16, 60

Sex ratio, 206, 238n. 5
Shore, Bradd, 219
Simmel, Georg, 109, 153
Smith, Carol, 234n. 26
Spain, Daphne, 153

Sperber, Birgitte, 122, 240n. 3
Strassman, Beverly, 128, 160–61
Strathern, Marilyn, 189

Tarlo, Emma, 94–95, 238n. 3
Tourism, 16, 28–30, 37, 44, 94, 113–16, 232–33nn. 19–23; foreigners' fantasies about Kalasha, 14. *See also* Anthropologists

Wilson, Elizabeth, 103
Wolf, Margery, 178
Work, men's, 74–76
Work, women's, 76–79, 93; for cash, 78, 110–11; distribution, 89–91; girls', 79–81; and marriage, 82–83; in the menstrual house, 128; productivity of, 86–87; underpinning women's agency, 74, 81, 83, 93